arbucks,

o Many,

Quick?

—The Wall Street Journal—

Th... anci
crisis in the US is lik
to be judged in retros
as the most wrenchi
since the end of the
second world war

—Alan Greenspan—

Starbucks
Goes from
nti to Grande

—Time—

A BITTER-
TASTING JOLT
FOR STARBUCK

—The Boston Globe—

ucks
rakes
store
th

s—

Is the Global Dominatio
of Starbucks Finally
On the Wane?

—The Independent—

—MarketWatch—

re living
h difficult
rtain times

ent Barack Obama—

Starbucks
sees tough
times ahead

I vividly remember my experience as a boy at the Horn & Hardart Automats in New York City, where I was amazed by the "magically" reappearing food. Even at a young age, I began to realize what it means to be a merchant.

Onward

Onward

How Starbucks Fought for Its Life
without Losing Its Soul

Howard Schultz
with Joanne Gordon

RODALE

Rodale books may be purchased for business or promotional use or for special sales.
For information, please write to:
Special Markets Department, Rodale, Inc., 733 Third Avenue, New York, NY 10017

Printed in the United States of America
Rodale Inc. makes every effort to use acid-free ∞, recycled paper ♻.

Book design by SYPartners

**Library of Congress Cataloging-in-Publication Data
is on file with the publisher**

Distributed to the trade by Macmillan
2   4   6   8   10   9   7   5   3   1   hardcover

We inspire and enable people to improve their lives and the world around them
www.rodalebooks.com

To my wife, Sheri, and my children, Jordan and Addison,
whose love and understanding has made all of this possible.

Yes, I want to tempt you to swim against the tide. I want to pass on to others, to younger folk, the taste of hard work, for improvement, for investing savings in the opening of a shop or workshop, and then to extend and enlarge it, not just for the sake of making money out of it but to give root to an idea, the idea of the vitality of things that are well made and being sold well.

If a man loses his workshop, his shop, his business, he loses his way, too.

Aldo Lorenzi
Proprietor, Coltelleria G. Lorenzi
Author, That Shop in Via Montenapoleone

Contents

Part 3: Pain

Part 4: Hope

Part 5: Courage

Introduction

"This date is very special to me," I said to the baristas and their store manager, who were seated around me in a small restaurant. "Exactly 28 years ago, on September 7, 1982, I began working at the first Starbucks store, your store, here in the Pike Place Market."

I reached into my pocket and pulled out a key. "I still have mine to the front door." It was not something they expected Starbucks' chief executive officer to be carrying around, but I kept it on my key chain as a constant reminder of the responsibility I have to honor the heritage of the company and all of the people who had come before me. Since it opened in 1971, the Pike Place store's front interior had remained unchanged, including the original logo.

A few weeks earlier, the store's manager, Chad Moore, had e-mailed me to praise his team for achieving eight straight weeks of record sales. Extremely impressed, I asked to take the entire team to dinner. So everyone could attend, baristas from other locations and several district managers offered to work at the Pike Place store while we celebrated. Now, on this warm Seattle evening, 27 of us had the restaurant to ourselves.

Throughout the meal, I sat and visited with people at each table. The group ranged in age from 28 to 40, and the conversations were easy and lively. At one point someone asked me to talk a bit about my own history. I could not help but smile.

* * *

I grew up in the poor projects of Brooklyn, New York, paid my way through college, and moved to Seattle, Washington, with my wife, Sheri, to take a job as head of marketing for a small coffee company called Starbucks. I spent my first weeks working at the Pike Place store, learning all about coffee, scooping fresh beans for customers and sealing them in small bags. But it was on a business trip to Italy that I unexpectedly discovered my true passion.

As I visited small espresso bars throughout Milan and Verona, I was taken by the power that savoring a simple cup of coffee can have to connect people and create community among them, and from that moment on I was determined to bring world-class coffee and the romance of Italian espresso bars to the United States. It was an experience I fervently believed could enrich people's lives. But many people did not believe in my vision—back then Starbucks stores did not sell beverages, only whole-bean and ground coffee. So I left Starbucks and started my own coffee company, Il Giornale. We opened two espresso bars in Seattle and one in Vancouver, Canada.

Then, in 1987, I found myself in a position, but without enough money, to buy my former employers' six stores and roasting plant. With the support of a few investors, I merged the two companies and chose to keep the name Starbucks Coffee Company. By the end of that year, we had 11 stores, 100 employees, and a dream to create a national brand.

In the fall of 2010, as this book goes to press, Starbucks has just posted its best financial performance in its almost 40-year history—despite critics' past predictions that our best days were behind us. Yet never has Starbucks' business been so healthy, primed to profitably grow not just by opening new stores around the world, but also through having deeper customer relationships, innovative offerings, and more places selling our products. Today, Starbucks has more than $10 billion in annual revenue and serves nearly 60 million visitors a week in 16,000 stores in 54 countries. More than 200,000 people, whom we call partners, represent Starbucks.

While these numbers are one measure of our company's success, they are not what make Starbucks truly successful, at least not by my definition.

As a business leader, my quest has never been just about winning or making money; it has also been about building a great, enduring company, which has always meant trying to strike a balance between profit and social conscience. No business can do well for its shareholders without first doing well by all the people its business touches. For us, that means doing our best to treat everyone with respect and dignity, from coffee farmers and baristas to customers and neighbors. I understand that striving to achieve profitability without sacrificing humanity sounds lofty. But I have always refused to abandon that purpose—even when Starbucks and I lost our way.

For decades Starbucks' shareholders and partners prospered. We were the first US company to offer both comprehensive health-care coverage as well as equity in the form of stock options to part-time workers, and we were routinely heralded as a great place to work. In

2000 I stepped down as ceo (since Starbucks' earliest days, we have lowercased all job titles) and became chairman, moving away from day-to-day operations to focus on global strategy and expansion. In the years that followed, we accelerated our store growth and our confidence, and our stock price soared as our sales and profits increased quarter after quarter after quarter.

Until the quarter they didn't.

By 2007 Starbucks had begun to fail itself. Obsessed with growth, we took our eye off operations and became distracted from the core of our business. No single bad decision or tactic or person was to blame. The damage was slow and quiet, incremental, like a single loose thread that unravels a sweater inch by inch. Decision by decision, store by store, customer by customer, Starbucks was losing some of the signature traits it had been founded on. Worse, our company's self-induced problems were being compounded by external circumstances as the world went through unprecedented change on several fronts.

Most significantly, the economy was hurtling toward a cataclysmic financial crisis that would destroy trillions of dollars in personal wealth; spur a credit crunch, a housing bust, and high unemployment; and, eventually, topple into a full-blown global recession.

At the same time, a seismic shift in consumer behavior was under way, and people became not just more cost conscious, but also more environmentally aware, health minded, and ethically driven. Customers were holding the companies they did business with—including Starbucks—to higher standards.

And then there was the digital revolution and the sea change in how information flows—the proliferation of online media and social networks, as well as the rise of the blogosphere. Too often, the real-time, worldwide exchange of opinions and news seemed to follow Starbucks' every move.

Finally, an onslaught of new coffee and espresso competitors—from multinational corporations to independent coffeehouses—swept into the marketplace and targeted Starbucks, often with unapologetic vitriol.

These would be daunting challenges for any company. And when it comes to Starbucks, I take every threat very personally. Starbucks is in my blood. It is such a part of me that letting it unravel simply was not an option. Too many people had worked too hard to create a company that rewarded its employees and investors and that, for years, had delivered a superior product and experience.

As chairman, I held myself responsible for the problems we ourselves had created. And although I did not know exactly how to address the variety of external pressures bearing down on us, I knew that, without daily control of the business, I was essentially powerless to stop Starbucks from sinking.

So in January 2008, I surprised many people by returning as ceo.

Onward is the story of what happened next.

Onward

Part 1: Love

Chapter 1

A Beverage of Truth

One Tuesday afternoon in February 2008, Starbucks closed all of its US stores.

A note posted on 7,100 locked doors explained the reason:

> *"We're taking time to perfect our espresso.*
>
> *Great espresso requires practice.*
>
> *That's why we're dedicating ourselves to honing our craft."*

Only weeks earlier, I'd sat in my Seattle office holding back-to-back meetings about how to quickly fix myriad problems that were beginning to surface inside the company. One team had to figure out how we could, in short order, retrain 135,000 baristas to pour the perfect shot of espresso.

Pouring espresso is an art, one that requires the barista to care about the quality of the beverage. If the barista only goes through the motions, if he or she does not care and produces an inferior espresso that is too weak or too bitter, then Starbucks has lost the essence of what we set out to do 40 years ago: inspire the human spirit. I realize this is a lofty mission for a cup of coffee, but this is what merchants do. We take the ordinary—a shoe, a knife—and give it new life, believing that what we create has the potential to touch others' lives because it touched ours.

Starbucks has always been about so much more than coffee. But without great coffee, we have no reason to exist.

"We looked at all the options," the team seated around me said. "The only way to retrain everyone by March is to close our stores, all at once."

I sat back in my chair. It would be a powerful statement, but no retailer had ever done such a thing. "That's a big idea," I replied, considering the risks. Starbucks would lose several million dollars in sales and labor costs. That would be unavoidable. Competitors would capitalize on our absence and try to lure away our customers. Critics would gloat, cynics would smirk, and the always-unpredictable media scrutiny could be humiliating. On Wall Street, our stock could sink even lower. Most dangerous of all, such a massive retraining event would be perceived as our own admission that Starbucks was no longer good enough. But if I was honest with myself, I knew that that was the truth.

I pursed my lips and looked at the team. "Let's do it."

* * *

There is a word that comes to my mind when I think about our company and our people. That word is "love." I love Starbucks because everything we've tried to do is steeped in humanity.

Respect and dignity.

Passion and laughter.

Compassion, community, and responsibility.

Authenticity.

These are Starbucks' touchstones, the source of our pride.

Valuing personal connections at a time when so many people sit alone in front of screens; aspiring to build human relationships in an age when so many issues polarize so many; and acting ethically, even if it costs more, when corners are routinely cut—these are honorable pursuits, at the core of what we set out to be.

For more than three decades, coffee has captured my imagination because it is a beverage about individuals as well as community. A Rwandan farmer. Eighty roast masters at six Starbucks plants on two continents. Thousands of baristas in 54 countries. Like a symphony, coffee's power rests in the hands of a few individuals who orchestrate its appeal. So much can go wrong during the journey from soil to cup that when everything goes right, it is nothing short of brilliant! After all, coffee doesn't lie. It can't. Every sip is proof of the artistry—technical as well as human—that went into its creation.

In the beginning of 2008 I deeply wanted people to fall back in love with Starbucks, which is why, even when bombarded by warnings against it, I decided to close all of our stores across America. I did not feel fear as much as a sense of the unknown, like I was flipping over a playing card. All I had was my belief that, even more than perfecting our coffee, we had to restore the passion and the commitment that everyone at Starbucks needed to have for our customers. Doing so meant taking a step back before we could take many steps forward.

* * *

When clocks struck 5:30 p.m. in cities across the United States, our customers were gently asked to leave our stores and the doors were locked behind them. Inside, our green-aproned baristas watched a short film our coffee experts had produced in a matter of days back in Seattle and shipped to all 7,100 stores, along with 7,100 DVD players. What our people heard that afternoon was pure and true:

> *If poured too fast from the spout into a shot glass, like water flowing from a faucet, the espresso's flavor will be weak and the body will be thin. A shot poured too slow means the grind is too fine, and the flavor will be bitter. The perfect shot looks like honey pouring from a spoon. It is dense and tastes caramely sweet.*

If the espresso was not good enough, I told everyone at the end of the video, they had my permission to pour it out and begin again.

And then there was the milk.

For our espresso beverages, steaming milk to create a creamy, sweet consistency is crucial. Unfortunately, in the name of efficiency, our company had created some bad habits among our baristas. Not only had we not trained many of them to steam milk correctly—the process requires aerating and heating the milk in just the right fashion— but some had also been steaming large pitchers of milk prior to customers' orders, letting the pitcher sit, and then *resteaming* the milk as needed. But once steamed, milk begins to break down and lose some of its sweetness. We had to correct these behaviors and return to higher standards.

Speaking to our people via the video, I had no script, just a heart-felt plea. "It is not about the company or about the brand," I said. "It is not about anyone but you. You decide whether or not it is good enough, and you have my complete support and, most importantly, my faith and belief in you. Let's measure our actions by that perfect shot of espresso."

Meanwhile, in city after city, news crews pointed their cameras at our closed stores as reporters interviewed baffled customers. "A World without Starbucks?" asked a headline in *The Baltimore Sun*. In New York City: "Starbucks Shutdown a Grande Pain for NYers." Online, opinions pro and con streamed in throughout the day, and on television, CNN, ABC, NBC, CBS, Fox News, and others covered the closings with an odd sense of wonder, as if it had snowed in summer. Late-night comedians also roasted us. At my home in Seattle, I watched Stephen Colbert's mock news report about his three tortuous hours without a caffeinated drink, which climaxed as he doused himself in the shower with coffee, foam, and cinnamon. I went to sleep laughing for the first time in months.

Not everything went well that day. As predicted, Starbucks lost money. Approximately $6 million. One competitor tried to poach our customers by promoting 99-cent cups of espresso-based beverages. Some critics were brutal, insisting that by admitting we were broken we had forever dented the Starbucks brand. But I was confident that we had done the right thing. How could it be wrong to invest in our people?

In the weeks following the closures, our coffee quality scores went up and stayed there as stories made their way to me, like this one from a barista in Philadelphia:

A gentleman came into my store this morning and told me he would like to try espresso but was afraid it would be too bitter. So I told him that I would pull some perfect shots for him and also make him an Americano. Together we talked about espresso, its origins, and how to enjoy the perfect shot. He enjoyed it immensely and said he would be back for more. . . . I think I now have a customer for life.

That was proof enough for me that we had done the right thing.

* * *

There are moments in our lives when we summon the courage to make choices that go against reason, against common sense and the wise counsel of people we trust. But we lean forward nonetheless because, despite all risks and rational argument, we *believe* that the path we are choosing is the right and best thing to do. We refuse to be bystanders, even if we do not know exactly where our actions will lead.

This is the kind of passionate conviction that sparks romances, wins battles, and drives people to pursue dreams others wouldn't dare. Belief in ourselves and in what is right catapults us over hurdles, and our lives unfold.

"Life is a sum of all your choices," wrote Albert Camus. Large or small, our actions forge our futures, hopefully inspiring others along the way.

Ultimately, closing our stores was most powerful in its symbolism. It was a galvanizing event for Starbucks' partners—the term we use for our employees—a stake in the ground that helped reestablish some of the emotional attachment and trust we had squandered during our years of focusing on hypergrowth. A bold move that I stand by today, it sent a message that decisiveness was back at Starbucks. No doubt, after that Tuesday, thousands of Starbucks espresso shots were poured like honey. But a symbolic act and three hours of education would not solve our mounting problems. We had a long, long way to go— further than I had imagined when I returned as ceo. In the winter of 2008, the fight began for our survival. What we faced was nothing less than a crucible, and I had spent the past year preparing for it.

Chapter 2

A Love Story

When we love something,
emotion often drives our actions.

This is the gift and the challenge
entrepreneurs face every day. The
companies we dream of and build from
scratch are part of us and intensely
personal. They are our families.
Our lives.

But the entrepreneurial journey is not for everyone. Yes, the highs are high and the rewards can be thrilling. But the lows can break your heart. Entrepreneurs must love what they do to such a degree that doing it is worth sacrifice and, at times, pain. But doing anything else, we think, would be unimaginable.

So it was with a heavy heart that, early one morning in February 2007, I sat at my long kitchen table, alone, and handwrote a memo to Starbucks' most senior leaders.

Outside, the morning would be dark for another two hours as rain drizzled down our kitchen windows. Sheri and I had been living in Seattle going on 25 years. Friends in New York had warned us about the foul weather before we moved. Their forecasts were not only overblown, but also overshadowed by the Pacific Northwest's rugged beauty and saner lifestyle. I actually enjoyed Seattle winters, which in truth were more gray than wet. Rainy winter mornings like this one were ideal for contemplation. I began to write.

"I want to share some of my thoughts with you."

Candidly expressing my business philosophies, feelings, and plans in writing to coworkers has been a habit of mine since 1986 . . . but I am getting ahead of myself.

The journey that brought me to that table, on that day, to write the memo that would trigger heated public debate and alter Starbucks' future as well as my own began many years ago.

* * *

My love of coffee developed when I first went to work as head of marketing for the four stores of a small coffee company named Starbucks. That was in 1982. I didn't truly discover coffee's magic, however, until one year later on a business trip to Italy. That visit was the seed of what blossomed into today's Starbucks Coffee Company.

Early one day in Milan, I was strolling from my hotel to a trade show when I popped into a small coffee bar. *"Buon giorno!"* an older, thin man behind the counter greeted me, as if I were a regular. Moving gracefully and with precision, he seemed to be doing a delicate dance as he ground coffee beans, steamed milk, pulled shots of espresso, made cappuccinos, and chatted with customers standing side by side at the coffee bar. Everyone in the tiny shop seemed to know each other, and I sensed that I was witnessing a daily ritual.

"Espresso?" he asked me.

I nodded and watched as he repeated the ritual for me, looking up to smile as the espresso machine hissed and whirred with purpose. *This is not his job,* I thought, *it's his passion.*

For a tall guy who grew up playing football in the schoolyards of Brooklyn, being handed a tiny white porcelain demitasse filled with dark coffee crafted just for me by a gracious Italian gentleman called a barista was nothing less than transcendent.

This was so much more than a coffee break; this was theater. An experience in and of itself.

After the espresso's rich flavors had warmed me, I thanked the barista and cashier and continued toward the trade show exhibit hall, stopping along the way at more coffee bars. There seemed to be at least one on every block! Inside, there was always a similar scene: a skilled barista or two behind a bar creating espressos, cappuccinos—and other drinks I had yet to taste—for people who seemed more like friends than customers. In every bar I felt the hum of community and a sense that, over a demitasse of espresso, life slowed down.

The blend of craftsmanship and human connection, combined with the warm aroma and energizing flavors of fresh coffee, struck an emotional chord. My mind raced. It was as if I envisioned my own future and the future of Starbucks, which at the time sold only whole-bean and ground coffee in bags for home consumption. No beverages.

After Milan I flew back to the United States, excited to share what I had experienced. But my bosses, the first founders of Starbucks, for whom I had tremendous respect, did not share my dream of re-creating the coffee bar experience in Seattle. I was crushed, but my belief was so powerful that, in April 1986, I left Starbucks and raised money from local investors to found my own retail coffee company. I named it Il Giornale, after Milan's daily newspaper.

That year, Il Giornale opened its first store in the lobby of Seattle's newest, highest office tower, Columbia Center. The store was 710 square feet, and I had to personally guarantee the lease, even though I had no assets at the time. To keep our labor costs down, my two colleagues and I—our chief coffee buyer Dave Olsen and Jennifer Ames-Karreman—sometimes worked behind the counter with the baristas. Pouring shots. Steaming milk. Blending beverages.

I also wrote my very first memo to employees. In it, I outlined the company's mission and the goals I expected us to achieve, as well as how we should achieve them. I was confident, especially because my passion was backed by conviction. I *believed*. The memo's tone captured the ambition and enthusiasm of the young entrepreneur I was:

> *Il Giornale will strive to be the best coffee bar company on earth. We will offer superior coffee and related products that will help our customers start and continue their work day. We are genuinely interested in educating our customers and will not compromise our ethics or integrity in the name of profit. . . . Our coffee bars will change the way people perceive the beverage, and we will build into each Il Giornale coffee bar a level of quality, performance and value that will earn the respect and loyalty of our customers.*

At the end, above my signature and in lieu of a traditional "Thank you" or "Sincerely," I wrote "Onward."

To this day, I am not sure if I had used the word prior to writing that memo. But at that moment the word struck me. It felt right, a call to arms that seemed to fit the daunting yet exciting adventure our little company was embarking on. Forward leaning. Nimble. Scrappy. An unquenchable desire to succeed, but always with heads held high.

It would, indeed, be quite a journey.

Sixteen months later, I found myself in a position to purchase my former employers' company. Starbucks' owners, Jerry Baldwin and Gordon Bowker, had decided to sell their Seattle stores and roasting plant, as well as the wonderful name. Buying the company that I had so much respect for seemed, to me, destiny, but I almost lost it in an emotional, contentious battle with another potential buyer. Had I not been able to quickly raise almost $3.8 million from investors who believed in me, Starbucks would have slipped through my fingers.

But it did not, and almost overnight the coffee company I founded went from five stores to 11.

Among our first big decisions was whether to keep the name Il Giornale, whose business model we would follow, or to adopt the Starbucks name and logo. Although I felt somewhat attached to the Il Giornale moniker, I knew that I had to let it go. Starbucks had established a respected reputation for high-quality, unique coffee. The name itself—after the first mate of the whale ship *Pequod* in Herman Melville's classic *Moby Dick*, Starbuck—harbored a familiar yet mystical quality, reflecting the essence of the products and services as well as the promise that we would be introducing to customers. We went with our gut, and from that point on the company that had started as Il Giornale would be known as Starbucks.

At 34 years old, I had 100 employees and a dream to create a national brand around coffee and what I came to call the "Starbucks Experience." I wanted to elevate the quality of coffee in America. Yet I also believed that Starbucks would thrive not just because of our coffee, but also because of our guiding principles. I was determined to create a different kind of company—one that would be committed to building shareholder value and to the fiscal responsibility of making a profit, yet all the while recognizing that, in order to do so and to do it well, we had to act through a lens of social consciousness.

★ ★ ★

With coffee, Starbucks inherited a grand tradition. For centuries the coffee bean has been at once poetic and highly political, romantic and, at times, rife with controversy. Coffee has survived, I believe, because of its inherent magic. A coffee cherry is a fruit born from some of the most exotic places on earth. Tremendous care must be taken to capture the rich, complex flavors of the beans beneath its skin.

By no stretch of the imagination did Starbucks introduce the world to coffee or espresso-based drinks, but I do think it's fair to say that Starbucks exposed many people to coffee's magic.

That, as I've said, is what merchants do. We take something ordinary and infuse it with emotion and meaning, and then we tell its story over and over and over again, often without saying a word.

If you are under the age of 30, you may not remember when coffee was only scooped out of a can, dripped from a vending machine or from a lukewarm stainless steel pot in an office break room, and served in a Styrofoam cup or a diner mug. Or when, at least in the United States, coffee was mostly inhaled for its caffeine jolt rather than savored for its exotic flavors, and the only customizations were cream and sugar.

Before the late 1980s, hardly anyone in the United States and dozens of other countries ordered an espresso or a non-fat latte with extra foam! Espresso was a treat most people indulged in only after dinner at four-star restaurants or on European vacations.

Harder to fathom is the fact that, in the 1980s and even into the mid-1990s, the only indoor public destinations where people in the United States went to read, catch up with friends, or relax after a harried day—assuming they even considered doing those activities outside their homes—were diners, a handful of local coffee shops, restaurants, and libraries.

The next time you walk by a coffee shop, peer inside. Take in the variety of people in line or seated. Men and women in business attire. Parents with strollers. College students studying. High school kids joking. Couples deep in conversation. Retired folks reading newspapers and talking politics. And, of course, scores of people sitting in front of laptops searching, downloading, listening, reading and writing books, blogs, business plans, résumés, letters, e-mails, instant messages, texts . . . whatever their hearts desire. Consider how many of those people furiously clicking away on keyboards and scribbling ideas on napkins might be working to create the next Google, Alibaba, or Facebook, or composing a novel or a piece of music. Maybe they're falling in love with someone sitting next to them. Or making a friend.

If home is the primary or "first" place where a person connects with others, and if work is a person's "second place," then a public space such as a coffeehouse—such as Starbucks—is what I have always referred to as the "third place." A social yet personal environment between one's house and job, where people can connect with others and reconnect with themselves. From the beginning, Starbucks set out to provide just such an invaluable opportunity.

So when some refer to Starbucks' coffee as an affordable luxury, I think to myself, *Maybe so.* But more accurate, I like to think, is that the Starbucks Experience—personal connection—is an affordable necessity. We are all hungry for community.

By 2000 Starbucks had achieved what I believed we could: We had evolved millions of people's relationships with coffee, from what they drank to where and when they drank it. We did so in a way that made me, as well as our partners and shareholders, proud. Even as we lost money in the early years, Starbucks established two partner benefits that, at the time, were unique: full health-care benefits and equity in the form of stock options for every employee. This was an anomaly. No company had ever extended these two benefits to part-time workers who worked at least 20 hours a week. To my knowledge, we were the only private company—and later the only public company—to do so. In addition to distinguishing us as a great place to work and helping us attract top talent, acting with this level of benevolence helped us build trust with our people and, as a result, long-term value for our shareholders.

Our intent to create a unique community inside the company as well as in our stores has, I think, separated us from most other retailers. Starbucks has always cared about what the customer can and cannot see.

Chapter 3

Surfacing

Work should be personal. For all of
us. Not just for the artist and the
entrepreneur. Work should have meaning
for the accountant, the construction
worker, the technologist, the manager,
and the clerk.

Infusing work with purpose and meaning, however, is a two-way street. Yes, love what you do, but your company should love you back. As a merchant, my desire has always been to inspire customers, exceed their high expectations, and establish and maintain their trust in us. As an employer, my duty has always been to also do the same for people on the other side of the counter. For our partners. This latter responsibility has driven me for many, many years.

When I was 7 years old, I came home from school one winter day and saw my father sprawled on a couch with a cast from his hip to his ankle. My dad was an uneducated war veteran, and while he was very proud, he never really found his spot in the world. He held a series of really rough blue-collar jobs to support our family, never making more than $20,000 a year. He'd been a truck driver, a factory worker, and even a cab driver for a while, but his current job was the worst. He drove a truck picking up and delivering cloth diapers. That week Dad had fallen on a sheet of ice and broken his hip and his ankle, and for a blue-collar worker in 1960 there was no worker's compensation. No health-care coverage. No severance. My dad was simply sent home after his accident and dismissed by the company. I never imagined I would one day be in a position to run a company a different way. But I did believe, even then, that everyone deserved more respect than my parents had received. By the time my father passed away in 1988 from lung cancer, he had no savings or pension. Just as tragic, in my mind, was that he never found fulfillment or meaning in his work.

As a business leader, I wanted to build the kind of company that my dad never got a chance to work for. But like crafting the perfect cup of coffee, creating an engaging, respectful, trusting workplace culture is not the result of any one thing. It's a combination of intent, process, and heart, a trio that must constantly be fine-tuned. Sometimes we've gotten it very right. Other times, we've faltered. People at Starbucks, in our offices as well as our stores, work very, very hard. The jobs can be stressful because we set a high bar, but at the end of the day I want each person to go home feeling that he or she made a difference.

By the year 2000, I was the one ready to take on new challenges.

After running Starbucks' daily operations for almost 15 years, something inside me had shifted. The company was performing exceptionally well. With 2,600 stores in 13 countries, our revenue was just shy of $2 billion. Since 1992 we had achieved a compounded annual growth rate of 49 percent. Yet I was feeling down. At times, almost depressed. I talked with Sheri about my change in mood and, after much soul-searching, concluded that my job was not as challenging as it had been for so many years. I was still passionate about Starbucks, but also a bit bored.

Leaving, of course, was not an option. But with my engagement less than it needed to be for the health of the company, I decided the time was right to step away from overseeing day-to-day operations. To replace me as ceo, the board of directors and I appointed our president and chief operating officer at the time, Orin C. Smith.

Wise, thoughtful, and affable, Orin had joined Starbucks in 1990 as chief financial officer. He shared my vision, was well respected by partners and investors, and had an admirably measured approach to solving complex problems. I trusted him, he trusted me, and we had a decade-long history of making decisions together. He knew the company inside and out, and would continue to strengthen the core business and invest in growth.

Orin committed to spending five years as ceo. I turned my attention to expanding Starbucks around the world. Since opening our first store outside North America in Tokyo in 1996, we had been deluged with requests to open Starbucks locations in other countries. Then, as now, the opening of a Starbucks was often viewed as a sort of "coming of age," a sign of arrival for a city as well as its inhabitants. At the time, Starbucks had 525 stores outside the United States, in such far-flung places as New Zealand and China. Soon we would bring Starbucks into Spain, France, and Russia.

My new role as chairman and chief global strategist was, in large part, to help select local companies that would operate our stores in each region. We chose these international partners very carefully, selecting only organizations whose leaders shared our values. As the ambassador of the brand, it was also my job to imprint our mission on our local representatives, to ensure the brand's consistency across cultures.

I was ecstatic about the possibilities that the future held for me as well as for the company, and during the next several years I officiated at hundreds of store openings throughout the world. Traveling exposed me to more innovative retailers and other merchants whose love for their products and professions was obvious the minute I walked into their shops.

During my years as chairman, we opened US stores at a rapid rate and continued to expand around the world, pushing toward a target of 20,000 stores outside the United States. We opened in Dubai and in Hong Kong. In Saudi Arabia and Australia. And we continued to build and open stores in our most promising growth market: China. In 2003 our new Beijing store was Starbucks' 1,000[th] store in Asia Pacific. The next year we opened the first Starbucks in Paris, followed over the years by stores in the Bahamas, Brazil, Egypt, Ireland, Jordan, Northern Ireland, and Romania.

One of my most touching moments abroad occurred in 2001 in Japan, the country where we opened our very first store outside North America in 1996. Japan was also the first market outside the United States and Canada where we gave full- and part-time partners equity, and I will never forget the day we announced it at a regional company meeting. As I looked out over the audience, I saw that some of our partners were actually crying.

Owning a piece of the company gave not just our partners in Japan, but so many of our partners a tremendous sense of pride, demonstrating that we respected our people enough to share our success. After the announcement, young people who worked in our stores in Japan approached me and explained, through translators, that they could not wait to go home and tell their parents because their mothers and fathers had never owned anything in their lives. It was an incredibly humbling and fulfilling day, the kind that reminded me that Starbucks is about so much more than coffee.

Ironically, my days spent working back home in Seattle were often when I felt most out of sorts.

Although, as chairman, I occupied the same office I had as ceo, with its expansive view of Seattle's ports and skyline, I felt somewhat lost inside our nine-story building on Utah Avenue. The role of chairman did not require me to be involved in day-to-day decisions. No longer was I part of the same meetings and planning sessions that had once packed my calendar. And while I felt comfortable, out of trust as well as respect, with leaving decisions to Orin and his team, there were times when, walking by closed-door conference rooms, I would peer through the windows, literally feeling like an outsider looking in.

* * *

During Orin's five years as ceo, there was a great deal of momentum as our store count almost tripled to just more than 9,000. The company was rapidly breaking into new markets and geographies, bringing our stores to smaller metropolitan areas and suburbs. Back in major cities, where we had always thrived, competitors were following our lead and exploding their own presences. Yet even as more coffee shops sprang up, the lines at our stores got longer and longer.

It was during this time that Starbucks began to better understand its customers, and what they wanted was convenience in all its forms. They didn't want to wait in line for their lattes, but they also did not want to walk a few more blocks or drive an extra mile to get it. Our way to reduce wait times was to open more stores, so we grew aggressively in urban markets, too. It was not easy and required hard work, but our growth felt manageable in large part because we had developed easily adaptable store designs. We also had adept real estate experts who took time to find just the right store locations, as well as skilled regional, district, and store managers who oversaw quality.

It was also during Orin's leadership that Starbucks capitalized on opportunities to bring our coffee to people outside of our stores. We signed an agreement to supply our coffee to guests at hotels owned by Hyatt and Marriott. Expanding our store-within-a-store concept—Starbucks was already doing business in Barnes & Noble stores—we opened stand-alone kiosks inside hundreds of national supermarket chains such as Safeway, Kroger, and Publix. These new sales channels provided another revenue stream.

But perhaps one of the most important, yet less publicized, strides that Starbucks made when Orin was ceo was to more fully and formally commit itself to social responsibility.

Going about our business in ways that were good for people as well as good for the planet is something Starbucks has always strived to do. It is part of our DNA. But beginning in the late 1990s, social responsibility also became a marketplace imperative. Most people, I have always believed, want to buy a product or a service from a company they respect and trust. Yet that respect and trust was getting harder to earn. In the United States, there had been a surge in education and media attention about environmental issues and human rights. The 2004 movie *Hotel Rwanda*, about that country's 1994 genocide, and popular films such as Al Gore's global-warming documentary *An*

Inconvenient Truth in 2006 increased awareness about global issues and helped to create informed consumers.

More than ever before, people wanted the goods they brought into their lives to be created, packaged, transported—and discarded—with respect for the environment as well as for all of the people associated with the products.

Our efforts came in many forms, from the reactive to the proactive. Between 2000 and 2005, the company and our individual partners committed more than $47 million to local communities around the world to support efforts such as youth and literacy programs in the United States and Canada like Jumpstart; improved education opportunities in rural China; and aid for the victims of disasters such as the September 11 terrorist attacks, the 2004 South Asian tsunami, and Hurricane Katrina in 2005. With donations and thousands of volunteer hours, our partners supported charities and improvement projects in the communities where they worked. As a company, we also joined with Global Green USA to raise environmental awareness. In 2005, when we acquired Ethos Water, we agreed to honor the brand's mission to increase access to clean drinking water for children around the world. We also began to take significant steps to reduce our stores' environmental impact by purchasing renewable energy, reducing water consumption, and conserving energy. And through ongoing partnerships with global organizations, most notably Conservation International, which works with businesses and policy makers to protect the earth's most valuable resources, we participated in and created programs to further protect ecosystems and educate our own customers about issues such as climate change.

Perhaps most significant was that Starbucks took more concrete steps to fulfill its commitment to ethically source premium coffee.

When it comes to buying coffee, I have always wanted Starbucks to be a company that gives back to farmers, not only with money but also by promoting healthy, sustainable farming communities. This has been our philosophy from the very beginning.

But in the late 1990s, we began to experience vocal push-back from special-interest groups. The company listened to their concerns and, while we were already doing a lot, we agreed we could do more to formalize our intentions. In addition to Conservation International, Starbucks established a relationship with Fairtrade advocates, the organizations that license products as Fairtrade certified. This is a certification system that aims to improve the livelihoods of small producers by, for example, guaranteeing them a minimum price and connecting them to global markets. In 2001 Starbucks committed to purchasing one million pounds of Fairtrade certified coffee; not long after, our Fairtrade purchases reached 10 million pounds, making us North America's largest purchaser, roaster, and retailer of Fairtrade green coffee beans.

But we went a step further. Also in 2001, in partnership with Conservation International, we created our own sourcing guidelines, setting out a comprehensive procurement process to ensure that the coffee we bought was ethically grown and responsibly traded. We called our verification program C.A.F.E. Practices, and it identified environmental and humanitarian standards that our coffee suppliers have to comply with to do business with Starbucks. Unique to our program is that quality and transparency are prerequisites to participating. What's more, independent verifiers are responsible for ensuring that our standards—from protecting workers' rights to conserving water and energy—are indeed being measured. More often than not, they are. And because Starbucks buys only the highest-quality arabica coffee and pays the higher prices that premium coffee commands, many farmers have agreed to participate in the program.

All the while, we continued to grow the business, and by the time Orin stepped down, Starbucks' market capitalization—the value of the company's outstanding shares—had grown from $7.2 billion to $20 billion.

* * *

The board of directors selected Jim Donald as the next ceo. His operational background—he had run Wal-Mart's grocery operations and later ushered in profitability turnarounds at Safeway and Pathmark—was impressive, but we were taken even more with his leadership style.

You cannot meet a kinder human being. Jim possesses a natural talent for building relationships at every level of an organization, and when we hired him to head Starbucks' North American operations back in 2002, everyone agreed that he embodied our company's values and brought to the job rare traits that could not be learned. Among them are heart, conscience, and emotional intelligence. In Jim's first two years at Starbucks, he seamlessly embraced the culture and our culture embraced him. Tremendously well liked, Jim's style fostered human connections. He routinely hand-wrote thank-you notes to partners for work well done. He enjoyed visiting stores and chatting with baristas. In the office, he had a habit of stopping one-hour meetings after 45 minutes and telling partners to use their extra 15 minutes to call someone they usually did not contact every day.

When he inherited the company as ceo, Starbucks' stock was at $25.83. We continued to set high bars for ourselves that Wall Street held us to, and every quarter, our people felt more intense pressure to maintain annual revenue and profit increases of at least 20 percent. It was an ambitious, some said unattainable goal that I was admittedly complicit in actively promoting.

During that time, we also extended our brand beyond our coffee core and into areas like entertainment. Where once we sold a couple of CDs—artful compilations of music we played in the stores—soon we were displaying kiosks packed with the music of an array of musicians. In a handful of stores, we experimented with music bars that let customers download songs and compile their own CDs. One of the albums we produced with Concord Records, Ray Charles's *Genius Loves Company*, won eight Grammy Awards in 2005, including Album of the Year. Of the 3.25 million copies that were sold in the United States, approximately 25 percent were sold in Starbucks stores. Outside the United States, the album sold more than two million copies.

We also sold books, creating several best sellers and helping to put unknown authors on the map.

This success led us to consider ourselves somewhat of a tastemaker, and in our confidence we wondered if Starbucks could do for movies what we were doing for books and music—create hits. With that, we enthusiastically ventured into the film business, heavily promoting family-friendly fare and then selling the DVDs. I was among the company's loudest champions, intoxicated by the groundswell of opportunities that came our way. Studios wanted to pay *us* to promote their products. The business deals looked great on our profit and loss statements.

It would be a while before I recognized that Starbucks' amplified foray into entertainment, while it had its upside, was another sign of hubris born of a sense of invincibility.

* * *

My relationship with Jim became complicated.

I tried to give him space to do his job by forcing myself to stay out of meetings and keeping some opinions, but not all, to myself. But backing off proved more challenging for me than it had been with Orin, given our long history.

In letting go of the ceo post, I had essentially agreed to trust in the decisions of others, even when my heart suggested those decisions were not wise. Like a parent standing back and watching his children make their own choices, the entrepreneur-as-chairman role had its unique emotional challenges.

What's more, as chairman I was not always familiar with specific operational decisions, such as where most of our new stores were being built or who we were vetting for executive positions. One of the ongoing disagreements Jim and I had was which people were best qualified to fill some of the company's most influential roles.

Eventually, toward the end of 2006, partners who had been with Starbucks for many years began coming to me in confidence. They expressed a variety of concerns about the direction of the company. People wanted something other than "Grow! Grow! Grow!"—a mentality that I, too, had helped to foster.

I was faced with a dilemma. On the one hand, I wanted to support Jim's decisions and forge ahead with our growth goals. On the other hand, the cracks I sensed in our foundation, such as deterioration in the store experience, greatly disturbed me—as did hearing concerns from third parties. I felt trapped between two poles. My quandary was intensified by my love of the company and my sense of responsibility to partners and shareholders.

As 2006 progressed, Starbucks' performance began its subtle slide. The amount of money each customer was spending in our stores began to dip. By summer 2007, the growth in our store traffic slowed to levels we had never in our history seen. That year our stock dropped by 42 percent.

It could not have been easy, and it probably was not fair, to expect a ceo who had spent only two years at Starbucks to operate unencumbered in the shadow of the person who had built the company and led it for years. Especially when that individual was as visible and influential as I had become inside Starbucks. In retrospect, I could have done a better job of preparing for Orin's inevitable departure.

I often think that the best person to have led Starbucks would have been someone who had been inside the company for many years.

As we had done from our early years, Starbucks was doing its best to invest ahead of the growth curve by, for example, building new roasting plants and distribution facilities before they were absolutely necessary to supply our stores. But as we opened more stores, it became almost impossible to effectively keep up the pace of investment. That reality, combined with the deteriorating customer experience I was witnessing in stores and the complaints I was hearing from colleagues, pushed me to act. That was why, in February 2007, as chairman, I sat down at my kitchen table to write a memo to Jim and Starbucks' leadership team:

> *Over the past 10 years, in order to achieve the growth, development and scale necessary to go from less than 1,000 stores to 13,000 stores and beyond, we have had to make a series of decisions that, in retrospect, have led to the watering down of the Starbucks Experience, and what some might call the commoditization of our brand.*
>
> *Many of these decisions were probably right at the time, and on their own merit would not have created the dilution of the experience; but in this case, the sum is much greater and, unfortunately, much more damaging than the individual pieces.*

It was never my intent to attack or to assign blame. We were all responsible for the problems I saw surfacing and was about to air. Our problems were, in large part, self-induced, and I desperately wanted all of our leaders to feel the level of distress that I felt knowing that Starbucks was under attack, mostly from within.

* * *

A well-built brand is the culmination of intangibles that do not directly flow to the revenue or profitability of a company, but contribute to its texture. Forsaking them can take a subtle, collective toll.

I always say that Starbucks is at its best when we are creating enduring relationships and personal connections. It's the essence of our brand, but not simple to achieve. Many layers go into eliciting such an emotional response. Starbucks is intensely personal. Aside from brushing their teeth, what else do so many people do habitually every day? They drink coffee. Same time. Same store. Same beverage. There's a special relationship millions have developed with our brand, our people, our stores, and our coffee. Preserving that relationship is an honorable but enormous responsibility.

In 2006, as I visited hundreds of Starbucks stores in cities around the world, the entrepreneurial merchant in me sensed something intrinsic to Starbucks' brand was missing. An aura. A spirit. At first I couldn't put my finger on it. No one thing was sapping the stores of a certain soul. Rather, the unintended consequences resulting from the absence of several things that had distinguished our brand were, I feared, silently deflating it.

In the memo, I spelled out my concerns.

New espresso machines that we had installed in stores, while effectively increasing efficiency, were too tall. This unforeseen barrier prevented customers on one side of the coffee bar from watching baristas on the other side create their beverages. The height also kept baristas from engaging with customers in the same manner that had enchanted me back in Milan. I expressed this concern in the memo:

> *When we went to automatic espresso machines, we solved a major problem in terms of speed of service and efficiency. At the same time, we overlooked the fact that we would remove much of the romance and theater that was in play. . . .*

Also in stores, the full-bodied, suggestive, rich aroma of freshly ground coffee had become weak to nonexistent, due in large part to how we shipped and stored coffee grounds. Without it, Starbucks lost a way to tell a story that transported customers out of their day to far-flung places like Costa Rica and Africa. Ever since I had been with the company, we had banned smoking and asked partners not to wear perfume or cologne to preserve the coffee aroma. It is perhaps the most sensory aspect of our brand, and it reinforces the core of who we are: purveyors of the world's highest-quality coffees. Again, I articulated this in the memo:

> *We achieved fresh roasted bagged coffee, but at what cost? The loss of aroma—perhaps the most powerful non-verbal signal we had in our stores; the loss of our people scooping fresh coffee from the bins and grinding it fresh in front of the customer, and once again stripping the store of tradition and our heritage.*

Finally, the stores' design, so critical to atmosphere, seemed to lack the warm, cozy feeling of a neighborhood gathering place. Some people called our interior spaces cookie-cutter or sterile:

Clearly we have had to streamline store design to gain efficiencies of scale . . . [but] one of the results has been stores that no longer have the soul of the past. . . .

Without these sensory triggers, something about visiting a Starbucks vanished. The unique sights, smells, and charms that Starbucks introduced into the marketplace define our brand. If coffee and people are our core, the overall experience is our soul.

"We desperately need to . . . get back to the core and make the changes necessary to evoke the heritage, the tradition, and the passion that we all have for the true Starbucks Experience," I wrote, adding that competitors of all kinds were breathing down our necks.

I could not allow us, or myself, to drift into a sea of mediocrity after so many years of hard work. I just could not do it. The time had come to speak up, from the heart:

I have said for 20 years that our success is not an entitlement and now it's proving to be a reality. . . . Let's get back to the core. Push for innovation and do the things necessary to once again differentiate Starbucks from all others. We have an enormous responsibility to both the people who have come before us. . . . our partners and their families who are relying on our stewardship.

I titled the e-mail "The Commoditization of the Starbucks Experience."

On Valentine's Day 2007, my longtime assistant, Nancy Kent, typed up my handwritten thoughts and, after I made a few changes, e-mailed it to Jim and his team. I hoped my impassioned plea would unleash an honest, provocative conversation, prompting us to look in the mirror and get back to our core.

Instead, the memo unleashed a public furor.

Chapter 4

Nothing Is Confidential

I was sitting at my desk on Friday, February 23, when a colleague stepped into my office and looked at me incredulously. "Someone leaked the memo." My jaw dropped. My forehead crinkled in confusion.

"What?" I was not sure I had heard correctly.

"It's on the Internet."

I swirled my chair around to face the three computer screens that streamed world news, market data, and e-mails to my desk throughout the day. A quick Google search and there it was: "The Commoditization of the Starbucks Experience" on a gossip website, for anyone to see. Investors. Competitors. Journalists. Starbucks' partners. Staring at the screen, I was speechless. Not because my criticisms were now public. What upset me, what felt like a blow to my gut, was *the leak*. I could not imagine who would do such a thing.

It was nothing less than a betrayal.

In my life I place enormous value on loyalty and trust. It is intrinsic to my personal relationships and to the integrity of our company's culture, essential to how we conduct business with one another and with our customers. And while Starbucks is not perfect, nor am I, and people may disagree with some of our choices, we make it our business to uphold that trust, and we make amends if we fail.

Unlike other brands, Starbucks was not built through marketing and traditional advertising. We succeed by creating an experience that comes to life, in large part, because of how we treat our people, how we treat our farmers, our customers, and how we give back to communities. Inside the company, there had always been an unspoken level of trust that, for more than two decades, had allowed us to empower partners and to communicate openly, always assuming that the information would be used to benefit the company.

Disloyalty was not part of our moral fabric. So for me to sit in my own office and discover that someone close to me, someone inside Starbucks, had acted with such blatant, premeditated disregard for me, Jim, and the rest of the leadership team was a tremendous disappointment. It took me a while to digest it.

But I had no choice. The deed was done.

News of the memo had already spread, and phones on our media hotline were lighting up with calls from reporters. Was the memo real? *Yes.* Can we interview Howard? *No.* I could not do a single interview. It would have been too emotional. Instead, I helped Valerie O'Neil, then our director of corporate and issues management, craft a statement that accurately expressed my thoughts:

The memo is legitimate. It is a reflection of the passion and commitment Starbucks has to maintaining the authenticity of the Starbucks Experience while we continue to grow. We believe that success is not an entitlement and that it has to be earned every day. We do not embrace the status quo and constantly push for reinvention. This is a consistent, long-standing business philosophy to ensure we provide our customers the uplifting experience they have come to expect.

We released the statement.

At one point amid the chaos, a welcome face unexpectedly appeared at my office door. Wanda Herndon is a straight-talking, fun-loving, wise woman who headed Starbucks' global communications from 1995 until 2006, when she left us to launch her own consulting firm, W Communications. As many ex-partners do, Wanda often returned to visit. She and I had our own rich history of honest conversations, and when she popped in to say hello I was relieved to see her. I asked her to close the door. "Did you hear about the memo?" I said, still emanating disbelief. Wanda said yes, she knew about it, and as she sat down in front of my desk, I shook my head and spoke about how hurt I was about the breach of trust.

"Howard," she said in the matter-of-fact tone I'd come to expect, and appreciate. "Nothing is confidential. This is the new reality."

It was not the first time Wanda had spoken these words to me. In the past she had even suggested I refrain from putting certain thoughts in writing. Yet Wanda also understood two things about me. First, that it is my nature to speak from the heart, usually unedited. Second, that I conduct my life with an expectation that people will do the right thing. Yet even with all my experience, I am still surprised when they do not.

"This too shall pass," Wanda told me. "Just hang in there."

She was a calming influence that day and helped me put the situation in perspective. With time, my hunger to find the person who leaked the memo—and fire him or her—faded as the source of the breach paled in comparison to its consequences, inside and outside Starbucks. Moving forward became more important than laying blame.

★ ★ ★

Every organization has a memory, a history of achievements, mistakes, even unintended consequences that contribute to an ongoing dialogue as people mold an event's meaning for themselves. The tapestry of interpretations informs, and often directs, the organization's future. That February, my memo became part of Starbucks' collective memory.

Some partners strongly disagreed with my opinions. After all, the company was soaring. In 1992, when Starbucks went public, our market capitalization had been $250 million. Now it was approximately $24 billion. People who invested with us in 1992 had experienced an almost 5,000 percent increase in the value of that investment. Every week, Starbucks' stores had 45 million visitors. We were the most frequented retailer in the world! Why complain? some murmured behind closed doors.

Other partners, even those who shared my concerns, could not help but feel confused or insulted because they had worked so hard to make the company better and meet our growth goals—the very growth goals that I had championed. Weren't we just doing our jobs? They wanted to know. Then there were partners who saw the memo as nothing new, just another one of Howard's impassioned commentaries.

But there was also a great deal of talk among partners that I was "right," that a dirty family secret had finally been aired. A secret that could no longer be ignored. Topics that had been taboo, such as our myopic push for efficient, rapid growth at the expense of the Starbucks Experience, were suddenly open for discussion. It was as if a collective sigh of relief rippled through the corridors.

As people at our Seattle support center—our name for Starbucks' headquarters—and in our stores interpreted my words, I had to reconcile my own emotions. I worried that Jim may have felt personally attacked, as if I had publicly reviewed his job performance. Assigning fault was never my intent, publicly or privately. I was as culpable as anyone for the direction we were headed in.

Plus, I had tremendous affection for Jim. Despite our differences, I wanted him to win and succeed, and after the leak I apologized to him for any embarrassment the memo may have caused him. Unfortunately, maybe inevitably, the leaked memo further complicated our relationship, widening the rift between us. In the months that followed, more partners e-mailed me and approached me in confidence to share their own concerns about the company. Others purposely avoided me, discounting me as little more than a cranky former chief executive who had lost touch with the business.

Neither of these situations was good for Starbucks.

* * *

Outside the company, the memo continued to take on a life of its own.

It had first appeared on what was, in early 2007, a little-known blog called Starbucks Gossip. One of many third-party websites that focused on Starbucks, it posted news releases, articles, and mostly anonymous opinion pieces about the company.

The day after the memo was posted, the mainstream media picked it up like a whirlwind. *The Wall Street Journal. The New York Times.* The Associated Press. Bloomberg, Reuters, the *Financial Times.* Online financial news sites and independent blogs. Articles quoted the memo and parsed my words, usually under dour headlines that implied, or stated outright, that trouble was brewing at Starbucks. Online, readers posted comments one after the other. Many of them stung.

Stunned as I was that the memo had been leaked, I was also astonished by the depth of conversation it unleashed, as well as the speed. It seemed that everyone—customers, partners, analysts, reporters, industry insiders, and business "experts"—had an opinion about the memo, its motive, what it meant for the future of the company as well as what it said about me as a leader.

Reactions swung to extremes. Some praised the memo as an entrepreneur's bold move to try to save his company. Others used my criticisms to support their own critiques. Yes, they agreed, Starbucks had expanded too far outside its coffee roots and was diluting the experience. Financial analysts acknowledged that our rapid expansion was necessary for growth, or they interpreted the memo as a strategic signal to Wall Street that we intended to slow our growth, which was not true at the time. Anonymous posts chastised me for not realizing that my words would get out; others insisted the leaked memo was a public relations stunt.

Amid the circus of speculation, we captured the company's quandary in an interview with *The New York Times*: "The question is always, How do you keep things in balance?"

That sentiment was, after all, the memo's point. Balance had always been Starbucks' challenge. Fiscal responsibility and benevolence. Shareholder value and social conscience. Profit and humanity. Local flavor on a global scale. Now our challenge was to restore proper balance between our desire for growth and the need to preserve our heritage.

Although the rush of news coverage, opinions, and false rumors was very frustrating, in retrospect it served two very important, and unexpected, purposes.

First, the avalanche of press and punditry pushed me to accept another reality: Nothing that Starbucks or I do can be presumed confidential. The Internet simply exacerbates that fact. Going forward, the company and I would have to be much more cognizant of what we said and where. While I would continue to strive to speak transparently, I would do it through a much tighter lens.

I also became more attuned to the true power of the virtual world.

The heated online conversations about the memo were beyond Starbucks' influence, more so than any other controversy we had experienced in the past. We were not perfect, but the good things about us, our values and the acts that distinguished us, these were getting lost in the public conversation. Our collaborative approach to working with farmers. The millions of dollars we invested in local communities. The health-care coverage and stock we extended to part-timers, at a considerable cost to the company. While we never put forth press releases about many of these initiatives—believing they were just the right things to do—we also were not getting credit for them.

It was clear: Starbucks did not have the tools to participate in the online debates on a scale that would make much difference.

Our website, with its beautifully designed pages that described our coffee and provided news and financial data, was primarily a one-way dialogue, inadequate in the digital age. Starbucks had no interactive presence online. No way to speak up quickly on our own behalf, to talk directly to customers, investors, as well as partners, or let them talk directly to us. To remind people of what we stood for. In short, we were losing control of our story, in the stores as well as in the world. I also began to reflect on new behaviors I was witnessing in our stores as well as in my own home, with my two teenage kids: the increasing number of young people on laptops and cell phones talking, texting, exchanging photos, downloading music, and watching videos, TV shows, and movies.

Personally, I was no technophobe. Just tactile. I prefer to visit stores in person rather than read spreadsheets. I like the feel of a pen between my fingers rather than a keyboard beneath my hands. And I always try to meet people face-to-face, to see their eyes instead of just hearing their voices. But other than using e-mail and reading the news, I was not as tied to a computer or a BlackBerry as so many others were. But I could not ignore what was happening around me.

The leaked memo helped me comprehend the enormous sea change occurring in how information was flowing as well as what was being communicated. Technology was redefining the nature of relationships and how people spend their time. This fundamental societal shift was affecting the psyche of our own people and our customers. But not until the memo leaked did it affect me, and none too soon.

Only a week before I had handwritten the memo, Apple introduced its first iPhone.

Four months earlier, in November 2006, Google bought YouTube for a reported $1.2 billion in stock.

And five months earlier, a website called Facebook officially invited anyone over age 13—not just select groups—to join its social network.

The times were changing, with or without Starbucks. I knew we could no longer tell our story only in our stores.

I sensed a second challenge on the horizon. In addition to tackling mounting problems inside our company, we also had to innovate in the digital domain, to discover new ways to reach out and be relevant to consumers. I was not sure exactly where to begin, but we had to do something.

★ ★ ★

Companies pay a price when their leaders ignore things that may be fracturing their foundation. Starbucks was no different.

The memo's content was never intended to be public, but once it was I did not view writing it as a mistake. Every thought I expressed came from a place of love. My critiques were honest expressions born of my passion for Starbucks and my deep desire to push for reinvention and self-renewal, especially at a time when we were still winning and our shortcomings had yet to become liabilities. I had written hundreds of memos during my 26 years at the company, and all had shared a common thread. They were about self-examination in the pursuit of excellence, and a willingness not to embrace the status quo. This is a cornerstone of my leadership philosophy.

Starbucks is in the business of exceeding expectations. That means we have to admit it when we are not as good as we think we should be. My role, my duty, is to initiate that discussion, to challenge us, as well as myself, to be better, especially when we are knocking the cover off the ball.

Our partners trust me to do so.

Only by not speaking from my heart do I betray that trust.

Chapter 5

Magic

I was just a young boy, no more than 10 years old, when my aunt took me to Radio City Music Hall in New York City. After the show, we walked to an Automat, a style of self-serve restaurant that I'd never seen anything like. I was immediately enthralled.

Rows of little windows stretched from wall to wall, and behind each window was a different food. A turkey sandwich. A bowl of Jell-O. And my choice that day, a slice of apple pie. My aunt put some coins into a machine and then lifted the window, which was hinged at the top, and removed my pie. Almost immediately a new piece of pie appeared, replacing the one we had bought. My aunt convinced me that a magician was working behind the scenes; back then, I had no idea there was a kitchen full of cooks and servers behind the vast wall of food, making and constantly refilling each item for new customers.

That experience crystallized for me what it meant to be a merchant. Since then, I have always looked for the magic.

It's not unusual for me, no matter where I am in the world, to hop in a cab or go walking to visit other retailers. I do not know how many times I have done this in my life. Hundreds. I love to experience different stores—sole proprietors' and large chains'—and to see firsthand how they present their products and communicate with customers. I am a sponge, always soaking up store design, layout, and salespeople's behaviors, and over the years I've been intrigued by many types of stores that have nothing to do with coffee.

In New York City, I once entered a soap store and was struck when the clerk invited me to wash my hands in a beautiful porcelain sink by the entrance. All customers were encouraged to wash their hands, and there was something about that simple act that elevated the shopping experience before it even began. In just seconds, I was seduced! The store had successfully transferred respect for the product to customers. Who wouldn't want to leave with something so special?

In Paris, one of my favorite places to visit is Colette, a spectacular three-floor specialty store that is owned and operated by a mother-daughter team. Colette delights customers with its whimsical collection of high-end, hard-to-find items from all over the world. Books. Sneakers. Toys. There is even a bar that serves 100 different bottled waters! The owners are curators, and shopping Colette is an adventure in discovery.

The merchant's success depends on his or her ability to tell a story. What people see or hear or smell or do when they enter a space guides their feelings, enticing them to celebrate whatever the seller has to offer. Intuitively, I have always understood this. So when, in 2006 and 2007, I walked into more and more Starbucks stores and sensed that we were no longer celebrating coffee, my heart sank. Our customers deserve better.

★ ★ ★

In the months after the memo was leaked, inside our company there were more open discussions about what was going wrong. To my relief, there was even general agreement that we were compromising too much in order to accommodate our ever-increasing size.

That spring of 2007, at an all-day brainstorming meeting with a cross section of leaders and partners at Seattle's Edgewater Hotel, I was pleased to hear others voice their own concerns and pose tough questions. Is the stock price and valuation a limiting factor to where we want to go? How do we improve how our store partners interact with customers? How blinded do we get when we are doing well financially? Are we willing to give up certain thinking for an uncertain future? How do we make good business decisions while still being aspirational? How do we participate in the conversation about Starbucks? How do we grow without losing our core? How do we stay small while growing big? What is the soul of Starbucks?

It was freeing to admit, collectively, that we had trapped ourselves in a vicious cycle, one that celebrated the velocity of sales instead of what we were selling. We were opening as many as six stores each day, and every quarter our people were under intense pressure from Wall Street—and from within the company—to exceed past performance by showing increased comparative store sales, or comps, which are the year-to-year differences in revenue generated by a retailer's existing stores.

Our answer had been to build more stores as fast as we could.

Our strategy was to do more of what had worked in the past.

But we were not pushing ourselves to do things better or differently. We were not innovating in lasting ways. We were venturing into unrelated businesses like entertainment. And we were pushing products that deviated too far from the core coffee experience. As one Starbucks partner expressed, it was as if we were running a race but no longer knew what we were running for.

During the Edgewater brainstorming session, as we sat in a circle and pondered our future, some of my colleagues said they recognized that Starbucks was at an inflection point or, as Jim put it, a "critical juncture." I believed our predicament was much more serious. Starbucks was on the verge of a defining test that we would fail if we did not look in the mirror, acknowledge our blemishes, and undertake transformative, even disruptive, change.

* * *

By summer 2007, it was no longer enough for me to talk about my frustrations with our executives in Seattle. I had to go out on my own and speak to our store, district, and regional managers directly, as well as talk with baristas. I considered the fact that it might have bothered Jim that I was talking to other partners about what I perceived was wrong with Starbucks, but still I took it upon myself to have these direct conversations about the deteriorating store experience.

For me, the most acute example of this, the most symbolic representation of how Starbucks was deviating from its heritage and losing its magic, was the breakfast sandwich.

Starbucks first began serving sandwiches in 2003. Over the years we had experimented with many types, from bagel sandwiches to, in 2006, warm combinations of sausage, turkey bacon, and ham and egg on English muffins. We called the latter warm or breakfast sandwiches, and most of them included cheese. I understood why sandwiches made financial sense. For years customers had come into our stores with competitors' food products, or only bought our coffee and then went elsewhere, or were buying lower-quality coffee where they purchased their breakfasts. The sandwiches met a need. As a result, they drove sales, drove profit, and drove comps.

But I had resisted the idea of serving hot food from day one. While I encouraged innovation, I never envisioned people coming into Starbucks for a sandwich. Many customers, however, embraced the warm breakfast sandwich, grateful for a tasty, more substantial food offering. In fact, they gained quite a loyal following. The more popular they became, the more our baristas had to heat them in our warming ovens. And when they did, the sandwiches' cheese would inevitably drip and then sizzle in the ovens, releasing a pungent smell. Whatever rich, hearty coffee aroma remained in the store was overwhelmed by singed Monterey Jack, mozzarella, and, most offensively, cheddar. The smell further chipped away at our narrative. Where was the magic in burnt cheese?

People who have known me for years will tell you that few things had ever piqued my ire as much as *that smell*. As far as I was concerned, nothing could be further from the romance of the Italian espresso bar.

I could not stand it.

One day I walked into a Seattle Starbucks and immediately felt frustrated because burnt cheese had, once again, enveloped the store. I spoke to the manager about it. But she did not understand my concern because, she told me, the store had already far exceeded its sales goals for sandwiches for that week. I left the store depressed. *What would be next? Hash browns?*

The breakfast sandwich became my quintessential example of how we were losing our way. "Get the sandwiches out!" I pointedly told Michelle Gass, then our head of global products, even as we continued to introduce them into hundreds of new stores. An hour later, Jim told Michelle that Starbucks needed the sandwiches and would not take them out. Research and anecdotal evidence had told him that customers liked them, bringing into our stores more people who now included our sandwiches in their morning coffee rituals.

Not surprisingly, Michelle and others felt uncomfortably pulled between two leaders. Both Jim and I had good intentions and similar goals, but differing opinions about how to achieve them. Removing the sandwiches would have cost the company sales and customer loyalty. I was willing to trade some short-term pain for longer-term gain. Jim and others were not.

My adamant stance was admittedly dispiriting for partners in our food department who had worked for years to create the new food offerings. Months of planning, research, and testing had gone into the sandwiches' development, including hundreds of hours trying to minimize the smells of sausage, bacon, and, of course, burnt cheese. At one point, an "aroma task force" was pulled together as the team wrestled to eliminate the offending smells.

They experimented with different ovens.

They retrained baristas to clean the ovens more often.

They replaced the parchment paper that held the sandwiches.

Cook times were narrowed to prevent dripping cheese.

Manufacturers were asked to rework their ovens' vents to keep aromas from entering the air, and our own operations people tried to improve the stores' heating, ventilation, and air-conditioning systems to pull odors from the air.

Nothing seemed to work.

Internal disagreement about the sandwiches' benefit to Starbucks as a business—versus their detriment to Starbucks as a brand—continued to heighten tensions within the company's most senior ranks. The debate was as divisive as the memo. Maybe even more so. The question at hand was whether the company should follow customer data or my intuitive sense. At the time, I was not interested in finding a compromise.

Adding to my frustration was the reality that the sandwiches were not alone in detracting from our stores' essence. There was also the loss of coffee aroma, the resteaming of milk, the too-tall espresso machines. The list was getting longer. Such negative incrementalization, like one thread after another pulling at our seams, could be the company's undoing.

I saw it. I felt it. I could not ignore it.

* * *

A founder's perspective is unique.

Entrepreneurs are builders, and the lens through which I view Starbucks and the marketplace is somewhat different from what it would be if I were a professionally schooled manager.

Such a lens, however, has its strengths and weaknesses.

On the plus side, founders know every brick in the foundation. We know what inspired the company and what was required to create it. That knowledge, that history, brings with it a high level of passion to do whatever it takes to succeed, as well as an intuition about what is right and what is wrong.

But sometimes we are too close to a situation. Entrepreneurs can be blinded by emotion, by our love of what we have built, unable to see it fresh and with the eyes of a more objective outsider.

Whether I was right or wrong about the sandwiches was less telling than my obsession with removing them, which was a manifestation of my mounting frustration. Twenty years after purchasing Starbucks, I felt like a former captain who could sense his ship slowly sinking. In a knee-jerk attempt to keep us afloat, I pushed to eradicate the sandwiches from our menu. But my efforts were only a gasping attempt to plug one hole when, in reality, there were so many other holes bringing us down.

By the fall of 2007, six months after I wrote the memo, I did not think anything substantial had changed inside the company or in our stores. Day by day my disappointment edged toward anger, and at times fear, that Starbucks was losing its chance to get back the magic. That's when I began to seriously consider if the time had come for me to return as ceo.

Chapter 6

Loyalty

I still remember what it was like when we started building the company. Every day we were fighting for survival, doing whatever we had to do. We rolled up our sleeves and left our egos at the door. Every small gesture mattered, and so much of what Starbucks achieved was because of partners and the culture they fostered.

We believed that celebrating coffee and creating connections mattered. And we believed we were capable of doing it, and that it was worth doing, on a grand scale. Confidence propelled us, and we went after audacious goals with enthusiasm. We did not take our success for granted.

Until some of us did.

If not checked, success has a way of covering up small failures, and when many of us at Starbucks became swept up in the company's success, it had unintended effects. We ignored, or maybe we just failed to notice, shortcomings.

We were so intent upon building more stores fast to meet each quarter's projected sales growth that, too often, we picked bad locations or didn't adequately train newly hired baristas. Sometimes we transferred a good store manager to oversee a new store, but filled the old post by promoting a barista before he or she was properly trained. This was the kind of operational rigor we let slip and then didn't attend to the subtle but negative cumulative effects, such as declining beverage quality, because every metric we were looking at said everything was fine. For years we were able to open new locations while sales continued to increase at the stores we already had.

As the years passed, enthusiasm morphed into a sense of entitlement, at least from my perspective. Confidence became arrogance and, at some point, confusion as some of our people stepped back and began to scratch their heads, wondering what Starbucks stood for. Music? Movies? Comps? And while our people worked hard to meet our goals, it was not always with the joy or innovation or pride that had once defined us.

I can recall popping in on meetings in mid-2007, sitting in the back of the room, a fly on the wall, and being struck by the lack of decisiveness and creativity around the table. It was incredibly tough for me not to jump in; I did not want to undermine Jim, but it also saddened me because I knew we were better than that. Back in the early days, just before our initial public stock offering in 1992, Orin, Howard Behar—a former leader at Starbucks who had been instrumental in helping to build the company—and I liked to say that a partner's job at Starbucks was to "deliver on the unexpected" for customers. Now, many partners' energies seemed to be focused on trying to deliver the expected, mostly for Wall Street.

This is why, I think, so many companies fail. Not because of challenges in the marketplace, but because of challenges on the inside.

That September in Boston, seven months after the memo leaked, I shared with the board what I was hearing from partners as well as what I continued to observe. In a private executive session the board and I openly discussed the concerns we had about what was going on in the business. For the first time I indicated that, if things got worse, if things continued to deteriorate, I would be willing to come back as chief executive officer. I also confided in Orin. When I told Orin what I was considering, he reassured me that returning as ceo was the right decision. I knew that if he thought otherwise, he would have said so.

It had never been my intention to return as ceo. But I have always said that people are responsible for what they see and hear. I could not be a bystander as Starbucks slipped toward mediocrity, especially since I had played a role in and bore some of the responsibility for our troubles.

* * *

Fiscal 2007 was not a terrible year for the company. But our internal problems, the toughening economic environment, and the rise of new competitors all hinted at a rougher time ahead—for our bottom line and our brand.

On November 15, Starbucks reported annual earnings for the 12-month period that had ended September 30. Starbucks had $9.4 billion in revenue, up 21 percent, and almost $700 million in net earnings, also an increase from the previous year. We hit the earnings per share target that we had laid out for the Street, and for the 16th straight year we had 5 percent or better comps. Under any scenario that would have been fantastic, especially in the tenuous economic environment. But Starbucks had such a long history of high performance that the bits of increasingly disappointing news we delivered that quarter—slowing store traffic, the cannibalization of old stores' customers by nearby new stores, and a contracting profit margin—worried Wall Street and drew more scrutiny.

The day we announced earnings, a *Wall Street Journal* headline rang out: "At Starbucks, Too Many, Too Quick?" "The growth in Starbucks same-store sales revenue and number of transactions in the U.S. has slowed," it read. The "'underlying fear is that Starbucks is finally seeing the signs of saturation in the US,' says John Glass, an analyst. . . . Some analysts say the chain has fallen behind on creating enticing new beverages and its breakfast sandwiches have created little excitement."

Meanwhile, every morning, just as I'd done almost every day for 20 years, I would wake up and, after making my coffee, go to my computer to look at the company's daily same-store sales data, the year-over-year changes in sales at stores open for at least 12 months. For most of my career, revenues, transactions, and comps had been nothing less than validations of Starbucks' health and momentum. But as November 2007 rolled on, I continued to shake my head at the screen, disappointed, as the comps dropped to levels we had not seen in years.

* * *

Eventually the board felt, and I agreed, that a change was really needed. Something had been lost at Starbucks, an ability to effectively execute at all levels: in our support center, at regional offices, and in the stores. The patient needed more than a face-lift. But the patient did not need a new heart. Starbucks was not that far gone. Our coffee beans' quality had not been compromised. In fact—and this was a frustrating irony— we were sourcing, buying, and roasting the highest-quality coffee in our history. In addition, the heart of our culture—its purpose and mission, our values—was still beating, albeit faintly.

But there were problems. The question was, how were we going to fix them?

Being a ceo during a turnaround situation was not something I had experience doing. My entire career had been about building something that had not existed, and, more often than not, having the wind at the company's back as we executed against our original vision. Now Starbucks needed another vision, and I had to come back with one. I had to come back leading. From day one, my return as ceo would have to resonate with our partners and shareholders as more than just a point of inflection. Starbucks had lost its point of view, and I needed to declare one, as well as a clear perspective about how we were going to change.

But whom could I talk to? Until we formally announced the change in leadership to the company and shareholders after the holiday season, it had to remain confidential. At the same time, I had to plan. I needed people I could confide in. I needed objectivity and tactical guidance to ensure we did more than just announce that I was back as ceo, but rather that I was back with confidence and vision.

Myron "Mike" Ullman was—and still is—Starbucks' lead director and the chairman and chief executive officer of JCPenney. Mike is not only one of the most respected retail executives in America, having also led R.H. Macy and Company and luxury goods manufacturer LVMH Moët Hennessy–Louis Vuitton, but also one of the kindest people I have ever met. This rare combination of qualities serves Starbucks well. During this period, Mike proved a supportive confidant and counsel for whom I was grateful. He knew I could not speak to people inside Starbucks about the upcoming transition, and he strongly recommended I work with an outside resource, a firm in New York City that he had worked with for many years.

In Manhattan I walked alone into a Midtown office building on Madison Avenue and took the elevator to the 19th floor, where Kekst and Company's offices were located. I sat in a conference room across from a tall, thin man with glasses whom I had never met. His name was Jim Fingeroth. When it comes to surrounding myself with people who can add value to the company, I look for experience and skill as well as people with like-minded values. I've always had a sixth sense about those who will be a good character fit, and as I began to explain the culture and values of Starbucks to Jim, I could see that this was someone who was going to understand and embrace them, as opposed to fighting them as someone else might. If Jim could not help me make changes in a manner compatible with the company's culture, and do so with a degree of sensitivity and humanity, then we would fracture our partners' trust.

I immediately felt comfortable with Jim. He was personable and smart, yet understated. As a principal of Kekst and Company, he had been with the firm for most of its almost 40 years, guiding large public companies and financial firms through crises, mergers, and abrupt shifts in leadership. Jim and his colleagues were often brought in by outside advisors, and they worked quietly with a board of directors or senior management, usually behind the scenes. During our conversation, he did not reveal any clients' confidences. I noted his discretion. There was a reason I had never heard of the firm. Being under-the-radar is part of its value.

Jim also had worked with and studied entrepreneurs, and he understood that the odds were against me. It is very unusual for a founder to be able to manage his or her company through all phases of its evolution, especially in a turnaround situation. He told me he had winced when he read about my leaked memo back in February 2007, and had been following the company's trials in the months since. I appreciated his honesty. At one point in the conversation, Jim introduced me to two of his colleagues, Molly Morse and Jeremy Fielding. I felt that Jim and his team were the right people to help me. Plus, he had been so strongly recommended by Mike that any trepidation I had about confiding in an outsider disappeared. I opened up, and we discussed in some detail the past few years, my mounting frustration, as well as my fears. Jim listened intently and asked important questions.

I had a lot of questions for them, too. What did I need to do in the weeks ahead to hit the ground running come January? How and when should we announce the change in leadership to our senior leaders? How should we announce it publicly and talk about it with shareholders? I knew there would be mixed reactions to my return. Some people would celebrate it, while others would question whether I was the right person for the job. I asked Jim how we could minimize the inevitable disruption and angst, but at the same time let people know that things at Starbucks were going to change. And what was the best way to communicate the many changes I was already thinking about?

One of my biggest concerns was how and when to inform Jim Donald. I dreaded the prospect of telling Jim. He is a good person, and I did not question his love for Starbucks. Upending his life was one of the most unsettling things I would have to do. In the coming weeks, Jim Fingeroth, Molly, and Jeremy would help me tackle these and other issues.

When I returned to Seattle, I shipped the Kekst and Company team a box full of background information about Starbucks. They immersed themselves in our history, watching DVDs of past speeches, reading transcripts of annual meetings, reviewing past memos, annual reports, and press releases. They also read my first book.

When they flew to Seattle for the first of several visits, I took them to Pike Place Market and to the original Starbucks store that had opened in 1971, 16 years before I bought the company and combined it with Il Giornale. As I walked in the door, I explained once again how it had captured my imagination more than 20 years earlier. We also visited several competitors, including some of Seattle's finest independent coffeehouses. Then I quietly brought Jim and his team to our support center so they could get a first-hand feel for the culture. The nine-story brick building just south of downtown Seattle was a former warehouse for Sears, Roebuck and Co's catalog division, and we had designed it to feel inviting and to inspire collaboration and community, much like a coffeehouse. Our kitchens have espresso machines. The walls are lined with art inspired by countries where our coffee is grown. Costa Rica. Guatemala. Kenya. As we walked to my office, through the playful maze of slanted hallways and exposed staircases, we passed coffee trees that grow year-round under skylights, a cupping room that hosts daily coffee tastings, and partners holding impromptu meetings on couches and chairs clustered throughout the building's open spaces. Again, much like a café.

I hold most small meetings in my office around a large rectangular coffee table, and when Jim Fingeroth sat down on the couch he voiced a specific request. Could I identify an internal Starbucks partner with whom he could coordinate? Someone I trusted, who knew our leaders as well as Starbucks' operations, but whose role would not be compromised by the knowledge of what was to come.

I sat back in my chair. There were many people whom I trusted and deeply respected. Two stood out as the most appropriate ones to confide in at the time.

* * *

One day I asked Chet Kuchinad to join me for a cup of coffee.

Chet was our number-two leader in partner resources at the time, and we had traveled together a great deal internationally. We often jogged together in the early morning hours through the streets of whatever city we were visiting. Back in Seattle, we would run at lunchtime, from our offices to Pike Place Market and back.

Chet had regular access to the board, and he was familiar with our senior leaders, our operations, and our day-to-day performance. I had always been impressed by his business acumen. He also did not shy away from speaking his mind with respect and conviction. He had a habit of telling me any number of things that I did not necessarily want to hear. At first I had been taken aback, but I came to value it.

During one of our runs, at a time when Starbucks' stock was doing well, Chet said half-jokingly, "Howard, you are making people too rich." Many Starbucks partners had seen their net worth grow as our stock rose and split several times over the years. "People are starting to think it will never end." There was truth in his statement. With time, I came to see the arrogance that the wealth of the company, and its track record for success, had created.

Whenever I spoke with Chet, I knew I was getting an honest perspective. That trait, coupled with his sensibility for Starbucks' culture, led me to seek his help.

I put down my mug and leaned forward. "I am coming back as ceo," I told Chet. "I could use your help, but I understand if it puts you in a delicate situation." Chet worked with and respected Jim Donald, and he understood the tension that had come to exist between the two of us. I did not give Chet much more detail. "Take the weekend to think about it."

On Sunday he called me on my cell phone. "Howard, I'm in."

The next day, we met in my office where, over another cup of coffee, I brought him up to speed and put him in touch with Jim Fingeroth.

The other person I wanted to bring on board was Wanda. A lot of the work Jim Fingeroth, Chet, and I had to do in the coming weeks involved crafting press statements and internal communications that would be released the day of the announcement. I thought Wanda would be the ideal candidate to assist. She was no longer a Starbucks partner, but she understood Starbucks' culture and my voice. After more than a decade of working together, I trusted her implicitly.

Wanda and I hadn't seen each other since February, when we had discussed the leaked memo, and in December I asked if she would meet me for breakfast at Lola, a restaurant in downtown Seattle. We hugged hello and settled into a booth inside the narrow, bustling restaurant. Over coffee and eggs, I asked Wanda how her family was doing and what projects she was working on. I updated her on the kids and Sheri. Then I casually changed the subject.

"Would you be interested in doing some work for Starbucks?" I asked, careful not to reveal the magnitude or nature of the project. "We might need some help at the end of the year with an announcement." I was not surprised, but I was pleased when Wanda smiled widely and, without hesitating, said she was available and would be more than happy to help.

I left Lola with a heightened sense of optimism. The team was coming together.

Chapter 7

Believe

At the end of December 2007, I joined my family for our traditional trip to Hawaii. Family has always been the most important thing in my life, and this was the only time of year when the four of us took time out from our busy lives to reconnect. But considering what I had planned for the New Year, it was hardly a vacation for me.

Every day I was on the phone with Chet in Seattle and Jim Fingeroth in New York, not only mapping out the logistics of the transition, but also planning for what would come in the following days, weeks, and months. There were no obvious answers, and together we thought through what a new management structure might look like and how a variety of people's roles had to change. One of the decisions I made was to eventually eliminate the newly created position of chief operating officer and, instead, to have Starbucks' most senior leaders report directly to the ceo. I wanted a clear line of sight into every aspect of our operations, from supply chain to store design to everything in-between. Reshuffling, as well as eliminating, some of Starbucks' leaders would be inevitable.

Given that I had spent the past two years observing and talking about what was wrong with Starbucks, it was invigorating to plan for how to make it right. Ideas and priorities had been percolating in my mind for so long. We needed to reignite our connection with customers. Replace the bureaucracy with a more efficient organizational structure. Slow our US growth to a more sustainable pace while ramping up internationally, focusing on countries like China. We would also have to close some stores, although I did not know how many.

My struggle, however, was with how to appropriately frame my priorities for our people in a manner that would instill confidence and elicit support while communicating that we could no longer do business as usual.

Fortuitously, I spent time in Hawaii with Michael Dell, founder of the PC company Dell, who was spending his holidays nearby. Michael and I had been friends for many years, and only 11 months earlier he'd returned to Dell as chief executive, replacing someone he'd selected to run the company two years prior. Our parallel circumstances were a bit uncanny, and although our respective businesses—coffee and computers—could not have been more different, Michael, as a returning founder, had a unique perspective and insight about what I could expect.

It was during one of our daily three-hour bike rides along the Kona coast that I first confided in him. "I think I have to come back as ceo."

Michael did not seem surprised, and together we talked through a host of logistical and strategic issues now in front of me: managing the

Street, maintaining morale, the teetering economy and the drop in consumer confidence, as well as the trepidation that came with reassuming responsibility for day-to-day operations. We rode to Michael's house, where he walked me through the chronology of what he had done at Dell one year earlier and graciously shared the very documents that had aided his own transition.

One tool stood out as particularly applicable to Starbucks. Michael called it the Transformation Agenda. Neither of these words was part of my or Starbucks' vernacular at the time. But they resonated with me. "Transformation" spoke to the scale of change that Starbucks had to undertake, but with a positive connotation. The word "Agenda" provided an actionable framework. This was key. I was intent on demonstrating, right out of the gate, a sense of immediacy and precision in decision making.

Yet just as the future of Starbucks was beginning to crystallize in my mind, its present circumstances were causing me great angst.

Every morning in Hawaii, I checked the company's daily sales reports.

It was extremely difficult for me to fathom what I was seeing.

Starbucks was reporting negative daily comps—meaning our sales were down compared to the same day a year earlier—in the *double digits*. Our comparable store sales had been negative before, but never had I seen performance this poor, and so consistently. Sales were in free fall! Every day, around the country, fewer and fewer people were coming into our stores. And those who did were spending less money than in the past. Starbucks was hardly alone. That holiday season in the United States, consumer spending reached its weakest level in four years. Still, I felt helpless. I was on the phone with our people in Seattle asking for comps from every region of the country. The numbers were so bad I felt paralyzed. I simply did not know what to do with myself. I couldn't eat breakfast. I couldn't enjoy my family. I could barely move. It was as if everything I feared was coming true.

As December 2007—and our first fiscal quarter of 2008—came to a close, I knew that Starbucks would not make its projected earnings. I was not only coming back as ceo, but also coming back to hold the mantle after the company's worst three-month performance in its history as a public company.

* * *

Immediately after the New Year, I returned to Seattle and reconvened with Jim Fingeroth and the few other people who knew of my return as ceo.

There was a disciplined, almost chesslike approach to the work we did in the days leading up to the public announcement on Monday, January 7, 2008. As the cold winter rains and gray skies engulfed Seattle, we hunkered down around my dining room table, comfortably dressed in jeans and sweatshirts, and engaged in very serious discussions about what and when to communicate to a variety of audiences. These included Jim Donald; Starbucks' most senior leaders; thousands of corporate and store partners; shareholders; the financial community; the business and consumer media; and customers who would likely come across the news online, in newspapers, or on television.

Everything had to be done with an eye toward disclosure regulations and legal formalities, as well as authenticity and sensitivity to our partners. I also wanted to personally touch as many people as possible, in person or by phone. It would be a logistical whirlwind that required precise execution. First, following my private meeting with Jim Donald, the board would have to meet and officially ratify the change in Starbucks' leadership. Before the announcement, Nasdaq, the exchange where Starbucks' stock trades, had to be alerted. After the announcement went out, a conference call with financial analysts had to be scheduled. For the Securities and Exchange Commission, we needed to prepare and immediately file an 8-K form documenting financial details of Jim's departure.

Although Starbucks' annual report was about to go to the printer, we still had time to revise the letter to shareholders so it came from me, as the new ceo, and reflected Starbucks' new vision.

I also needed to resign from my board position at DreamWorks to convey to everyone my complete commitment. I had already given up my board seat at eBay.

How our partners received the news was of utmost importance to me. Without their support, we would not succeed. Many people would be very sad to see Jim Donald leave, that I knew. To temper reactions and allay uncertainty, one-on-one meetings needed to be arranged between our top leaders and myself, and a larger gathering

Part 2: Confidence

Chapter 8

A Reservoir of Trust

In the predawn hours of Monday, January 7, 2008, I drove along Seattle's hilly, tree-lined streets to Starbucks' very first store. Vendors along the narrow alleys of Pike Place Market were just waking up to their day as I took out my personal key and unlocked the door to the dark shop. It was so quiet.

The espresso machine was still asleep. Bags of coffee beans lined the shelves alongside rows of porcelain mugs and coffee tumblers. I ran my right hand over the original wood counter, feeling more than three decades of history beneath my fingertips. Nostalgia washed over me. In this store I'd learned how to make espresso as a young man. That was so long ago. Long before my kids and Il Giornale. Before I bought Starbucks, before the initial public stock offering, and before Japan and hundreds and then thousands of stores and legions of partners.

I stood there in the dark and made two commitments to myself.

One, I would not return to the role of ceo dwelling on our storied history. Instinctively I understood that we had to return to our roots, but if that heritage was not linked to a willingness to reinvent and innovate, then we would fail.

Second, I would not cast blame for the mistakes of the past. Not only would it be unproductive, but also, given the accelerating slide of the company's sales and its stock, there was simply no time to point fingers. As chairman I shared responsibility for the crisis that Starbucks faced at the onset of 2008, and I had lessons to learn from our errors. But the number-one priority in the next weeks and months was to instill confidence in our future. Without confidence, people could not perform.

The collective doubt that had emerged within and around Starbucks was palpable. I saw it on partners' nervous faces and in their body language. I heard it in customer feedback. And it was embedded in our sinking stock price. Letting that doubt linger inside the company would chip away at the resolve required for the hard work ahead, stifling creativity and sapping the courage to make bold moves.

Strategies and tactics were not enough to get us out of this mess, particularly in the early days of my return. Passion, that intangible concept many businesspeople belittle, was also essential, and as I locked up the Pike Place store I considered what needed to be done, starting that day: muster a collective faith in the original Starbucks Experience—our purpose and reason for being—and then refocus the company on customers instead of breakneck growth. But that faith was not something I could demand. I had to ask for it and, ultimately, earn it, day after day.

Fortunately, both Starbucks and I had history on our side, and something I referred to as our reservoir of trust. Unlike other organizations or, say, a start-up with no past, Starbucks had a long past in which values and winning were part of the culture. The memory of

how we historically tried to behave as a company and as individuals—
going the extra mile for a customer or a colleague, for example—was
not so far gone that it could not be tapped. Over the years, Starbucks
and I had made deposits into the reservoir in the form of exceptional
employee benefits and the respect with which we treated people. We'd
made enough deposits that I could draw from it. But not forever.

Resetting a beaten, dubious mind-set to an impassioned, confident
one required, in my estimation, communication that was authentic,
decisive, and concrete and came from all of Starbucks' leaders. Not
just me.

I took a deep breath and exhaled before I got back in my car and
drove to work.

* * *

Later that day, at 12:45 p.m., behind the closed doors of our corporate
boardroom, I stood at the head of a long conference table and
addressed Starbucks' chief financial officer, chief operating officer,
and the senior leaders responsible for US and international store operations, our consumer packaged goods business, marketing, partner
resources, supply chain, and legal affairs.

"I am absolutely confident that we will turn the company around.
It is going to be hard, and I am going to ask more of you than has ever
been asked before. And you must ask yourself whether you believe in
Starbucks' mission, whether you believe we can do this. Whether you
are up for it."

My tone was serious and stern. I wasn't returning to the chief executive post intent upon being liked. In fact, I anticipated that many of
my decisions would be unpopular with various constituents. "I don't
need a vote of approval from you. I just need one thing from you, and
that is to fix the house because the house is on fire! And let me be
absolutely clear," I said. "This performance will not stand." I went on
to say that I had no tolerance for anyone in that room who did not
believe in the company and our core mission. "If you do not, then let's
have a private, respectful conversation, and you can leave the company
with no hard feelings." This was not one of my more aspirational
moments, but it was still an honest one.

The day before, early Sunday evening, Nancy had called members
of the leadership team at home and asked them to be at my house at
precisely 9 p.m. for an extremely important, confidential meeting.

"Please do not tell anyone," Nancy had requested, but that was all she had let on.

Most on the team were settling in for a final weekend evening with their families when the phone rang. I disliked disrupting that time, especially without explanation. But to maintain confidentiality, Nancy could not explain the urgency or say that the rest of the team was also being asked to attend. To my surprise, one individual refused to come until after being called three times.

One by one, Starbucks' senior leaders pulled up to the front of my house, their car tires crunching on the driveway's stones as they parked. As they descended the few steps into the living room, they were taken aback to see their fellow team members. By five after nine, everyone was seated, wondering.

I got straight to the point.

"I have something important to tell you. I am going to come back as ceo, effective tomorrow." It was as if a pile of bricks had hit the floor. "And Jim Donald has left the company."

The room was silent and serious. I think everyone was in shock. There was no hearty congratulating or obvious anger. Perhaps my tone made it clear that this decision was not up for discussion. It was done. Locked and loaded. The only option was to forge ahead in unison, and I handed each member of the team the press release, the next day's schedule, and an outline of his or her individual responsibilities over the next 48 hours.

They had one night to prepare what they would say to their own teams before the news went public, as well as to reflect on what Starbucks' new course meant for them. Several leaders had been hired or promoted by Jim and almost everyone liked him, so feelings about my return were definitely mixed.

But in the boardroom the following day, the prevailing sentiment seemed to be united resolve. "We're in," was a repeated refrain. Nonetheless, I considered the fact that climbing a mountain is not for everyone. Some people would not have the fortitude for the kind of journey I needed them to embark on, or the skill to make tough, quick decisions. Others simply would not have the faith in the brand or in me.

* * *

Forty-five minutes later, at 1:30 p.m., I stood in front of more than 1,000 Starbucks partners who had crowded into the large communal space that spans our eighth and ninth floors, an area connected by an open staircase and brightened by skylights. The space is typically filled with pods of partners discussing business; now it was wall-to-wall with people gathered for an all-hands meeting—at Starbucks we call them open forums—that had been announced that morning, sparking curiosity throughout the building. The forum would be broadcast to our offices and roasting plants around the world.

I had no prepared speech, just an intuitive sense of what to say.

"Good afternoon," I began. "I'm sorry to have you all abruptly gather here in the middle of the day and interrupt your schedules, but I have an important announcement to make." The room was quiet except for shifting feet and the shuffling of latecomers arriving. "Yesterday, Starbucks' board of directors had a meeting in executive session, and in that meeting it was concluded that I would be coming back as chief executive officer." I paused and the abrupt sound of clapping filled the space, filling me with relief. "Thank you," I said, and broke into a wide grin. "You always wonder when you make an announcement like that what the reaction could have been." There were trickles of laughter as both the crowd and I relaxed.

My goal during the next 30 minutes was, in large part, to ensure that people understood that Starbucks' very survival was at stake, while at the same time helping them feel safe. I had to demonstrate my own confidence in the resiliency of our brand as well as my belief in our collective ability to rise above our own missteps. But beyond rhetorical cheerleading, I also discussed the plan I'd formulated.

First, of course, I acknowledged Jim.

* * *

The previous day at my home, Jim Donald found out that I would be coming back as ceo. Weekend meetings at my house were quite common, but asking colleagues to come there at the last minute was not something I did regularly. Still, despite the short notice, Jim readily agreed to come by without knowing why. When the bell rang, I opened the front door and we exchanged hellos and, while walking through the front hall, inquired about each other's family vacations. He followed me down the two steps into the living room, where we sat across from each other.

This scenario had repeatedly played out in my mind.

I knew what needed to be said: *The board has been closely monitoring what has been happening at the company and feels that under the circumstances, we must act to restore shareholder value. The board feels it is my obligation, as chairman and founder, to take direct responsibility for doing so, and returning as ceo is the most direct way for me to have the authority to make the needed changes and see them through.* More difficult to articulate given my inevitable discomfort with the situation would be my feelings. I wanted Jim to know how much I regretted that this conversation had to happen, that I think he is an exceptional professional and a wonderful man, and that I hoped he knew how deeply appreciated and liked he was throughout Starbucks. In the end, our conversation happened so quickly that I cannot recall the exact words I spoke to Jim before he looked at me with what I perceived as disappointment and surprise, accepted several legal documents that had been prepared for him, and left my house.

Saying good-bye to people when they leave Starbucks never gets easier, even when I think it is the right choice for the company, and especially when I truly respect the individual. If I share a friendship with the person beyond work, this kind of career-altering event pretty much severs our personal bond, a cost I have reluctantly come to accept but never fully reconciled. Of course, as difficult as this process is for me, it is undoubtedly worse for those who leave.

I went to the kitchen and made a fresh cup of coffee. Soon the Starbucks leadership team would arrive to hear the news.

* * *

"Let me first acknowledge and pay special tribute to Jim Donald, who will be leaving the company," I spoke into the microphone at the open forum. "It is very difficult and emotional when you have a business partner and a close friend who you work next to for five years, especially someone so well liked and admired, and for whom you have so much respect. Unfortunately, the business and responsibility we have is bigger than any one person—whether it's Jim or myself or anyone in this room. We have a greater responsibility to the 200,000 partners and their families and shareholders. And the board felt, and I agreed, that a change was really needed."

I'd conducted open forums throughout the world for two decades, and whether I spoke to hundreds of partners in Seattle or the staff of a single store in London, I usually had no script, just a general idea of what I wanted to say on that given day. Before I spoke, Wanda had asked me if I had talking points. I told her I didn't. I just wanted to speak honestly and share my own emotions and show that I truly understood what people were feeling. Everyone had to leave the forum believing that Starbucks would be okay, that I could lead us out of the quagmire. As I spoke, I strove to subordinate the company's problems to our collective ability to overcome them. Much more than just an announcement of new leadership, this open forum was my rallying cry:

If you're really honest with yourself, as I have tried to be with myself, along the way in building the company, there has been something we have lost. And it's no one's fault and there's no punishment or blame. We are what we are—but the question is, What are we going to do about it and how are we going to fix it?

I want to express to you that this is not an interim situation for me. And I will tell you as I told the board that I'm in this 100 percent. My passion. My commitment. This is the most important thing in my life other than my family. This is 25 years of my life, and I don't like what has happened.

It is not going to be good enough to go "back to the future," but there is a piece of that past we need; we have to find and bring the soul of our company back, find our voice.

Soon I'm going to share with the leadership team a restructuring of the organization, and I promise you I will do everything in my power to restore the company to the greatness we have known in the past. But understand that this is not a one-person job. We have to lock arms with one another and recommit ourselves to the things that are important.

The worst thing that could happen is that you spread out with fear and trepidation. That's not the purpose of this meeting—the purpose is to be honest and open that we have serious challenges, and we need serious people to help solve them. And I commit myself to being in the front of the line leading the way.

As I spoke, a flurry of internal and external communications was being unleashed. Just as the stock markets stopped trading for the day on the East Coast, our press release hit the newswires ("Starbucks Announces Strategic Initiatives to Increase Shareholder Value; Chairman Howard Schultz Returns as CEO") and a memo from me ("The Transformation of Starbucks") was e-mailed companywide. Simultaneously, the voice message that I'd prerecorded landed in every partner's voice mail and a letter to customers was posted on our website.

Meanwhile, Nancy and Tim Donlan—my other assistant, who first worked for Starbucks as a barista in 1991 and, like Nancy, is an invaluable asset to the company—sent dozens of international vice presidents and the regional organizations that operated our stores in other countries an invitation to join me for a conference call. Nancy sent another letter to a collection of individuals who were not formally connected to the company, but were considered friends and family. Also, on the eighth floor, Valerie O'Neil and her team were busy scheduling one-on-one interviews with journalists, responding to media requests, and answering the questions that were flooding in from news outlets.

Overall, the news we issued that day strove to balance humility about our missteps with self-assurance about our ability to self-correct.

The open forum ended as open forums always do, with an opportunity for partners to ask questions. Nothing was vetted beforehand, partners were free to broach any issue. I surveyed the crowd, and one person raised a hand. His question was not about Jim, me, or the impending restructuring or new strategies I'd touched on. His question was about another elephant in the room. Competitors.

That very day, *The Wall Street Journal* had run a front-page article about McDonald's move into the specialty coffee market and the effect it might have on Starbucks. At the time, only 800 McDonald's franchises in the United States served espresso-based beverages, and they were made by machines that automatically mixed espresso and milk. The offering would soon spread to all of its 14,000 US stores, accompanied by a sprawling, $100 million advertising campaign. McDonald's also had $1 billion in capital to reconfigure many of its stores into what it was calling McCafés.

Starbucks' ills were not the result of competitors of the likes of McDonald's or Dunkin' Donuts. Yet, as the economy continued to put pressure on consumer spending, McDonald's would no doubt capitalize on convenience and price. And despite what we perceived as the stark differences in the quality of our brewed coffee and espresso drinks—Starbucks sources and roasts its own beans in its own roasting plants, while McDonald's and Dunkin' Donuts outsource those processes—we could not ignore the fast-food chains.

I answered the question. "We have never had a major threat from a national company that has the resources, muscle, and commitment that McDonald's appears to have to coffee—and we have to get ready."

The one thing we could not and should not do was dismiss the ability of any competitor to capture our customers. It was going to be hand-to-hand combat as we tried our best to differentiate ourselves in the marketplace. "I strongly believe that if we protect, preserve, and enhance the experience to the point where we really demonstrate that the relationship we have with our customers is not based on a transaction, that we're not in the fast-food business, and then let the coffee speak for itself, we're going to win."

We also could not allow competition to define us. We had to play offense, proactively defining ourselves by sharing the full story of Starbucks' value proposition: Behind every cup of Starbucks is the world's highest-quality, ethically sourced coffee beans; baristas with health-care coverage and stock in the company; farmers who are treated fairly and humanely; a mission to treat all people with respect and dignity; and passionate coffee experts whose knowledge about coffee cannot be matched by any other coffee company.

"If we can't do all that," I concluded, "then shame on us and they deserve to take our business." I hoped that fear of a company like McDonald's could actually motivate the organization, giving us something to fight against, someone else to point to, instead of just ourselves.

A bit to my surprise, there were no other questions and so I wrapped up the forum with a heartfelt thanks and a final emotional boost. "We earned our respect and recognition because of one reason: the quality of our people. Thank you for all you've done in contributing to the success we have enjoyed. I ask that you do everything you can to support the new initiatives and help get this company back, find our voice, find our soul, and make our customers and partners proud to be associated with Starbucks."

There was a palpable, positive buzz in the air as I headed to a 2:30 p.m. conference call with financial analysts, a group that was sure to have no shortage of questions.

★ ★ ★

Unlike the enthusiasm I was experiencing at our support center in Seattle, I anticipated a high degree of cynicism from some of the analysts and institutional shareholders who covered the company; they would come to the call with a preordained view that Starbucks' cup was half empty given that our stock was down almost 50 percent in the past year.

As I saw it, Starbucks had three primary constituencies: partners, customers, and shareholders, in that order, which is not to say that investors are third in order of importance. But to achieve long-term value for shareholders, a company must, in my view, first create value for its employees as well as its customers. Unfortunately, Wall Street does not always see it the same way and too often treats long-term investments as short-term dilution, bringing down the company's value. Adopting this mentality was, in large part, how Starbucks had become complicit with the Street: For the past two years in particular, we—and I say "we" because no one person had led the charge—chased the pace of growth by building stores as fast as we could rather than investing in sustainable growth opportunities. The top line grew fast, but in a way that, for a variety of reasons, was impossible to sustain, especially when combined with the macrofactor of a tightening economy.

In the conversation with the financial community, I had to be careful not to perform as a salesman. I would not overpromise, but rather would be realistic about the problems at hand and that they would take time to fix. I was not coming back with a solution up my sleeve, but a road map and commitment in my heart to create long-term value.

For about an hour, I fielded queries from financial institutions whose influence had the power to raise or lower Starbucks' value.

"Your [business] started to slow around the same time as other retailers'," said Sharon Zackfia of William Blair and Company. "How do you try to disaggregate what's economic versus self-inflicted . . . and what do you think you have in your arsenal to protect the company [from the economy] going forward?" Few brands would be immune from the impending economic downturn. Consumer confidence had been declining since July, except for a slight rise in December after hitting a two-year low that November. I told Sharon—as well as everyone else on the call, which also included partners, customers, and the media—that I would not use the economy as an excuse and that we would fight the economic headwinds and rising commodity prices by reinvigorating customers' attachment to our brand and creating highly relevant new products.

David Palmer from UBS asked if our new-product pipeline had some "triples or home runs" in it. "It seems like it's been a while since your innovation has resonated," he said. David was right. During the past five-plus years, our new product offerings either had nothing to do with coffee or were simply line extensions rather than exciting ideas that had significant impact, such as Frappuccino and the Starbucks Card. I responded with what I believed to be true. "What we have to do [now] is bring new opportunities to the marketplace that are consistent with the heritage of the company." I stopped short of offering details about what was on my mind. But I was thinking of something very specific.

The billion-dollar question came from Joe Buckley of Bear Stearns, who essentially asked how we planned to grow the company at the same pace it had grown at in the recent past—20 percent top-line growth as a public company for 15 years—especially since we were going to slow new store openings in the United States. I did not have a specific, tactical answer for Joe that day. I had not come back as ceo with some silver bullet that would restore the company's value. But I had come back with a navigational framework for how we were going to do it. And faith. But Wall Street doesn't buy faith.

"It's very strange to hear about so much change and not have it financially dimensionalized at all," countered Deutsche Bank's Marc Greenberg. "What can investors, after hearing this call, really sink their teeth into? What about margins, profits, costs, improved returns? We're numbers guys, and you're not giving us any numbers." Because Starbucks was in the so-called quiet period of the quarter—we were restricted in what information we could say publicly—there were limitations on how much detail we could provide before we announced fiscal first-quarter earnings on January 30:

Let me try in my own way to answer this. I've been here more than 25 years. I've seen every aspect of the growth and development of the company, and I am dissatisfied, perhaps more than anyone else on this call, with where we sit today. I have as much at stake personally, as well as my own reputation. . . .

I am here to say that I'm making a commitment and a promise that we are going to do everything we can to make sure that the relationship we have with you, from a financial standpoint, is one in which you will be a proud shareholder of the company and recognize that we're making the right strategic decisions over the long term and going to take decisive action to put in place those things that have not been done before.

Had I polled the analysts that day about how they felt about Starbucks and me after the call, I would venture to say that most of them did not come away believers. In the end, my words to them didn't really matter. The financial community only cared about how we executed and performed in the months and years to come. They are numbers people and they wanted numbers, and I was intent on delivering. But it would take time.

In contrast, my words to Starbucks' partners that day did matter because they gave them confidence, the fuel required to execute and perform.

* * *

Every communication Starbucks issued that day—the press release, the companywide memo and voice mail, conversations with partners, journalists, and Wall Street—included three strategic initiatives that Starbucks would immediately undertake. I had come up with them during my time in Hawaii over the holidays, when I'd had time to plan.

First, Starbucks had to *improve the current state of its US retail business.* This was our burning platform. The US stores provide the bulk of the revenues for the entire business, approximately 70 percent in 2007. Plus, their performance molds perception around the world. We are a global brand, and what happens in the States never stays in the States. We needed to be more cognizant of that fact and to act swiftly to deliver flawless execution and improve economics at the store level. To do that, we would immediately slow the rapid-fire pace of new store openings. We would also evaluate and then close underperforming locations. This was dramatic. Never before had Starbucks closed more than a handful of stores.

My second strategic emphasis was less tangible than the first but equally vital: We would *reignite the emotional attachment with customers.* Unlike other retailers that sold coffee, the equity of Starbucks' brand was steeped in the unique experience customers have from the moment they walk into a store. The aroma. The sense of community. The familial relationships customers establish with their local baristas. And the pride they feel knowing that their purchases support our high standards and socially responsible practices. Reinvigorating the Starbucks Experience could provide the meaningful differentiation that would separate us from competitors.

Third, we would immediately begin to *make long-term changes to the foundation of our business*, closely reexamining our organizational structure, including our leaders, and digging into operations, revamping in ways that would significantly reduce costs and improve customer service. Everything from information technology—Starbucks' antiquated checkout system in stores dated back to the early 1990s—to our bloated supply chain was ripe for overhaul. The only sacred cows, the two elements I'd refuse to strip from the company no matter how much others pushed me, were our employee health-care program and the quality of our coffee.

These three strategic pillars were not definitive keys to success, but rather a near-term navigational blueprint from which a more comprehensive, easy-to-understand Transformation Agenda would soon take shape. The pillars also gave meat to the announcement of my return as ceo, positioning the move as far more than just a transfer of power—it was the serious first step in the company's holistic restoration.

* * *

The day had flown by, and before I knew it the sky outside my office was dark with the Northwest winter's early nightfall.

I spent the final hours at work talking to journalists and partners and reading e-mails that had begun to come in. I was pleased to see congratulatory notes from shareholders and comforted by sentiments of support from friends and other CEOs. One e-mail included that iconic photo of James Dean walking in a rainy Times Square. "It's going to be lonely in the rain for a while, but you can make it," a friend who understood this particular reality of leadership wrote. That type of encouragement meant a lot to me.

Most of all, I liked reading the e-mails from Starbucks partners. Many welcomed me back, but not blindly, and were quite pointed in acknowledging the company's problems and my responsibility to address them.

Sandi Torrente, a regional coordinator in South Florida, wrote:

I am an eight-year partner who started as a barista and this has been a tough year. I have always loved my job, but this year, not so much! I watched tenured partners leave the company and my optimism has been whittling away. I know how hard our partners in the stores work. We would not have a job if it were not for them. But it saddens me when I walk into our stores and don't receive legendary service or a greeting. It is not the fault of the baristas working behind the counter. It is the responsibility of the leadership team to keep our culture alive, growing and thriving.

It will be a long hard road back; I am proud to count myself among those willing to do whatever it takes. Thank you for providing me with an uplifting day!

That evening I drove home alone.

Passing the city's massive, hollow stadiums and rows of sleeping railcars, I felt humbled but also energized. Eager to get started. I'd had so much time before January to get my head around what needed to happen upon my return that I wasn't nervous, but instead antsy to act. Like a player who'd finally come off the bench, I was hungry to win, confident that we would, and grateful to no longer be so alone in that conviction.

Chapter 9

A New Way
to See

Feeling somewhat skeptical, I entered
the large event space of Seattle's Palace
Ballroom for a three-day brainstorming
retreat being conducted by a consulting
firm from San Francisco. Historically,
I was not a fan of business consultants.
Rarely had I looked to outsiders to tell
Starbucks what Starbucks needed.

It was only weeks after I'd returned as ceo, and as I walked into the hotel's ballroom someone handed me a black Sharpie, a white iPod, and a packet of index cards. Instead of the murmur of small talk I was expecting, the dozen or so people already in the room, most wearing jeans and sweaters, were hushed. Following instructions, I clipped the iPod to my belt and put the earphones on. The familiar rhythm of "Come Together" was a jolt of joy on the chilly January morning. *Interesting*, I thought, and made my way to a large table covered with what looked to be a collage of posters. Familiar faces hovered over the table, each listening to his or her own music and scribbling notes on the cards. I leaned over to see what was so engrossing them.

A Hard Day's Night.

Yellow Submarine.

Abbey Road.

Meet the Beatles!

Laying across the table were enlargements of more than a dozen bright album covers and photos from The Beatles' remarkable career, which spanned a decade as well as musical genres. For the second time that morning I was pleasantly surprised. I looked down and read what was written on one of the cards I'd been given: "What does it mean to reinvent an icon?"

Wow. There could not have been a more apt question for Starbucks at this juncture in our existence. And I was not sure I knew the answer.

* * *

On my second day back as ceo, Starbucks' stock jumped 8 percent from the previous day, to $19.86. The media coverage, in a reprise of its reaction to the leaked memo, was a circus of opinions and speculation about what lay ahead for the world's largest coffee company now that its founder had retaken the reins. A *BusinessWeek* story headlined "Howard Schultz's Grande Challenge" noted that, while a returning founder has more freedom to play with the formula, nostalgia can also be dangerous. True, I thought. When the *Financial Times* asked other business leaders what our management change meant for our strategy, one banker I had never heard of chimed in that I might reposition the company for sale to a larger entity. That was way off. Selling the company was absolutely, positively the last thing I ever wanted. Ever.

In Herb Greenberg's column on Dow Jones' *MarketWatch*, the oft-quoted Yale School of Management professor Jeffrey Sonnenfeld opined on the three qualities of returning CEOs who are ultimately successful. First, he said, they come back reluctantly, with no intention of undermining the sitting leader. Second, even though their reputations may be at stake, they aren't trying to fulfill some unmet ego need. And third, according to Sonnenfeld, effective second-time CEOs recognize that what they built the first time was not a religion. They accept that change is inevitable. The column also recalled companies whose former CEOs had triumphed after returning to their posts, such as Steve Jobs of Apple and Charles Schwab, as well as chiefs whose comebacks did not go so well, like Gateway's Ted Waitt and Xerox's Paul Allaire.

Which kind would I be?

That was the overriding question—for all of us.

Aside from perusing a daily summary of news to take the temperature of the marketplace and Wall Street, I didn't spend much time reading the omnipresent coverage that followed Starbucks like lint. Not only do I hate reading about myself, but also there simply was too much for me to do.

In fact, almost immediately, my work habits shifted as my level of discipline heightened. I could no longer be as freewheeling with my daily schedule, especially as I learned just how deep Starbucks' internal problems went. I began spending quiet time alone early in the morning, either at home or at the office, preparing for the day, something I had not done as chairman or in my previous years as chief executive. Now, after skimming the news before 6 a.m., I'd make calls to our overseas offices, read e-mails from partners—hundreds were streaming in with suggestions and observations about the business—and then sit back to consider what I needed to do that day to be as productive as possible and have the most impact on the business. I asked Nancy to be very discriminating with my schedule, and it helped that I'd shed outside distractions, such as my corporate board positions.

By 7 a.m. for the first two weeks in January, I welcomed one or more senior leaders into my office or the boardroom where, using the three transformational pillars as a guide, we decided the company's most immediate next steps.

One of the first organizational changes I'd made was appointing the equivalent of a chief of staff, someone who would work closely with me to craft our vision and a more comprehensive, long-term Transformation Agenda. The person I turned to was Michelle Gass, a 12-year Starbucks partner who at the time also happened to be the youngest member of the leadership team. An engineer by training, Michelle is an energetic, hard-charging, creative leader who embraces risk and bold thinking as well as details. In the 1990s, she led the strategy that took Frappuccino from a two-flavor product to a $2 billion brand platform.

I had a lot of confidence in Michelle's analytical thinking and recognized in her a rare duality: an embodiment of the values of our culture and a fierce, quantitative understanding of the world. Plus, she did not shy away from respectfully disagreeing with me.

Prior to announcing Michelle's new role, I'd asked for her input on my first draft of the Transformation Agenda—again, the three pillars—and 24 hours later, she had come to my office with solid suggestions. A few days later, we brought others into the planning process, and for the first time in a long while, Starbucks' leaders debated, disagreed, and occasionally laughed as we envisioned a future that involved much more than opening new stores.

We had a delicate balance to strike.

A balance between heritage and innovation.

Between meaningful tradition and modern-day relevance.

What elements about Starbucks, we asked ourselves, are ritual and what elements are merely habits? Not everything required overhauling or needed to be discarded. But what, specifically, had to go, such as the movie promotions, and what was core to our soul, like healthcare coverage, Bean Stock—our term for the equity in the company that we gave our partners—and ethically supporting our coffee farmers? Before we could challenge the status quo, my colleagues and I had to see it in new ways, reframe our existing ideas, and move beyond self-imposed constraints to imagine new possibilities.

Before we began the tough work of defining Starbucks' future, we had to spend time just *seeing*.

To help us, I asked Michelle to organize an off-site retreat to flush us out of our familiar spaces and help us freely consider how we had lost our way, and then embark upon fresh thinking. To lead the retreat, Michelle suggested we look for someone outside Starbucks, and she asked me to interview SY Partners, a consultancy that Howard Behar had recommended and that Michelle had already vetted.

"They're different," Michelle promised as I raised an eyebrow. But, in the spirit of being open to new ideas, I agreed, and a few days later the firm's founders, Susan Schuman and Keith Yamashita, flew to Seattle with their colleague David Glickman.

"Put down your pens. Don't take notes. Just listen," I instructed after we shook hands. Then I summarized for them the past year at Starbucks, from the leaked memo to my gut instinct that the company had to get back to its core in a way that also embraced change and renewal. "I want to convene a summit not just for our top executives, but also 20 or so people with different histories that can enrich our perspective." I told them the meeting was about much more than making money or putting bandages on old wounds. We needed to rediscover who we were and imagine who we could be.

The discussion that followed was intriguing, not the PowerPoint presentation or jargon-laced dialogue I'd anticipated. Susan, Keith, and David asked probing, thought-provoking questions, and as they told me stories of various clients—Nike, Gap, Procter & Gamble— they spoke Starbucks' language, from the word "partner" in their company's name to their philosophy: "See. Believe. Think. Act."

I was impressed, enough to override my long-held bias. If Starbucks was going to bring in strategic consultants, SYPartners seemed to be the firm for us. My ultimate decision to hire them was greatly influenced by my confidence in Michelle.

"Let's give it a shot," I conceded, having no idea what to expect given that they had only a few days to organize the retreat.

*　*　*

The iPods were put away, and we sat in chairs around a sea of Beatles' posters that had been spread out on the floor. The group included members of the leadership team as well as a select group of diverse voices from throughout the company. There were also a few people from outside the company whose ideas I respected.

Another question was posed: "What did John, Paul, George, and Ringo teach us about the art of reinvention?"

Everyone was deep in thought, but playfully so. The meeting had begun on such a sensory note with the music, the effervescent posters, even the writing with pens instead of keyboards, that it immediately transported our minds to a different place, in some cases back in time. Cliff Burrows, a Brit and seven-year partner and our regional president for Europe, the Middle East, and Asia, had flown in from Amsterdam to be here at my personal request. Tall and lean in a crisp white-collared shirt, Cliff enthusiastically held up a poster of a brick building splashed with a psychedelic painting, his eyes dancing behind rimless glasses. "This building is on Baker Street, only two blocks from my old home in London and near the Starbucks where I would stop on my way to work every morning."

While it would have been audacious for any of us to compare Starbucks' cultural impact to that of The Beatles, one thing was clear from comments like Cliff's: Both are icons that play memorable roles in people's lives.

Others piped up with observations about The Beatles' career.

"The band took risks," someone said.

"They took us on a journey at a time when the world needed cultural leaders."

"They didn't compromise."

"They led with their hearts."

"The Beatles believed. And if you believe, you can change anything."

"They kept reinventing themselves, but at the same time they stayed true to their music," I offered, recalling their 1967 album *Sgt. Pepper's Lonely Hearts Club Band.*

Using The Beatles as a metaphor for an iconic brand was, I thought, brilliant. It swept us into a creative process, providing fresh context for us to examine and speak about ourselves and the company. Most of us were enthused (although I noticed a few who were lost or rolling their eyes at the exercise), and, like Cliff, we got up out of our seats and walked across the posters to pick up our favorites.

We considered other brands that had also evolved, some radically, but had still preserved their stature, some even after taking a hit. Brands such as Apple, Gucci, Mini Cooper. Even New York City. Then, with guidance from SYPartners, we looked for parallels that could inform Starbucks' own challenges and touched on several themes.

- **Icons make sense of the tension of the times, offering hope and even mending a culture in turmoil, much as The Beatles did for my generation in the 1960s.** In what ways could Starbucks help bridge the political divides, environmental concerns, and economic uncertainties that were sweeping the country, particularly during a tumultuous election year in the United States and a recession that seemed inevitable?

- **Icons assert a "cultural authority," helping to frame the way people view the times they live in.** How was the concept of "community" changing, online and offline, and how did we want to react to it—or drive it?

- **Icons don't confuse history with heritage, and always protect and project their values.** How could Starbucks continue to grow through the lens of ethical behavior, global responsibility, and human connection?

- **Icons disrupt themselves before others disrupt them.** With competitors and critics breathing down our necks as never before, how could we tell our story, reassert our coffee authority, and perhaps change the industry—again?

- **Enduring icons are willing to sacrifice near-term popularity for longer-term relevance.** For Starbucks, that would mean making tough choices and experimenting with new concepts at the risk of ridicule.

These were profound questions that could not be answered that day, but at least they were being planted in our brains. I suggested something to the group as ideas began to percolate. "The only filters to our thinking should be: Will it make our people proud? Will this make the customer experience better? And will this enhance Starbucks in the minds and hearts of our customers?"

Those questions, I figured, provided focus, but left lots of room for creativity.

★ ★ ★

In those early days after I returned, as we talked long-term strategy, we also focused on tactics. Real actions that would yield visible results, and fast. The company had already announced that it would slow US store openings, close some stores, and accelerate growth in other countries. But we also needed to innovate and dramatically improve the in-store experience. A number of projects were already in the pipeline and, if pushed to completion and positioned right, held a great deal of potential.

In my head I knew that no silver bullet would transform Starbucks overnight, but in my heart I was on the lookout for a big idea—What would be the next Frappuccino, the most successful new product in Starbucks' history?—that would solve our problems. In truth, I was also impatient, a weakness I needed to curb.

Yet there was another reason to insist on immediate, tangible improvements to the business. The annual Starbucks shareholders' meeting loomed. On March 19, less than two months away, more than 6,000 investors and partners would pack Marion Oliver McCaw Hall, Seattle's grand arts auditorium nestled near the towering Space Needle, and the nearby pavilions we use for overflow. For the first time in our 15 years as a public company, many people in attendance would not be happy with Starbucks' performance. Nor should they have been.

Rather than apologize for the past, I viewed the 2008 annual meeting as a chance to move us forward. It would be a seminal event, an unparalleled moment with tremendous potential to reassure shareholders and partners that Starbucks was committed to—and, more importantly, already embarking on—real change. As ceo I would host the two-hour presentation, and secretly I was a bit worried about what the reaction would be when I stepped onstage to face thousands of people whose investments had lost almost half of their value in the past 14 months. Would they welcome me back? Would they boo? Anything was possible.

My instinct was to take as much control of the situation as possible by infusing the meeting with honesty and optimism. To do so, I would need to deliver more than a compelling speech and a business plan. I would need proof of our progress.

At the same time that I was working with others to imagine the company's future, I was also meeting with people in our operations, financial, partner resources, supply chain, and real estate departments to address our mistakes of the past. In those meetings, I more fully realized not only that I'd have to significantly change the makeup of our leadership team, but also that there were myriad questions that needed to be answered. What were the stores' trending unit economics, our term for the financial performance of individual stores? Exactly how many stores were underperforming, why, and where? How many stores could we open, and in which markets, without risking further cannibalization? How far was our supply chain operation being stretched? Where were we spending more money than necessary to achieve the same or better results? Did we have the right people with the right skills in place for everything that needed attention?

Perhaps the most important step in improving the faltering US business was to reengage our partners, especially those on the front lines: our baristas and store managers. They are the true ambassadors of our brand, the real merchants of romance and theater, and as such the primary catalysts for delighting customers. Starbucks desperately needed baristas and managers to be genuinely friendly, enthusiastic, and willing to go the extra mile millions of times a week.

Unfortunately, I continued to learn via e-mails from people in the field and through my own observations that many of our retail partners were unmotivated and uninformed about our coffee and the company. Our turnover rates in stores were too high, and a new generation of baristas had not been effectively trained or inspired by Starbucks' mission. It was not their fault. New hires were often handed a thick, three-ring binder of rules, techniques, and coffee information and simply told to "read it." Employee reviews and pay raises could be inconsistent, and the scheduling of shifts was also inefficient, sometimes burdening one employee with the work of several. For some, being a barista was just a job.

Part of the problem was that we did not have the proper incentives or the right in-store technology to help store managers operate like owners, taking more control over their stores' destiny. Because we were opening new stores so fast, a barista could easily have a new manager every few months. Much too much inconsistency. In addition, our compensation and benefit plans, while generous compared to almost any other retailer, no longer rang revolutionary. Reinventing compensation and benefits for a 21st-century retail organization, and for a younger generation, was crucial. Unfortunately it would take time, likely more than a year, to put in place meaningful new programs.

In the near term, however, we had to do something to inspire and improve performance.

I made two quick decisions.

First, we would retrain 135,000 baristas in espresso beverage preparation, from pouring a perfect shot to properly steaming milk. And we would do it before the annual meeting. I had long maintained that our training was inadequate, and giving baristas more tools and knowledge to do their jobs well would improve the experience for them as well as customers. I asked a team to figure out how the company could take on such a large task in a matter of weeks, and they came back to me with the radical idea of closing all of our US stores on one day. Espresso Excellence Training was set in motion, and on January 11 we issued a press release announcing that, on February 26, we would close stores for a "historic in-store education and training event." Rather than trying to hide our deficiencies and teach people in private, we publicly celebrated espresso, loudly asserting our coffee authority.

Second, I committed to hosting a 2008 leadership conference for our 8,000 US store managers and almost 2,000 more partners. Starbucks had a history of holding these mass meetings every few years in a different city as a way to inspire and reward our managers. But the company had not held one for several years. I did not know where we would hold the 2008 conference or how I would justify to Wall Street the millions of dollars it would undoubtedly cost, but I intuitively knew that such a massive gathering, if executed right, would infuse the people who managed our stores with the emotional capital they so desperately needed to reconnect with the company.

* * *

The first day of the brainstorming summit neared its end, but instead of sending us home or back to the office, we were split into smaller groups and sent out into various corners of the city to visit some of Seattle's most compelling homegrown retailers. Our assignment was to observe and report back on what we saw, heard, tasted, smelled, and felt. The merchant in me was hungry to explore.

In the Fremont neighborhood, Theo Chocolate is a cozy store connected to the company's only factory in a flat brick building. The smell of warm chocolate wafts through nearby streets, while factory tours and free candy bar tastings let customers experience confections like Coconut Curry and Vanilla Salted Caramel. Plus, Theo's status as the only organic, Fairtrade certified, bean-to-bar chocolate factory is inspiring to customers and a source of pride for the staff we met.

We also crowded into Top Pot Doughnuts, where a two-story, floor-to-ceiling wood bookcase, coupled with the shop's slogan, "hand-forged doughnuts," elevated sugary cake to a level beyond fast food.

And in Pike Place Market I ventured inside Beecher's Handmade Cheese, where founder Kurt Beecher Dammeier makes natural cheese on the premises. I love cheese, and chatted easily with an enthusiastic woman behind the counter. "How did you get to be such an expert on cheese?" I asked, and was floored when she told me that she had known nothing about the subject before she was hired—just six months earlier!

Leaving the cheese shop, which is located just yards away from the very first Starbucks, I couldn't help but think about our baristas. About how knowledge can breed passion. And about how our company had to do a much better job of sharing our coffee knowledge and communicating our mission. Pride in purpose would help give our partners a sense of ownership. These were not new insights, for me or for most of my colleagues, but revisiting them helped us—or at least it helped me—see our priorities more clearly. My eyes were wide open.

My thoughts wandered back to the iconic nature of The Beatles, as a band and as a brand. What courage they had had, staying true to their musical talents while maintaining relevance in the world. One reason I believed that the Starbucks brand would be resilient was because our founding values still resonated, perhaps now more than ever as anxiety and distrust seeped into the popular zeitgeist, and not just in the United States. In addition to our values, Starbucks' core product would also continue to be relevant. Coffee will never lose its romance. It will always bring people together and be part of conversations in every language, even as the conversations change. Coffee will forever connect.

Our ongoing challenge is to creatively nurture coffee's essence, keeping it personal despite our size. I do not want Starbucks to be defined solely by its thousands of stores or millions of customers. More than our scale, the brand can and should be defined by the quality of its coffee as well as its values. Community. Connection. Respect. Dignity. Humor. Humanity. Accountability.

It is our mission to make sure the world sees us through those lenses.

* * *

The retreat did more than just spark creative thinking. It also took us to a new level of decisiveness. One thing in particular was absolutely clear to me: Starbucks had to advance its position as the undisputed coffee authority. Without great coffee, Starbucks had no reason to exist. In the weeks ahead, I would intensify our focus on coffee quality and innovation. Espresso Excellence Training was already in motion, and at the retreat we locked in on more specific initiatives that Starbucks could move forward with immediately, including projects already under way inside the company.

Two projects in particular intrigued me, but if they were to have a material impact, each needed to be seized, accelerated, and amplified, ideally in time to share with investors at the annual shareholders' meeting.

Chapter 10

Playing to Win

Starbucks' top coffee experts watched with bated breath as I tasted their newest coffee blend for the first time.

I put my nose to the cup and inhaled deeply before bringing the liquid to my lips. Next, in traditional coffee-tasting fashion, I made a loud slurping noise as the coffee sprayed across my palate. My eyes opened wide. The taste was significantly different from anything Starbucks had ever brought to market.

"It's smooth, like butter," I remarked. "Really balanced. Somewhat acidic and bright. Drinkable. Easy."

While the flavor was a bit light for my personal preference, I thought it was fantastic because of what the coffee represented: Starbucks' renewed effort to play to win as opposed to playing not to lose. For the past few years, Starbucks had been acting out of fear, mainly a fear of failure. So much of what the company had done was defensive, done to protect itself. Our primary goal had been to avoid missing our earnings projections rather than to actively engage our customers. As ceo, it was my job to reignite our partners' courage and to foster an aggressive desire to once again swing for the fences—as if our lives depended on winning.

This mentality had been ingrained in me as a kid.

Growing up on what was literally the wrong side of the tracks in Brooklyn, my afternoons and weekends were usually dedicated to playing sports. It was an era before video games. Before Wii and the Internet. A time when, from dawn until dusk, if kids weren't in school, they were at the school yard playing every kind of ball. Baseball. Basketball. Football. Punchball. Slapball. These were the games of my youth, and I took them quite seriously.

For the rough-and-tumble boys in my neighborhood, team sports were a chance, often our only one, to escape our cramped apartments and the stress of struggling families. Few kids would grow up and make it out of Canarsie, but every time I smacked a baseball high and clear across the asphalt yard and crossed home plate, or powered my way to a touchdown, passing boys who were bigger and stronger and faster than me, anything seemed possible. These neighborhood victories were among the few times I tasted glory and felt the potential of my life, and I always took big, bold swings. I wanted nothing less than a home run.

The coffee I had just sipped had the potential to be just that.

* * *

On any given day in a warehouse adjacent to one of Starbucks' five roasting plants, rows of 154-pound burlap bags are stacked floor to ceiling, waiting patiently. Inside each bag are hundreds of thousands of raw green coffee beans shipped by boat, plane, or truck from all over the world. Running my fingers over the sacks' thick, prickly fabric, I can still feel a twinge of amazement knowing that, not long before arriving at our door, the beans had been at a coffee farm in a remote village, perhaps on an island or atop a mountain.

No doubt about it. Coffee's journey from soil to cup is quite amazing.

Coffee beans come from a coffee cherry, a red-skinned fruit that, when ripe, is not much larger than a cranberry. Inside every cherry are two green coffee beans, each made up of hundreds of compounds whose composition—and potential flavor—varies based on where and how the cherry was grown. Harvest coffee atop a steep mountain in Latin America, for instance, and its friendly flavor is reminiscent of nuts or cocoa. Coffee grown in other regions can be more assertive, earthy, and herbal in the mouth.

Wherever the location, the best beans—the ones with enchantingly complex flavors and compelling characters, known as arabica—grow under some degree of stress, like high altitudes, intense heat, or long dry periods. Such harsh weather conditions can produce high-quality beans, but also fewer beans per tree. This makes arabica coffee more costly, which is why most mass coffee producers opt to buy cheaper robusta beans. Produced in more predictable and mild climates, robusta beans are less expensive because they deliver a higher yield per tree. But most robusta beans also taste harsh and rubbery, sort of like sucking on a pencil eraser.

In its almost 40-year history, Starbucks Coffee has never used a single pound of robusta beans in our products.

Once the cherries are picked by hand, one of two things happens. Their skin is either removed and the remaining fruit and bean are fermented, or thousands of cherries are laid out on concrete patios to dry naturally before their beans are extracted. Then, prior to being packed in sacks, our coffee experts taste, or "cup," small batches of coffee to ensure that their flavor meets our standards.

Only 3 percent of the world's highest-quality arabica beans are good enough to make it into one of our burlap bags.

* * *

While most companies have access to the same high-quality arabica beans that Starbucks insists on purchasing, it is what happens to beans after they are harvested that further sets coffee companies apart from one another. No organization has the same combination of original technology and knowledge as Starbucks, and thus none can match the uniqueness and consistency of the coffees that we roast, blend, and serve on a global scale.

Roasting coffee beans is a delicate process requiring a thoughtful, exacting balancing act of time and temperature. Any coffee producer that truly cares about quality has a roasting philosophy, and at Starbucks our philosophy is to roast every bean to its peak of flavor in a manner that extracts its maximum potential. This means Starbucks roasts beans for longer than most commercial roasters for a so-called Full City roast that pulls out the beans' honest richness, flavor, and acidity, or brightness.

Our professional roasters are constantly refining our roasting process. Over the years, they have customized our machines and developed proprietary software to help control and replicate their techniques. We take tremendous pride in knowing that no one in the coffee business has more control over the roasting process than Starbucks.

Like roasting, blending specialty coffee is also an art form, and our blenders' culinary talents are akin to those of master chefs. Most coffee companies mix different types of beans together as a way to mask inferior coffee, but Starbucks has always used blending as an opportunity to elevate coffees from different parts of the world. Sometimes, in order to capture each bean's peak flavor, we won't even roast different beans together; only after roasting do we combine them. And when beans from multiple regions are blended just right, they create a unique symphony of flavor that does not exist by itself.

By 2007 our dark roast and original blends had created legions of loyal fans, and most days our stores rotated their brewed coffee offerings so customers could experience different types. Unfortunately, as we eventually learned through market research, many people did not realize that our stores switched brewed coffees daily. So, if someone ordered a "tall drip" each morning on the way to work and the coffee tasted different every day, that person may have assumed our coffee was inconsistent. Other people thought Starbucks' coffee was too intense, especially compared to the lesser-quality coffees they'd grown up drinking in diners and restaurants or at home. This was a reason many longtime brewed-coffee drinkers in the United States perceived Starbucks' coffees as "burnt" instead of bold. But just as a master chef would not change the ingredients to his signature recipes if a few customers disliked them, Starbucks could not abandon what made Starbucks Starbucks: that signature *bold* experience.

Still, some people at Starbucks wanted to reconcile our taste standards with consumers' perception of inconsistency and the fact that Starbucks' coffee did not appeal to every palate. The need to address this issue took on new urgency when, in 2007, a *Consumer Reports* taste test rated Starbucks' coffee behind McDonald's. I was not the only one stunned. How could an organization that goes to such lengths to procure and produce high-quality coffee be bested by a fast-food chain?

In the fall of 2007, our coffee and marketing departments went out and conducted their own taste tests to gain a definitive understanding of what many consumers really wanted in lieu of a bold brew—not what we assumed they wanted, which was a weak, inferior coffee. What we heard, what many people told us, was that they wanted Starbucks to sell a more consistent, balanced brewed coffee. Every day. Some of our partners became convinced that we could deliver without compromising our brand.

Not all of our partners agreed. Many coffee purists—as well as partners who had come to appreciate the special nuances of a darker roast—worried that selling a milder roast was kowtowing to inferior competitors, diluting our brand. Yet no one could deny that Starbucks was losing potential customers. The time had come to create a coffee with the right balance—and then hit it out of the park.

In November 2007, a team of coffee and roasting experts, led by Andrew Linnemann, one of our most talented master blenders, wiped their schedules clean and buckled down to develop a more well-rounded blend. They dug deep, taking all of their passion and knowledge, and, using Starbucks' roasting technology, tried to create a unique blend that was bold and authentic, yet more approachable. A smoother taste that a population of brewed-coffee drinkers would embrace *and* that was worthy of our heritage. A coffee Starbucks would be proud to serve. As Andrew would say, "The more you know, the better your technology, the more you can tweak." He fervently believed that no other coffee company had the capability to achieve the balanced flavor profile his team was after—and then replicate it worldwide. A brewed coffee our customers could count on day after day.

The project's code name was Consistent Brew.

They'd set up camp in the tasting room across from my office on the eighth floor, and through the room's large viewing window anyone could stop and watch their trials. For two weeks, shot glasses were lined up along countertops as our tasters blended, roasted, cupped, and commented on sample after sample. Their first coffees used beans from Colombia, Guatemala, and Sumatra, which they roasted at a combination of temperatures to discover the perfect match between time and heat, a relationship called the roast curve. During the first two weeks, the team created more than a dozen combinations.

Some were too tart or sour.

Others metallic or aggressive, papery or acidic.

By the end of the month, after experimenting with almost 30 recipes and roast curves, most had been eliminated.

Then, in a consumer taste test on December 3, one sample stood out as superior. Consistent Brew 19 was round, smooth, and balanced and exhibited a mild, sweet finish. Jackpot . . . almost. It was not yet perfect, so throughout the 2007 holiday season, right up until New Year's Eve, the team roasted Consistent Brew 19 again and again and again.

Finally, in January 2008, they hit the mark with a flavor profile that did not abandon Starbucks' roasting philosophy but, whether it was served black or with cream and sugar, delighted more people's palates. The winning blend was balanced but rich in flavor.

We named it Pike Place Roast, after our first store. I thought the name should be as symbolic as the coffee. In theory as well as in flavor, Pike Place Roast was a nod to our past while embracing our future. It was one of the most transformative blends we had ever created, in part because it spoke to an audience that had yet to become part of the Starbucks community. And we were excited to welcome them.

Our challenge, however, was to elevate Pike Place Roast so it would not be perceived as just another new product. No, Pike Place had to come out of the gate screaming not only that it was a new brew, but also that Starbucks was back and dead serious about recapturing our coffee authority.

We positioned Pike Place Roast as nothing less than our reinvention of brewed coffee, and to further back up that claim we did indeed reinvent our brewed experience.

Once again we would grind beans in our stores, a ritual we'd abandoned in order to serve customers more quickly. Now, in lieu of being ground at the plant and delivered to stores in sealed bags, all beans for brewed coffee would arrive whole and be scooped and ground by baristas. To further improve upon freshness, no more would batches of brewed coffee sit for up to an hour before being served. Thirty minutes was the new maximum "hold time." Any coffee that remained after half an hour was to be thrown out. Finally, to give customers the consistency they desired, Pike Place Roast—regular and decaffeinated—was to be the first brewed coffee we would offer every day, 365 days a year, always alongside a rotating bolder alternative.

These were significant changes that were sure to jolt our operations in ways that we could prepare for but not fully predict. Our roasting plants needed to adopt Pike Place's new roasting technique. Our supply chain had to establish a new system for packing and delivering whole beans, and our baristas needed to be trained how to scoop, grind, and introduce customers to the new roast, effectively communicating its special qualities. Meanwhile, the marketing and communications department had to coordinate a coast-to-coast coffee-tasting campaign for the scheduled launch day, April 8, 2008. We only had a matter of months, and our partners went to work to deliver on their respective mandates.

Losing was not an option.

Strategically, Pike Place Roast had the potential to be a powerful catalyst for and symbol of our transformation. For partners, the new brew was an accomplishment, the first in a while, to rally around, savor, and celebrate. For customers, Pike Place Roast ushered back in some of what had been missing in our coffee experience. Aroma. Freshness. A little theater. And for shareholders, Pike Place would be proof that the company was actively reclaiming its coffee authority.

I was determined to demonstrate to our partners that Starbucks was going to push for self-renewal and reinvention. Pike Place Roast was just the beginning.

Chapter 11

Elevating the Core

"You would have to agree that the consumer is in a recession," I stated on the afternoon of January 30, 2008, during Starbucks' first-quarter earnings conference call.

I had seen this difficult day coming since the end of December and now, as I sat at the head of our boardroom conference table having returned only three weeks before as ceo, I mustered optimism in the face of so much discontent.

Only 1 percent. That was how little our same-store sales—that all-too-important measure of retail success—had gone up by in the first three months of our fiscal year. *One percent* after 16 years of 5 percent or better comps. It was Starbucks' worst performance since the company went public in 1992. At the office, my personal frustration was fueling my desire to put Starbucks back on top, yet every day brought new challenges. I felt as if the team and I were racing to fix a sinking ship while at the same time charting its course and setting sail. And it didn't help that the economic waters were getting rougher.

Outside our walls, seemingly fail-proof financial institutions were doing what had seemed impossible: failing. Amid staggering losses, America's largest mortgage lender, Countrywide Financial, was being taken over by Bank of America in a risky $4 billion deal. On January 15, banking giant Citigroup posted the largest quarterly loss in history, a staggering $9.8 billion. Less than a week later, stocks had their biggest one-day loss in six years. These and other daunting trends—the tightening credit crunch, foreclosures, rising food and gas prices, an uptick in unemployment—fostered more uncertainty. Consumer confidence continued to slide and people started limiting spending to essentials.

Starbucks was hardly the only retailer suffering. Home Depot was closing locations. Sales had crumbled at high-end department stores like Nordstrom. Even consumer favorites Target and Wal-Mart posted lower than expected same-store sales.

In addition to Starbucks' disappointing comps, I was about to make two unexpected announcements on the earnings call—news that was sure to alienate customers as well as investors.

The first was a choice I had made unilaterally.

"By the end of fiscal 2008, we will discontinue warm breakfast sandwiches in our North American stores," I said into the speakerphone somewhat triumphantly. This was, after all, a move I had wanted to make for more than a year but had been unable to bring about as chairman. Despite the sandwiches' loyal following, and disagreement among Starbucks' top managers, I was convinced that this was right for the business. "We are committed to a replacement category," I reassured the analysts who asked about the sandwiches' impact on sales, which was about 3 percent per store for the 3,700 stores that sold them.

The second unanticipated announcement that day was even more contentious, at least among the financial community: Starbucks, I said, would no longer report its same-store sales. Our comps would no longer be made public. Had the analysts not had their phones on mute until they wanted to speak, I likely would have heard a collective groan, not to mention a few four-letter words, of irritation.

"I would really love to know," asked David Palmer of investment bank UBS, not mincing his words, "why you think it would help your stock, the company, investors, or anybody to remove disclosure at a time like this?"

I agreed with David that comps were an appropriate measure for gauging a retailer's health. But for Starbucks, comps did not take into account the company's revenues from packaged whole-bean coffee in grocery stores or beverage sales at thousands of our licensed store-within-a-store counters in supermarkets and bookstores and in airports. This gap did not matter much during times when our stores were thriving, but if our US comp store sales continued to decline, we would not get any credit for sales in other venues.

But there was an even more important reason that I chose to eliminate comps from our quarterly reporting. They were a dangerous enemy in the battle to transform the company. We'd had almost 200 straight months of positive comps, unheard-of momentum in retail. And as we grew at a faster and faster clip during 2006 and 2007, maintaining that positive comp growth history drove poor business decisions that veered us away from our core.

The fruits of this "comp effect" could be seen in seemingly small details. Once, I walked into a store and was appalled by a proliferation of stuffed animals for sale. "What is this?" I asked the store manager in frustration, pointing to a pile of wide-eyed cuddly toys that had absolutely nothing to do with coffee. The manager didn't blink. "They're great for incremental sales and have a big gross margin." This was the type of mentality that had become pervasive. And dangerous.

Eliminating comps from the radar was my attempt to send a message to Starbucks' partners: We will transform the company internally by being true to our coffee core and by doing what will be best for customers, not what will boost comps.

The financial community was not pleased with this latest wrinkle because it made it more difficult to assess our present performance and predict Starbucks' future. Many assumed we were hiding. But contrary to perception, I was not trying to be arrogant or obtuse or slick. I was, however, attempting to establish new priorities inside the company.

Both decisions—eliminating the sandwiches and the comps—were worth risking public backlash. Especially the comps! It is difficult to overstate the seductive power that comps had come to have over the organization, quite literally becoming the reason to exist and overshadowing everything else. Releasing us from their shackles, especially at this very fragile stage of my return, demonstrated to our people that things really were changing, that "transformation" was not just a word I was throwing around. It was a grand gesture that freed everyone to enthusiastically focus on our coffee and our customers. And there was so much in that arena that demanded our immediate attention. In addition to the upcoming national launch of Pike Place Roast, I had elevated another internal coffee-related initiative that, at the time of the earnings announcement, was in a very private process of unfolding.

* * *

Back in March 2004, a young engineer in Seattle set out to improve how brewed coffee is made. Zander Nosler was 32 when he quit his job at an industrial design firm and asked investors to fund a dream. Zander wanted to invent a coffee machine that brewed the best cup of coffee possible—one that equaled the quality of a French press. Even more ambitious, the machine and the brewing process had to be enchanting, even beautiful, something worth watching and waiting for. It was a niche wide open for innovation.

Zander heard "no" many times before finding a few investors who believed in him. Together with his partner, Randy Hulett, a multitalented engineer who oversaw the small product development team, they built a lab in the back of a friend's woodworking shop in a garage in Ballard, one of Seattle's oldest, most eclectic neighborhoods, about six miles from Starbucks' support center. Together his team began to build a high-end machine. After several false starts, they had their prototype. Made out of particleboard and hoses, it was the reverse of a French press, with a plunger that pushed ground coffee up instead of down.

They named their machine the Clover brewer.

By 2007 the company had sold 150 Clovers, all handmade. With its creative mix of automation and manual attention, the sleek Clover machine was beloved by its customers, which were mostly small, independent coffeehouses. It began to amass a loving following.

* * *

I was with Sheri in New York City when I decided to do a round of impromptu pop-ins at independent coffeehouses I'd been hearing about. We jumped in a cab and hopped out on a tree-lined block, where we walked to a small shop with a charming wood and brick façade.

We ducked inside for a look.

The space had a bohemian feel and in general I was underwhelmed. But one thing did intrigue me. There was a long line of people waiting for brewed coffee that cost, according to the sign, up to $6 a cup. A tall brewed at Starbucks was $1.50. I decided to try it.

For me, the best way to brew coffee has always been in a French press. That was how I'd brewed it at home for 25 years. Unlike the drip method, where water passes over coffee grounds and drips through a filter, the coffee grounds in a press pot are continually steeped in water; the full immersion brings out a taste that just cannot be achieved with a drip brewer.

As I stood in line and waited my turn, I watched the barista. I did not recognize the machine she was using, but it was fascinating to watch as she weighed and ground the beans for each order and then poured the grounds into the top of a stainless steel, black-sided machine. A silver spout on top added hot water and then, like magic, the resulting grounds unexpectedly materialized atop the machine in a thick, precise, pancakelike formation. It was beautiful.

When it was my turn at the counter I ordered, watched, waited, and finally took a sip. I was stunned. This coffee was as rich and flavorful as coffee from my French press. Sparkling.

"What's the name of the machine?" I asked the barista.

She looked up at me as she prepared the next customer's cup. "Clover," she said, and went back to her work.

I walked outside and on my cell phone dialed our coffee department back in Seattle. "Who makes the Clover?" I wanted to know. Less than an hour later, I received an e-mail. Unbelievable. The machine was made by a company in Starbucks' own backyard.

I did not recall that I'd actually seen a Clover brewer in action, tasted its coffee, and met its inventor in mid–2007 as part of a demonstration at Starbucks. At the time, as Zander recalled, I told him that I had never tasted such a good cup of brewed coffee from a machine. About a month after that tasting, unbeknownst to me, Starbucks ordered one Clover and put it in one of our stores to test.

The next time I saw Zander was in his makeshift laboratory not long after I rediscovered Clover and only three weeks after I had returned as ceo.

This time when we met, I wanted Starbucks to acquire Clover.

It interested me for several reasons.

First and most important, Clover makes a terrific cup of brewed coffee. A cross between a French press and a vacuum pot, Clover sucks water through the bottom of finely ground coffee instead of pressing water through the top, using a very fine filter that lets the coffee retain its best-tasting oils. By no means did I see Clover as a replacement for our brewed coffee, but it would complement Pike Place Roast in our attempt to elevate coffee and the coffee experience. Nor was Clover a big revenue play to immediately spike sales. Rather, Clover would add depth to our menu, offering customers more options while supporting our mission to be the undisputed coffee authority.

Second, because of Clover's inventive engineering and graceful design, it treats brewed drinkers to a level of customization and personal attention that had, historically, been reserved for our espresso drinkers. When someone ordered a brewed beverage at Starbucks, our barista poured the already brewed coffee into a cup with his or her back to the customer and then handed the drink over at the register. For espresso beverages like lattes or cappuccinos, the experience is intrinsically more elaborate and personal: The barista pours the shot, steams the milk, and customizes the drink facing the customer, then announces the order and presents the beverage on a high, uncluttered counter, much like a stage. All in all, there was not much theater for the drip drinker.

Clover presented an opportunity to help solve that. Like an espresso machine but much more compact, a Clover could be positioned on a counter in front of customers, who could then watch the barista and the machine brew their coffee in a way they had never witnessed.

What's more, Clover's technology would allow us to serve more specialty, small-batch coffees whose complex flavors are often lost using traditional brewers.

Clover's quality and beauty not only were thrilling, but also posed a very real competitive threat, even at its premium price per cup—so much of a threat that I believed Starbucks needed to own it. Now.

* * *

I was a bit taken aback when I walked, alone, into the large garage that was home to the Coffee Equipment Company.

"Zander," I said, a smile on my face and a hand outstretched. A slight, soft-spoken young man in glasses smiled back and welcomed me. Although we had met before, I did not recognize him. (Throughout my years at Starbucks, I have always met so many new people in the course of even one day that, as much as I wish I could recall every face, it's almost impossible.) Zander and I chatted for a bit next to a few half-built Clover machines before walking to Brouwer's Café to eat lunch outside.

Listening to Zander, I was tremendously impressed. Here was an articulate, highly intelligent young man who is passionate about coffee and had educated himself about the industry. Respectfully, I told him why I had come. "Zander, we would like to acquire your company," I said. "I think Starbucks can offer you something that you'll be quite happy with." By "something" I was alluding to not just the purchase price, but also to the respect and opportunity Starbucks would give Zander, his team, and Clover.

It was obvious from his expression that selling was not in Zander's immediate plans.

"And what would we do with our current customers?" he asked me, clearly concerned.

"You'll have to take great care of them," I answered, knowing that, even if we bought Clover for Starbucks' own proprietary use, Clover's current coffeehouse customers could continue enjoying the machine.

"And what about our team? We have 11 employees."

I said they could come work for us and stay with Clover.

After a handshake, I left Ballard rejuvenated.

During the next month, I met with Zander several times to negotiate the broad strokes of the deal. Often it was just the two of us, across the table in my office or at my home, and with each meeting our mutual trust increased. It was important for me to stay closely involved with him. I never wanted Zander to regret trusting us, trusting me, with his dream.

Meanwhile, back at Starbucks, our senior vice president of global finance and business operations, Troy Alstead, and his financial team worked diligently on the nuances of the Clover acquisition. Troy had been with Starbucks for 15 years. He is not only extremely intelligent, possessing a keen understanding of our global business, but also an excellent communicator. When Troy speaks, he never hides behind accounting jargon or numbers. His integrity, knowledge, and personal style garner a high degree of trust.

Thanks in part to Troy's round-the-clock dedication and ability to work well with the young entrepreneurs we were acquiring, I had faith that the Clover deal would come together in a remarkably short period of time.

As for launching Clover machines in Starbucks stores, that was *not* something we would do at a rapid pace. In light of the country's receding consumer spending as well as Clover's manual manufacturing process, it would take time for Clover to realize its full potential inside Starbucks and for Starbucks to see the financial fruits of the marriage. But I was okay with that. More important, in my view, was the message of confidence that Clover's acquisition would send to partners, customers, and shareholders, reassuring everyone that Starbucks was once again committed to decisiveness and coffee innovation.

Chapter 12

Get In the Mud

I have long believed in the power of a word or a single phrase to effectively communicate a business imperative— and to inspire people. The best words are never big or complicated, but are packed with emotion and meaning, leaving no question of what I expect of myself and others.

Rarely in my career have I actively searched for the right words. They tend to find me, often in a poignant moment, maybe minutes before addressing a roomful of people; during an impassioned, unscripted speech; in a private conversation; or when sitting alone in my kitchen, drinking a cup of coffee. The concepts that my words convey may be strategic in their intent, but the words themselves are spontaneous manifestations of my love for Starbucks. I feel them before I voice them.

Mike Ullman, our lead director and an experienced CEO, has said that communication is always important, but it is even more essential when things are not working. Ensuring that communication is narrow, clear, and repetitive to set expectations wins people's trust. During this tumultuous period in Starbucks' history, what I said and how I said it was, I believe, key to tapping into our partners' passion, recapturing their faith, and redirecting their talents.

* * *

In any well-run retail business there is, by definition, a maniacal focus on details. Especially in the beginning. Young companies must produce results every day or risk closing their doors. Anything with the slightest potential to add or detract from sales or earnings—the quality of each item, every customer interaction, the attitude of each employee, every dollar spent—is attended to with steadfast concern.

In 2008 I felt very strongly that many of us at Starbucks had lost our attention to the details of our business. While there exist obvious limitations to what the leaders of a multibillion-dollar global organization can be expected to attend to, we had, as a group, strayed too far in the opposite direction. We had defaulted, for example, to talking about national or global comps and rapid expansion, and when our comps went up we assumed that individual parts of the business—distribution, partner resources, entire geographic regions—were also healthy.

Like a doctor who measures a patient's height and weight every year without checking blood pressure or heart rate, Starbucks was not diagnosing itself at a level of detail that would help ensure its long-term health. We predicated future success on how many stores we opened during a quarter instead of taking the time to determine whether each of those stores would, in fact, be profitable. We thought in terms of millions of customers and thousands of stores instead of one customer, one partner, and one cup of coffee at a time.

With such a mind-set, many little things dangerously slipped by unnoticed, or at least went unacknowledged. How could one imperfect cup of coffee, one unqualified manager, or one poorly located store matter when millions of cups of coffee were being served in tens of thousands of stores?

We forgot that "ones" add up.

Grounding our leaders as well as myself in a more disciplined, detail-oriented mind-set—down from the 30,000-foot view and way of thinking about the business—was one of my earliest challenges. It was all too easy to assume that an almost $10 billion company could not operate with the perspective of a single merchant fighting for its survival. But wasn't every Starbucks store a single merchant? *Yes*, was my position, and I was adamant that we should think of ourselves as such.

"When you start a business, you do not operate from a lofty place, because you cannot afford to," I explained to a roomful of our top leaders one day. "It is so vitally important that we get back to the roots of the business, that we get back in the mud," I declared spontaneously. "Get our hands in the mud!" I literally pleaded, holding my hands out in front of me. I held on to this analogy because it made so much sense, and from that day on I repeated it over and over and over, to people at every level.

In fact, one day when I was walking through the offices of Starbucks' architects and designers, I stopped in my tracks when a poster caught my eye. A pair of dirt-smudged hands, palms up, framed the words "The world belongs to the few people who are not afraid to get their hands dirty." I asked to borrow the poster and marched it to the eighth floor, where I placed it on the wall of our boardroom so Starbucks' executive team would see it every time we met.

The words—Get *dirty*. Get in the *mud*. Get back to the *roots of the business*—cascaded down through the organization. I think that people could relate to them at a visceral level and immediately understand what they had to do differently. Not that they always did it, but an expectation had been set.

* * *

Words, of course, in and of themselves are not enough. I also sensed that people inside the company needed to see and connect with me.

Often. I had to be accessible, almost ubiquitous, more than I'd ever been throughout my Starbucks career.

Showing up, listening to, and talking with Starbucks' partners was one way I got my own hands dirty.

One of the first things I did when I came back as ceo was invite people to e-mail me directly, and in my first month I received about 5,600 e-mails. I personally responded to as many as time allowed. Sometimes, instead of sending e-mails, I would call Starbucks partners throughout the country to respond to their notes or just ask how they were doing, and more than once I had to convince the person I had dialed that, yes, it really *was* me on the phone. I also visited our stores and our roasting plants, and almost daily I made a point of walking the floors of our home office, up and down the stairs multiple times, saying hello to people working at their desks, often stopping to chat.

To more formally involve our partners, I reinstated regularly scheduled open forums. Similar to a town hall meeting, an open forum has always been an opportunity for partners to hear directly from me or other senior leaders, especially on the heels of major public announcements. Our open forums are brief and unscripted, and anyone can ask any question with no fear of retribution. They bring all of us together face-to-face, which helps to establish some of the emotional connection lacking in phone calls and e-mails. Over the years, our forums have yielded creative tension and critical feedback, which is good for the organization. But in the past two years, open forums had become less frequent. Now they were back, at least once a quarter.

Whether I was in front of one person or thousands, I remained extremely conscious of how people might interpret anything I did or said. Who I talked to. My body language. Whether I was smiling or pursing my lips in frustration. There was an inevitable spotlight on me, and I wanted to use it as an advantage. I strove to be authentic and frank while threading optimism into every communication. Yes, we had hard work and challenges ahead of us, but we would get through this difficult time.

In these early days, no one could predict the extent of our challenges, especially with regard to the economy. Any fear I had was overshadowed by my own enthusiasm and morning-to-night activity. As with all new beginnings—a marriage, a baby, a presidency—the inevitability of future hardship was buried by the momentum and possibility of it all.

Writing helped me stay in touch with myself as well as our people, and I resurrected one of my favorite modes of communication: composing frequent memos to Starbucks' partners. Sometimes these memos apprised people of the latest decisions being made, like changes to the leadership team. Other memos, which I composed with input from others—including Wanda, who I had asked to remain with Starbucks for a while to temporarily oversee our global communications—reiterated our strategy, restating the company's three pillars of immediate focus: fixing the US business, reigniting the emotional attachment with customers, and making long-term changes to the foundation of the business.

Every once in a while, I penned a memo out of a spontaneous desire to share what I was thinking.

Dear partners,

As I sit down to write this note (6:30 a.m. Sunday morning), I am enjoying a spectacular cup of Sumatra, brewed my favorite way—in a French press. It's been three weeks since I returned to my role as ceo of the company I love, and I wanted to share with you what I know to be true:

Since 1971 we have been ethically sourcing and roasting the highest quality arabica coffee in the world . . . we are in the people business and always have been . . . our stores have become the third place in our communities—a destination where human connections happen tens of thousands of times a day . . . we have a renewed clarity of purpose and we are laser-focused on the customer experience and returning to our core to reaffirm our coffee authority.

There will be cynics and critics, all with an opinion and point of view, but this is not about them or competitors, although we must humbly respect the changing landscape and the many choices facing every consumer. I will lead us back to the place where we belong, but I need your help and support every step of the way. My expectations of you are high, but higher for myself.

I am proud to be your partner. I know this to be true.

I titled most of my memos using two words that articulated the journey we were on and the work we had to do during this make-or-break period in the company's history. Those two words were "Transformation Agenda."

My first memo, "Transformation Agenda Communication #1" was e-mailed January 7, 2008, the day I took over as ceo. By early March I had written more than 10 such memos. All of them concluded with the same word. A word that alluded to the power of our past as well as the potential of our future. A word that implied passion as well as planning and spoke to the confidence with which we had to forge ahead, despite daunting hurdles. And a word that implied a willingness to dig deep and get hands dirty, but always with heads held high.

A word I had first written more than 20 years before: "Onward."

Chapter 13

A Reason
to Exist

By early March 2008, the fact that
I had returned to run Starbucks was
no longer news. People outside the
company—shareholders, analysts,
journalists—had stepped back, moving
on to other things and waiting to see
if we could reverse the tide. Most
doubted we could.

I was busy every hour of every day. Ushering through the Clover deal. Planning for the launch of Pike Place Roast. Dissecting the company's cost structures. Realigning senior leaders. Conceiving a new vision and strategy. It was all a bit overwhelming, but there was no time to waste. With the disappointing first quarter behind us and a worsening second quarter already under way, a very real sense of urgency propelled me. The window for rallying thousands of partners, for rekindling their passion and belief in the company's future, would not remain open long.

We were already planning to call together 200 of our most senior leaders from around the world for a global summit, the first time in the company's history that our vice presidents and leadership team would convene in one place. The unprecedented gathering was long overdue. Fortuitous in its timing, I saw a chance to recast and heighten the importance of the meeting. No agenda was circulated prior, and there was a high degree of secrecy surrounding the event, which began at 8 a.m. sharp on Tuesday, March 4.

Starbucks' department heads and regional presidents flew in from Asia Pacific, Europe, Canada, Latin America, and throughout the United States, or drove from their homes in and around Seattle. It was quite a sight. The head of Starbucks Greater China, Jinlong Wang, was within shouting distance of the head of Canada, Colin Moore. Logistics experts sat next to architects. Our top coffee experts mingled with marketing executives. Each person came to the summit with his or her own Starbucks history and questions about its future.

Standing on a small stage no more than a few feet high, I could not discern a cynic from an optimist. Who believed in Starbucks—or, for that matter, who believed in me? All I saw seated before me were partners from every region and discipline of the company, and all I could do was speak from my heart.

"I read a quote," I said, "that was attributed to Paul McCartney when he was asked to identify the beginning of the end in terms of The Beatles breaking up." I then recounted the story about the first time The Beatles played New York's Shea Stadium in the summer of 1965 to 55,000 screaming, hysterical fans, the largest crowd the band had ever performed for live. Amidst the clamor and chaos, as the story goes, The Beatles could not even hear their own music. Their art was drowned out by their popularity. It was massive shows like this that were, Paul had said in retrospect, the beginning of the band's end.

A palpable anxiety hung in the ballroom. It was almost a year to the day that my infamous memo lamenting the erosion of Starbucks' soul had leaked. Our stock's value continued to fall, and day by day our comps dipped further into negative territory; even though comps were no longer our obsession, they were still a measurement of our health and could not be ignored.

My tone was somber as I wondered aloud, "When did we stop hearing our own music?"

Was it in the march to 40,000 stores? When did we forget that our business is about the customer and our love and passion for the coffee? As we got tangled in bureaucracy and quarterly comp growth? And why did we stop holding our business operations to the same standards that we hold our coffee?

There was no one right answer, of course, but what was more important was that we all accept that Starbucks had strayed.

A tiny microphone clipped to my white shirt amplified my voice throughout the hushed ballroom. "We looked in the mirror and we said, 'Ladies and gentlemen, let's be honest with one another. We are not doing this as well as we once did, and the mediocrity that we have been embracing cannot stand any longer.'" As proof of the company's newfound commitment to dramatically shift behavior, I cited the more than 7,000 US stores that had closed for espresso training just a week earlier. "I do not know in the history of retail anywhere in the world that a company would have the courage to make that kind of a step. It cost us millions of dollars, and there were people in multiple constituencies who questioned whether or not it was the right thing to do. But we are going to look back on it as not only the right thing to do, but also as a turning point."

Just as it is when a coach has one shot to get his team ready for the biggest game of their lives, this was not a time for a vacuous pep talk or to rehash past mistakes, but a moment that required honesty about our situation as well as sincere optimism that we would get through it. And I still believed that we would. But by the end of this three-day summit, everyone in attendance—the people who oversaw Starbucks' business—also had to believe.

They had to believe in our brand. In our purpose. And they had to believe in the comprehensive plan we were about to unveil, the Transformation Agenda, which would not come to fruition unless our most senior leaders stepped up, understood their personal roles in executing it, and then shared it with their teams. Yet I could not demand that they follow my lead. All I could do was state the case for change, then ask for and earn people's fellowship.

That morning, I wrapped up my remarks with this:

A week before I came back as ceo, both my children asked me, "Dad, why are you going back? You don't need this." I told them that if I think about the two things I love in my life, it is our family and this company. There is not anything I would not do for my family, just like everyone in this room. And there is nothing I would not do for this company.

I will hold myself to the highest level of accountability. I will walk through and climb over every wall to make sure that we get to the place that we deserve . . . but no one in this room, including myself, can do this alone. There has never been a time in the history of the company that we needed each other more than we need each other now.

Looking back at me were partners like Dub Hay, a former commodities trader and wine enthusiast who had spent 25 years steeped in the coffee business, traveling to far-flung regions of the world; and Peter Gibbons, a pragmatic problem solver born in Scotland who, after 22 years at a global chemical company and turning down job offers from Starbucks three times, finally joined us in 2007 as head of manufacturing. Everyone in the room had his or her own story and point of view. Now it was time for all of us to get on the same page. "The reason I think we are here for these three days," I said, "is to make sure that we level set the reason why we exist."

* * *

Later that day, after lunch, Michelle Gass stepped in front of the group to introduce and explain our more fully realized vision.

In the past eight weeks, thanks to much discussion and debate, the Transformation Agenda had evolved from the three pillars that had marked my return into a much more comprehensive yet compact document. It was a clear, concrete plan that framed the company's bold goals and articulated exactly what we would do to achieve them. All on one page. Perhaps most important, at least from my perspective, was that the Transformation Agenda had been written in approachable language so anyone at the company—part-time baristas, store managers, regional directors, division presidents—could read it, quickly grasp our priorities, and understand how they could effect productive change. My intent with the agenda had always been to create a sound navigational tool with tangible objectives that could deliver measurable results. I felt pretty sure that we were almost there.

Michelle had been spearheading the Transformation Agenda's evolution, working closely with me and other members of the leadership team as well as with SYPartners. Since the first brainstorming summit, the firm has helped us distill our ideas and communicate on many levels. In addition to Susan Schuman and David Glickman, Dervala Hanley, a strategic thinker, had joined the team.

The Transformation Agenda, in its present form, began with a compelling strategic vision.

OUR ASPIRATION

To become an enduring, great company with one of the most recognized and respected brands in the world, known for inspiring and nurturing the human spirit.

Following the vision was the plan's backbone, seven goals that we identified as our Seven Big Moves, each with specific tactics for achieving it.

SEVEN BIG MOVES

1. Be the undisputed coffee authority. Starbucks could not possibly transform the company if we did not excel and lead in our core business. We needed everyone to recognize the quality and passion we exhibit in sourcing, roasting, and brewing coffee. To accomplish this we would tell our story, as well as improve the quality and delivery of our espresso drinks, reinvent brewed coffee at Starbucks, deliver innovative beverages, and increase our share of the at-home coffee market.

2. Engage and inspire our partners. Every partner should be passionate about coffee, from soil to cup, and possess the skills, enthusiasm, and permission to share that expertise with customers. Going forward, we would significantly improve training and career development for our partners at all levels of the business, and, once again, Starbucks would develop meaningful and groundbreaking compensation, benefit, and incentive packages for partners.

3. Ignite the emotional attachment with our customers. People come to Starbucks for coffee *and* human connection. We would put our customers back in the center of the experience by addressing their needs, providing "value" in a manner congruent with the brand, and developing programs that recognize and reward our most loyal customers. In our stores, we would achieve operational excellence, finding new ways to deliver world-class customer service and perfect beverages while keeping costs in line and our retail partners engaged.

4. Expand our global presence—while making each store the heart of the local neighborhood. We'd continue to grow our retail presence around the world—Starbucks had less than a 1 percent share of the global coffee market—but also strive to connect with and support the neighborhoods and cultures that each store serves. Enhancing our local relevancy would mean redesigning existing and new stores, offering new products that reflected the tastes of particular cultures, and reaching out by volunteering or fund-raising to support local programs and causes.

5. Be a leader in ethical sourcing and environmental impact. Starbucks has led the way in treating farmers with respect and dignity, working directly with organizations such as Fairtrade and Conservation International. Now we would expand our efforts, strengthen those partnerships, and forge new ones, as well as reduce each store's environmental footprint. We also had to do a much better job of sharing with others our extensive efforts on this front.

6. Create innovative growth platforms worthy of our coffee. Starbucks would grow not just by adding stores and selling coffee, but also by extending its brand and/or expertise to new product platforms expanding or complementing coffee, such as tea, cold beverages, instant coffee, food, and the booming health and wellness market. Innovation that was relevant to our core and values would be a hallmark of our transformation.

7. Deliver a sustainable economic model. Without a profitable business model, Big Moves 1 through 6 would not be possible. It was imperative that as we refocused on our customers and our core, we also improved upon how we operated our business by reducing costs and building a world-class supply chain, as well as creating a culture that drove quality and speed and managed expenses on an ongoing basis. Big Move 7 would likely be the most painful, least sexy, and most difficult part of transforming the company.

By discussing the agenda at the summit, we also hoped to put many previously announced initiatives into a larger context so they did not seem like random decisions from above, but rather thoughtful initiatives connected to a larger goal. Pike Place Roast and Clover, for example, were our answers to reinventing brewed coffee.

The Transformation Agenda was no quick fix. It was a mind-set dictating the company's primary focus until we were in a healthy position, ready to refocus on profitable growth. It was also a one-page road map designed to be willingly and creatively followed.

More than a business plan, the Transformation Agenda gave us all something concrete to believe in.

* * *

The day before the summit, Starbucks made an announcement that took many of our people by surprise: The head of our damaged US operations was leaving the company—after only six months in the role—and her replacement was Cliff Burrows, then the head of Starbucks Europe, Middle East, and Africa. Cliff is an exceptional operator and an affable leader with a deep understanding of the retail business.

But he had never lived in the United States, which had several people in the company and even on our board doubting my choice. How could a Brit who had never lived in America run America, the company's most important business, given that about 70 percent of the company's revenues came from our US business? But I'd spent a good deal of time traveling with Cliff since he had joined the company in 2001, especially in the past year, and had learned a lot about his character.

Cliff had grown up doing the unexpected. Born in a small steel town in Wales, Cliff probably would have followed his father and grandfather to work at the blast furnaces had his parents not decided that they wanted a better life for themselves and moved to Zambia in southern Africa. At age 10 Cliff traveled, alone, 5,000 miles to the United Kingdom to attend boarding school, returning home only twice a year until his parents returned to the United Kingdom when Cliff was 13. Cliff's father died in an industrial accident and, fiercely independent, Cliff shunned college after a semester for a career in retail. His very first job back when he was 15 had been at a Woolworth store where, every Saturday, he began the day in the basement peeling mice off the sticky mousetraps and ended the day setting the traps for the following week. By age 23, he was running his first store.

I was impressed by the organizational clarity he had brought to the regions under his lead. To the United States, the region that demanded immediate attention, my intuition told me that Cliff could bring discipline as well as a skill set that we did not have: the ability to translate and execute our renewed coffee- and customer-focused strategy at the store level.

I offered Cliff the job over lunch at a popular Vietnamese restaurant near Seattle's Starbucks support center, and he, like others, was a bit surprised but clearly intrigued. As I talked about what he would be doing—I assumed he would accept the offer—Cliff was pondering just how he would tell his wife back in Amsterdam that they were about to move halfway around the world to Seattle, a city many Americans still considered off the grid.

This shuffling of senior leaders was further proof that I would not hesitate to make significant changes at all levels of the organization, and it no doubt contributed somewhat to the angst and uncertainty that hung in the air at the beginning of the summit. But over the next two and a half days, that tension dissipated as the company's new strategy became clear and partners were given opportunities to hear directly from me and share in the Transformation Agenda's evolution.

Our leaders spent the majority of their time at the summit actively participating. Just as a smaller group of us had done a few weeks earlier, they ventured out of the conference room and into Seattle's most inspiring retail shops. Pike Place Market. Beecher's Handmade Cheese. Rocky Mountain Chocolate Factory. Zanadu Comics. Their instruction during this "seeing" exercise was to consider each retail experience not as a merchant or an operator, but from the point of view of a customer. What did they witness, smell, and hear? What nonverbal cues enhanced the experience? All the partners had notebooks to record their observations in, which they later shared with each other.

That journey helped put our leaders back in customers' shoes, providing an enlightening and for some emotional exercise that underscored just how critical it was that all of us place the customer at the center of every meeting and business decision. If we had any hope of reigniting their emotional attachment, we had to replace our comps-at-any-cost mind-set with a customer-centric one.

★ ★ ★

By late Thursday afternoon, the summit's tours, working lunches, and breakout sessions were over. We'd spent three days together talking about reinvention, fine-tuning the Transformation Agenda, and discussing how to execute it at the operational and regional levels. We had also stepped outside ourselves to see great customer experiences in action, and we had heard from two inspiring individuals—Marty Ashby and Bill Strickland—who nurture the human spirit in their own ways. Through jazz. Through social change. By seeing potential in people and giving them opportunities to excel. All in all, it had been an emotional, intellectual journey. Many people in the group were rightly exhausted. Exhilarated, but a bit wiped.

From side conversations I'd had over the three days and snippets of conversation I'd overheard, I sensed that something had taken hold, that most of our people recognized the scope of change required and what they needed to do. My optimism about Starbucks has always come from knowing that when we relegate responsibility to our partners and give them the right tools and resources, they will exceed expectations. After watching our top people work together and embrace our new agenda over the past few days, I felt more optimistic than ever and could only hope that others had been similarly moved and were ready to recommit to Starbucks' future.

There was only one more thing to do before everyone went home.

I walked back onto the stage, informal in jeans and a dark gray sweater, and took a seat on the first of several red-cushioned chairs. On the seat of the stool to my left, I placed some important papers. Behind me, as a backdrop, was an oversized version of the Transformation Agenda—our Aspiration statement, the Seven Big Moves outline, and the tactics that we would execute—updated with changes from the past few days. I sat back comfortably, rested my forearms on my legs, and clasped my hands in front of me:

When we started here two days ago, I said that the key to all this is to embrace the work that we have done over the years but at the same time recognize the need for constant innovation and to challenge ourselves not to embrace the status quo and push forward.

The pressures of today—economic and competitive, local and regional, national and global—are substantial, and we have to, I think, look within ourselves and try to be different types of leaders and demonstrate a different view of the world than we have in the past.

So, over the last few weeks, when we examined all the things that we wanted to talk to you about these last couple of days, we began to look at a piece of paper that has been in place now for 25 years, and that is the mission statement of Starbucks.

Starbucks' mission statement had never been just some framed piece of paper posted on our offices' walls. Perhaps more than any other company, we had for years used our mission as a touchstone to make sure the guiding principles of how we run our business are intact and as a measuring stick for whether or not the company is aligned with its founding purpose, which at the highest level is to inspire and nurture the human spirit. Our mission provided guardrails for the company as we ventured down new roads, and every once in a while we looked in the rearview mirror to make sure we were being consistent.

It was from our mission that we had strayed:

Thinking about the transformation, we came to a consensus that the mission needed to be updated, and updated in a way that would capture the passion we have for the future and the respect we have for the past, but give the people who are with us today as well as new people who will join us in the future a new way to look at the company.

At that very moment, I realized that, of all the people in the room, only one had been with me, with Starbucks, when the original mission statement was written in 1990. Dave Olsen. I always refer to Dave as the conscience of the company, and for more than two decades Dave's pride in and knowledge about our coffee and roasting processes has inspired thousands of partners and customers. Dave lives our mission in every way, the quintessential Starbucks partner.

I was pleased to see his face as the company introduced a new, bolder mission that reflected our heightened ambitions in a world that had changed so much since Dave and I had first begun working together.

I would like to try, in a serious way, to share with you the words that we believe are right for this time: our new mission that will replace the existing one. And I think that when you hear it and read it and live with it for a while, you will agree that the group of people who have been assigned the very important responsibility for rewriting it have done it very well, representing the value and the history and the heritage of the company in a way that is consistent with our past and present, but most importantly the future and where we are going.

I picked up a paper from the chair next to me. "I am going to read to you the overarching theme that will frame the document, and then I'm going to get some help from others." I stood up and read the first line aloud.

The Starbucks mission: To inspire and nurture the human spirit one person, one cup, and one neighborhood at a time.

Then, without a cue, a vice president of store design stood up from her chair in the audience and read the next line of the mission statement into a microphone. Her smooth voice filled the room.

Our Coffee: It has always been and will always be about quality. We're passionate about ethically sourcing the finest coffee beans, roasting them with great care, and improving the lives of people who grow them. We care deeply about all of this; our work is never done.

As she sat down, our UK vice president of partner resources stood up and read the next line aloud in a distinctive Scottish accent.

Our Partners: We're called partners, because it's not just a job, it's our passion. Together, we embrace diversity to create a place where each of us can be ourselves. We always treat each other with respect and dignity. And we hold each other to that standard.

Then, one by one, four more partners stood up, took a microphone, and read aloud.

The president of Asia Pacific: *Our Customers: When we are fully engaged, we connect with, laugh with, and uplift the lives of our customers—even if just for a few moments. Sure, it starts with the promise of a perfectly made beverage, but our work goes far beyond that. It's really about human connection.*

The director of marketing for Canada: *Our Stores: When our customers feel this sense of belonging, our stores become a haven, a break from the worries outside, a place where you can meet with friends. It's about enjoyment at the speed of life—sometimes slow and savored, sometimes faster. Always full of humanity.*

The vice president of our south-central region in the United States: *Our Neighborhood: Every store is part of a community, and we take our responsibility to be good neighbors seriously. We want to be invited in wherever we do business. We can be a force for positive action—bringing together our partners, customers, and the community to contribute every day. Now we see that our responsibility—and our potential for good—is even larger. The world is looking to Starbucks to set the new standard, yet again. We will lead.*

A partner from our Hong Kong field office: *Our Shareholders: We know that as we deliver in each of these areas, we enjoy the kind of success that rewards our shareholders. We are fully accountable to get each of these elements right so that Starbucks—and everyone it touches—can endure and thrive.*

I didn't smile as each piece of the mission was being read, but rather listened as if I were hearing it for the first time, pondering this transitional moment in our history. At the end of the reading, I stood up and offered a somber "Thank you." There was applause, but it was an emotionally subdued moment. I even saw several people crying. We would not reveal the new mission to the entire company until the timing was right; for now, it had to sink in with our top leaders.

Then, in the back of the room, huge sliding panel walls slowly opened to reveal a scene that no one had expected or knew quite what to make of at first glance. SYPartners had created a remarkable interactive display that took the words we had just heard to another level. "Please, walk through it and enjoy," I said gesturing toward the back of the room, "and hopefully embrace it, because it is ours."

People rose from their seats and, with The Beatles' "Lady Madonna" playing over the speakers, walked curiously toward seven 11-foot-high, three-dimensional displays constructed of stacked cardboard boxes and words in black type that simply yet viscerally represented each of the mission's themes.

For the display representing "Our Partners," excerpts from letters and e-mails I had received from our people were posted next to a stack of green aprons and photos of baristas working in our stores.

At the "Customers" station, more than 100 grande coffee cups had been attached to the display wall in perfect alignment. On each cup was written a hypothetical moment of connection that anyone might experience over a cup of Starbucks coffee. "I felt like someone understood me," read the sentiment on one cup. "I worried about the future." "I came up with an idea for dinner." "I played peekaboo with a wandering child." "I wrote a love letter." These kinds of moments are what Starbucks is all about.

People mulled the larger-than-life displays as if at a museum, talking in hushed voices or silently studying the words. They pulled out cameras and snapped photos. People smiled to themselves.

What happened next was one of the most unexpected and touching events I've ever had at the company. Someone approached and asked me to sign his copy of the new mission statement. Then another person asked. Then another. A line began to form. Rich Nelsen, a regional vice president of the mid-America region, was fourth in line. Behind him was Rossann Williams, a three-year partner who had relocated to Amsterdam from Texas. With all of the requests, I shook hands with and thanked partners old and new. In the end, I must have written my signature on more than 150 mission statements, the entire time somewhat slack-jawed at the emotional display of commitment unfurling in front of me.

Eventually the line ended, the music stopped, and the partners who remained began filtering out of the room, bound for families, international flights, or rush-hour traffic.

The summit had been a success. I felt it had inspired many of our people, and in the following days I received e-mails that said as much.

Ultimately, the summit helped align our top global leaders around two very important pieces of paper: the Transformation Agenda, which outlined what everyone at Starbucks needed to do, and the mission statement, which reminded us why.

Chapter 14

Benevolence

Inside a narrow Starbucks in Tokyo, the store's manager, Mayumi Kitamura, was telling me through a Japanese interpreter about the coffee-tasting parties that her store's partners host for customers who are visually impaired. Twice a year, a group of blind men and women join the baristas to cup coffee and learn about the beans' origins. Mayumi's colleagues Chihiro Ogawa and Yukiko Fukuda came up with the idea after a blind customer came to the store and mentioned that he only orders drip coffee because that was all he knew to order.

Realizing that their store is located near the Tokyo Metropolitan Welfare Association for the Blind, as well as the Japan Braille Library, Chihiro borrowed a Braille kit from a family member and hand-made a Braille menu, which is kept next to the register for use by customers with sight problems.

I rubbed my thumb across the bumpy card and looked up, shaking my head. Extraordinary. "This is something I wish everyone at Starbucks could experience with me," I said to half a dozen of our Japanese partners in green aprons who had gathered around the table.

Seven days a week, Starbucks' partners give of themselves in ways big and small. One of the most touching examples I'd heard of was when Sandie Andersen—a mom, wife, grandma, and Starbucks barista—found out that one of her regular customers, Annamarie Ausnes, was on the kidney transplant list. Sandie went and got herself tested. "I'm a match," she said, grabbing Annamarie's hand when she came into the store for her daily cup of drip coffee. "And I want to donate to you." Not long after, the two women checked into Virginia Mason Medical Center in Seattle. The transplant was a success. "Life is just too short not to live it," Sandie explained when asked about her motivation. "And if I can help someone else do that, then it's a good thing. . . . It is the ultimate human connection."

Admittedly, the gifts our partners give usually are not organs, but their generosity of spirit comes from the heart. We have store managers who send their own Christmas cards to customers' homes. Many baristas pen personal notes—"Christina rocks!"—on cups of morning coffee. Our partners' attitude and actions have such great potential to make our customers *feel* something. Delighted, maybe. Or tickled. Special. Grateful. Connected. Yet the only reason our partners can make our customers feel good is because of how our partners feel about the company. Proud. Inspired. Appreciated. Cared for. Respected. Connected.

I do not mean to imply that Starbucks is by any means a perfect place to work or the ideal retailer, somehow above reproach. We have made many mistakes over the years, and we will continue to make them. But we do aim high. And we do have high expectations of ourselves as we try to manage the company through the lens of humanity.

Starbucks' coffee is exceptional, yes, but *emotional connection* is our true value proposition.

This is a subtle concept, often too subtle for many businesspeople to replicate or cynics to appreciate. Where is emotion's return on investment? they want to know. To me, the answer has always been clear: When partners like Sandie feel proud of our company—because of their trust in the company, because of our values, because of how they are treated, because of how they treat others, because of our ethical practices—they willingly elevate the experience for each other and customers, one cup at a time.

I could not believe any more passionately than I already do in the power of emotional connection in the Starbucks Experience. It is the ethos of our culture. Our most original and irreplaceable asset. And every time I see it come to life, I ask myself if, as leaders, we deserve our people. People like Sandie.

In my own work at Starbucks, I will never pull shots or pass drinks over the counter or create great experiences for our customers day after day. But I can pull the right levers to create great partner experiences, identify products, green-light new projects—or fast-track ones already in the pipeline—that will make our people feel good about the company they work for. Instinct, quite honestly, guides many of my choices about where to focus the company's energy, and it was especially so during my first few months back. But every customer-facing initiative we pursued, from Espresso Training to Pike Place Roast, was also intended to reconnect our partners, emotionally, to Starbucks. Trying to make our partners proud was constantly on my mind.

* * *

Because of our founding mission to achieve the fragile balance of profit with social conscience, Starbucks has long had a reputation for being a "different kind of company." But if you ask people about it, they'll be hard-pressed to identify exactly what we do. Yet we do so much! Our partners' individual actions are accompanied by more concentrated, expansive efforts.

After years of research with our suppliers, Starbucks began using hot-coffee cups in the United States and Canada that were made from material containing 10 percent postconsumer recycled fiber, saving an estimated 78,000 trees and removing three million pounds from the solid waste stream every year. This is significant because the Food and Drug Administration had never before given a company a favorable safety review to use postconsumer recycled fiber in packaging that comes in direct contact with food. On other fronts, the Starbucks Foundation has, over the years, given millions of dollars to support local initiatives in our retail and coffee-growing communities. For every bottle of Ethos Water sold in our stores, five cents goes toward providing children with access to clean water. In an unprecedented move, we extended health-care coverage to thousands of part-time workers. Starbucks is also one of the largest buyers of Fairtrade certified coffee in the world, supporting thousands of farmers and their families.

I am proud of these and other initiatives, but too few people inside and outside the company appreciate our efforts. We do good, but we have not done a good job of telling this chapter of our story. Our marketing department had been trying to fix that, and in 2008 it was on the cusp of formulating a campaign that would, with a singular, cohesive voice, publicize our ethical sourcing, environmental stewardship, and community support. But the campaign had yet to launch.

As ceo I recognized just how critical our social and environmental stewardship was to recapturing our partners' pride in the company, so on January 10, 2008, I met with Ben Packard. An intelligent, mildmannered partner, Ben had been one of those kids who loves the outdoors. Every job he'd held since college had focused on conservation, and after earning an MBA and a certificate in environmental management, he joined Starbucks in 1998. I felt lucky to have his passion and expertise working for us.

"Ben," I urged when I named him our interim chief of corporate responsibility that day, "we have got to tell our story!" There was a lot to accomplish, but right away I asked Ben to firm up our flatlining relationships with Conservation International and Fairtrade.

Ben left my office and, with Terry Davenport, our senior vice president of marketing, set their first meeting with Conservation International. Our 10-year relationship with the environmental nonprofit had lost its relevance, and in the meeting, the first high-level one between us in a long while, Conservation International's people enthusiastically explained their most pressing concern: climate change.

Unfurling a map, they pointed to geographic regions clustered around the equator; all were endangered areas that are home to irreplaceable plant and animal life. These biodiversity "hot spots" are climate change's ground zero. The trouble is not only that these ecosystems are at risk for destruction by human deforestation, but also that the burning and clearing of forests contributes 20 percent of the world's carbon emissions—twice as much as *all* the world's vehicles combined. Twice as much!

Coincidentally, these hot spots are also located in areas where farmers grow some of Starbucks' most precious coffees.

A lightbulb went off. A new deal was in the works.

Starbucks would re-up its partnership with Conservation International with a $7.5 million commitment over three years. In this next phase of our partnership, we would, one, measure the impact of our C.A.F.E. Practices to ensure that we were making a positive difference for the people and places we intended. Two, we would link small farmers to global carbon markets. And three, we would stand shoulder to shoulder with Conservation International and more actively and vocally share our efforts.

I was thrilled. With just a few strokes, Starbucks was ready to launch another powerful catalyst to use our scale for good. I knew our partners would be extremely proud, and I was eager to tell them as well as our customers what we were up to. But the news would, I felt, be more appreciated if it came from someone else. I picked up the phone and called Conservation International's well-respected cofounder Peter Seligman to ask if he would personally announce our enhanced relationship.

* * *

When it came to reigniting emotional connections to our coffee, the bold moves I asked our people to make required courage. The company's biggest financial and logistical bet to date, however, was upgrading our almost 20,000 espresso machines. A prototype had been years in the making and was almost ready to roll out. Someone just had to hit the switch.

The debate over manual versus automatic espresso makers can get pretty heated. Independent coffee shops covet their manual espresso machines, but for a company with Starbucks' high traffic flow, superiorly engineered semiautomatic machines provide an unmatchable level of consistency, delivering high-quality shots millions of times a day despite multiple variables—temperature, humidity, barometric pressure—that affect espresso's quality from bean to cup.

Manual espresso machines have a rich, romantic history, and our much-beloved La Marzocco machines were part of the Starbucks Experience and had a passionate following. But as more and more customers crowded into Starbucks and espresso orders increased, the repetitive motions our baristas had to perform with the manual machines caused some physical issues for them. I will never forget a meeting I had with several store managers in our boardroom. They were insistent, and rightly so, that we go to a more automatic machine. The choice was clear. Changing to semiautomatic machines was the right and only option. Our challenge would be to preserve the quality of the shot.

In 2000 our stores swapped the La Marzocco for the Verismo 801, a state-of-the-art semiautomatic machine manufactured by Thermoplan, a family-owned Swiss company in Weggis, Switzerland, a quaint little town of less than 5,000 on the green, sloping shores of Lake Lucerne. I had come to know the generous, hardworking owners, Domenic and Esther Steiner, who began Thermoplan in 1974. Thermoplan is a respected force in the small community, donating funds for buildings, parks, and even a temporary arena for the Brazilian national soccer team to train in before the 2006 World Cup, a move that brought Weggis international attention.

Thermoplan's Verismo 801 is a fantastic piece of technology, but I had always been frustrated by how high the machines sat on our counters.

For a while, a small team in our equipment development department, headed by Paul Camera, had been collaborating closely with Thermoplan to invent a next-generation espresso machine for Starbucks. They set high standards, and during our company's growth-focused period the development process was fraught with delays and false starts. But by the end of 2007, they were very close, and before my return as ceo, I had seen a prototype. In January 2008, I approved its rollout, but because I wanted our espresso machines to be a more prominent, elegant part of Starbucks' in-store coffee experience, I asked that it be more artfully designed.

Thermoplan delivered with a beautiful espresso machine called the Mastrena.

With its dusted copper and shiny metal skin and ergonomic design, the Mastrena is truly elegant. On top, a clear chalice holds fresh espresso beans waiting to be ground. Inside, every component had been engineered with Starbucks' beans in mind. The Mastrena also, to my great joy, sits four inches lower on our counters, so baristas and customers can visually and verbally connect. What's more, the Mastrena gives our baristas a sense of control. By perfecting the coffee's grind size and pour time, a barista can proudly "own" every shot. A retooled steam wand also lets him or her slowly ease a pitcher of milk into steaming to create the dense, creamy foam our customers love.

Being a barista is not an easy job. On their feet for hours, juggling multiple, complex drink orders as the line at the register grows longer, baristas do strenuous, exhausting work. That's why it's imperative that they take pride in the process. With the Mastrena's world-class technology at their fingertips, I truly believed they would.

I was antsy to announce the Mastrena to the marketplace, but the time to share it was not yet quite right. The Mastrena's introduction, as well as news of our stronger relationship with Conservation International, would have to wait.

Chapter 15

Beyond the Status Quo

It was December 23, 2007, just weeks before I returned as ceo, and Michael Dell and I had just finished the 30-mile bike ride we took with a group of friends almost every morning in Hawaii over the holidays. More than just exercise, these daily rides had become therapeutic for me, especially as Michael and I got into the habit of talking about our individual challenges at work.

This was the morning I finally revealed to him, in strictest confidence, my intent to return as Starbucks' ceo. When we went back to his home after the ride, Michael first took me through Dell's Transformation Agenda, which I would soon adapt for Starbucks. He also showed me a site he called up on his computer screen, IdeaStorm: "Where Your Ideas Reign."

The Dell site invites PC users to post their ideas for the company. Michael explained that Dell built IdeaStorm to reengage with its customers online—the very place, it occurred to me, where Starbucks also needed to show up. I was intrigued.

I've always believed that innovation is about rethinking the nature of relationships, not just rethinking products, and as Michael explained how IdeaStorm was helping Dell listen to customers and improve its products and services, I nodded. There was definitely something here for Starbucks. A chance to reconnect with customers we had lost touch with.

Michael immediately e-mailed Marc Benioff, the founder and CEO of Salesforce.com, the company whose customer relationship management applications were the foundation for Dell's site. Marc was also vacationing with his family in Hawaii, and the next morning, even though it was Christmas Eve, he and I met for breakfast. I was impressed by Marc's intelligence and foresight as he gave me a cursory education in the power of online customer communities, and we agreed that there were definitely elements of IdeaStorm that could benefit Starbucks.

By the end of breakfast, I had taken the conversation with Marc as far as I could, but I knew who could take it further. I grabbed my cell and dialed a Seattle phone number.

★ ★ ★

Inside our company, there is a standing joke. Whenever a partner tells someone he or she works for Starbucks, the other person's response is, more often than not, a to-do list. "You know what you guys should do?" is followed by a litany of new ideas. Everyone, it seems, has a suggestion for us. Capturing this instinct, it seemed to me, was another way to reignite our emotional attachment with customers.

While it seemed bizarre to some of our people that a brick-and-mortar coffee company might get a lot of traction from online social networks, we would have been foolish not to explore their hidden opportunities. The barrier to entry was not that expensive, almost nothing compared to national advertising, which Starbucks historically avoided. The risk with social media was showing up inappropriately; if not done thoughtfully, it could damage our brand.

Starbucks did, of course, have a website, but it represented a status quo that we needed to move beyond. Our real journey into the virtual world—and in developing our own social media and digital muscles—began December 24, 2007.

Back in Seattle, it was already dark when Chris Bruzzo's cell phone rang. A dedicated, energetic leader, Chris had recently come to Starbucks from Amazon.com to help us better understand the web. "Hello?"

"Chris, this is Howard. Do you have a minute?"

Hearing adrenaline in my voice, Chris generously excused himself from a family gathering and went into his home office. "I just had a fantastic meeting with Salesforce.com's Marc Benioff," I explained. "Chris, you've got to talk to Marc. Today!" My tendency to let enthusiasm morph into impatience was a trait widely known throughout the company—generally appreciated, but occasionally a cause of frustration. But Chris got it. He had helped Amazon build its interactive community beyond its book and product reviews by finding new ways for customers to participate on the site. Chris knew a movement was already under way as more and more consumers connected with their favorite brands online. And he understood that Starbucks' customers were already inclined to share their thoughts, ideas, and experiences with the company, as well as with each other.

After we hung up, Chris dialed Marc in sunny Hawaii. The seeds of their Christmas Eve conversation would blossom just days into the New Year.

* * *

One week later, the same week I put Ben Packard in charge of corporate responsibility, I appointed Chris Bruzzo Starbucks' interim chief technology officer. My first directive to Chris was concrete: Build IdeaStorm, Starbucks style.

Chris asked Alexandra Wheeler, his newly named director of digital, to oversee what they dubbed Project Greenstorm. A half dozen engineers from Starbucks and another dozen from Salesforce.com immediately signed on to bring Project Greenstorm to life. Fast. Of all the new initiatives that people inside Starbucks were working on—Pike Place Roast, rolling out the Mastrena—this was one project I felt certain we could and should announce at the annual shareholders' meeting in 63 days.

The digital team dove in, and very quickly one overarching notion became clear: More important than customers' *ideas* would be the *discussions* that followed. Each idea was a door, an opening line for conversations on topics our customers cared about, like recycling or low-fat food. By using suggestions as opportunities to learn from and inform our customers, the new website would be more than a mere one-way suggestion box; instead, it would be a genuine opportunity to connect.

Understandably, inviting uncensored, real-time conversations and criticisms made some people inside the company nervous. What if people posted false information? What if people maligned us? What if a partner wrote something inappropriate? What if we set expectations we could not meet? Conversations about Starbucks were already taking place online, we countered, on sites where we had little or no chance to contribute to the discussion.

The digital team made two key decisions up front.

First, instead of assigning one or two people to moderate the site full-time, they enlisted 50 partners from throughout the company to spend eight hours a week monitoring posts in their area of expertise—coffee, food, conservation, etc. Putting our corporate partners in direct contact with customers seemed risky, but it was the most authentic, honest way to communicate.

Yet even with a posse of 50, Starbucks still wouldn't have enough manpower to personally respond to all the posts, let alone implement every good idea. But we also didn't want to alienate customers by asking for ideas and then ignoring them. The solution? Let the site's community vote on which posts would get our people's attention. Anyone who signed on to the website could literally give someone else's suggestion a thumbs-up. The ideas that racked up the most points, and that garnered a high degree of conversation, would cue our moderators to chime in, answer a specific question, or begin the process of making the idea a reality in our stores.

Ironically, the toughest challenges were not technical. They were human, like convincing leaders throughout the company to dedicate resources to the new site. And allaying fears that Starbucks was opening itself up to unbridled criticism, which was reaching a fever pitch in the marketplace, or that the site would be hijacked by so-called haters. The digital team also had to train our 50 moderators so they would not inadvertently offend or reveal proprietary information when they posted replies.

There simply was no time to debate every what-if scenario and, in the end, there was only so much we could affect—or, for that matter, should affect. Starbucks just had to go for it with faith that the site's participants, like guests at a dinner party, would act with decency and police themselves, encouraging excellent ideas and shunning ugly chatter.

The Greenstorm team plugged away day and night on the seventh floor. Inevitable glitches arose, but they were overcome by the camaraderie among the Starbucks and Salesforce.com partners. They all believed that the team was building something fresh and fun to connect with Starbucks' customers and that the site just might, using the influence of social media, drive more traffic into our stores, even as that traffic was dwindling. I wasn't privy to the project's daily hurdles— micromanaging usually is not my style, especially when it comes to technology—and I gave them freedom to innovate, but held them accountable. "I do not want this to be a jump ball," I'd told Chris early on. We had one shot to get it right.

By mid-March 2008, Chris felt confident that Starbucks' first virtual community, no longer named Greenstorm, was just about ready to launch, both online and onstage at our annual shareholders' meeting.

Chapter 16

Bold Moves

Spring was just around the corner, but the chill on March 19, 2008, held little promise that winter was on its way out. I'd arrived at McCaw Hall in the predawn darkness and spent time rehearsing. Now, just minutes before 10 a.m., I was alone backstage, thinking.

On the other side of the massive curtains, thousands of people were streaming into the auditorium to secure seats for Starbucks' annual shareholders' meeting. In the first few rows the company's leadership team, board members who had flown in from around the country, and members of my family were settling in for the two-hour program. Behind them, in row after row all the way to the far reaches of the auditorium, to the last aisle in the balcony, were thousands of shareholders and Starbucks partners. There were people in the room—moms and dads with kids in college, retirees, widows, and customers—who had owned our stock since the day we went public, plus a handful—Arnie Prentice, Cynthia Stroum, Steve Ritt, Carol Bobo, Jack Rodgers, and Harold Gorlick—who had invested in me back in the 1980s.

For me, each annual meeting was sort of like an episode of the 1950s television series *This Is Your Life*, with people from my past hidden in a sea of faces. Never just business, these gatherings were inevitably quite personal.

Unlike those of other publicly held companies, Starbucks' shareholder events were far from stodgy, formal meetings to elect directors or vote on proposals. I had, over the years, used them as brand-building opportunities because the company's passionate, engaged shareholder and customer base flocked here, so much so that in some years we had to seat thousands of overflow attendees in Seattle Center's neighboring Exhibition Hall, where they watched the show on huge screens. And for years, it was a show.

The company's stellar performance had always given us a tailwind going into each meeting. We'd created so much value for shareholders that most of us at Starbucks got swept up in the adulation and joy. Our biggest challenge was topping the previous year's meeting to thank and surprise people. Usually we brought out a surprise entertainer whose music we sold in Starbucks stores. One year Tony Bennett sang. Another year Paul McCartney joined us live via satellite. Today it would be my good friend K. D. Lang.

Yet the meeting also had strategic purpose. In addition to being a brand builder, it also had a forcing function, pushing the company to bring various projects to fruition.

Never had that push been more necessary than in 2008.

This year I intended to use the stage to rebuild confidence in our future. We would announce six new consumer-facing transformation initiatives. Each fell under one of the seven Big Moves that formed the backbone of the Transformation Agenda. On their own merits and collectively, the six would, I hoped, illustrate Starbucks' laser focus.

Backstage I felt anxious. This was the first time that the company's earnings as well as our share price were lower—the stock was down 44 percent!—than at the same time the previous year. Starbucks was crashing, and shareholders had a right to be disappointed. Given our uncharacteristically dismal performance, I couldn't predict the audience's reception.

My refusal to stick to a script that day made some of our people nervous—anything that was said onstage could be picked up by journalists and bloggers in the audience and plopped online immediately—but my rationale was simple. I wanted to react naturally, whether I was greeted with contempt or kindness. Letting my words flow according to the mood rather than a teleprompter freed me to connect sincerely with this important constituency in a very delicate period.

A female's voice filled the quieting auditorium. "The meeting is hereby called to order, and the inspector of elections has advised us that we have a quorum." She read the required disclaimer statement that begins all shareholder events, and for a split second, as I do every year while waiting in the wings for my cue, I thought of my parents.

Without a doubt, this was the most important annual meeting in Starbucks' history. I had prepared for the worst but hoped for the best.

* * *

"Wow."

That really was all I could say. It might have sounded sophomoric, but it was my gut response to the loud applause and even whistles as I walked somberly to the center of the stage in a dark navy suit and tie. It was nearly impossible to see the entire audience with the bright stage lights. "Thank you," I said calmly, shocked as well as relieved. "Thank you very much." I felt myself getting emotional and tried to quiet the crowd. "Wow. I really didn't know what to expect." People laughed, and that's when I knew. I knew that Starbucks and I had our shareholders' support—at least for the next two hours.

It was time to get down to business.

I'm not quite sure we've ever had a meeting like this before. On one hand, you have an economy that really is in a tailspin, and many would say the consumer is in a recession. Just this week Alan Greenspan said that the economy is in its worst shape since World War II.

On the other hand, you have a company's performance that has not met your expectations, nor mine. And let me say at the outset that I humbly recognize and share both your concern and your disappointment in how the company has performed and how that has affected your investment in Starbucks. And I promise you this will not stand.

There are many challenges inside and outside the company that we have to address. But we are on it with relentless focus on the customer, the customer experience, and doing everything we can to differentiate Starbucks from everyone else attempting to be in the coffee business. . . . It's time to convince you and many other people who are not represented here, to give you all reasons to believe in Starbucks again. And that is exactly what we will do today.

I took a moment to introduce the members of our board of directors. Each stood as I announced his or her name. Next, I recognized Starbucks' retiring chief financial officer, a loyal 12-year partner, Michael Casey.

"We have almost 200,000 partners around the world. They are obviously not all here today, but many of them are. Would the Starbucks partners please stand to be recognized?" Heads and bodies popped up to deserved applause.

"Okay," I said. "Let's gets started."

* * *

I stood in front of a large object covered with a mysterious black cloth.

"What we want to unveil to you," I explained to the audience, "is a new piece of equipment that we believe will advance the quality and consistency of Starbucks to a level that is second to none."

The cloth was lifted to reveal the Mastrena. To demonstrate it for our shareholders, I'd requested that Ann-Marie Kurtz, a 17-year partner who started her Starbucks career as a part-time barista, join me on stage. Now a manager in our coffee education department, Ann-Marie is a pro at pulling shots. Her eyes smiling under her red-framed glasses, she handled the Mastrena with grace and placed two shot glasses under the spouts.

"Would you like to taste a shot?"

"Love to," I said as the glasses filled with espresso. "What is that sound I am hearing?"

"That's the sound of the grinder," Ann-Marie answered over a gentle whirring. "So every time shots are poured, coffee is ground fresh just beforehand. That's the biggest difference. With the Mastrena, as opposed to old-style machines, I am delivering freshly ground coffee every time."

She handed me a glass, and I took a sip.

The Mastrena would give Starbucks a differentiated edge in the marketplace, and by the end of 2008 the Swiss-made machine would be in 30 percent of our company-operated stores in the United States, and in the majority of our stores by 2010. I gave a nod to Domenic Steiner and his family, who were seated in the first few rows, and asked them to stand. "It's not just a piece of equipment," I said. "It's an unbelievable tool that will provide us with the highest-quality consistent shot of espresso that will be second to none and will transform the espresso experience in our stores."

I thanked Ann-Marie for her help and switched gears.

* * *

"So I've talked about the coffee," I said to the audience. "I think it's time to go back to the soil and really explain to you the relationship that we have had with farmers and growers in developing countries around the world, and our relationship, our unique relationship, with Conservation International. Please join me in welcoming the chief executive officer of Conservation International, Peter Seligman." I embraced Peter as he walked onstage to address Starbucks' shareholders in his own words.

We joined with Starbucks in 1998 to demonstrate that a company could help protect biodiversity with shade-grown coffee produced with fair compensation and safe working conditions for coffee farm workers. I am proud to stand here with Howard to announce that we are building on the successes of the collaboration to address the most pressing issue facing our planet: global climate change.

Protecting forests is an essential first response to climate change. The CI and Starbucks partnership is going to focus on protecting the land, water, and forests that surround and nurture the most important coffee-growing regions in the world by working with and providing incentives for farming communities to leave forests intact.

We are at what historians call an "open moment," when societies come together and real change is possible. Starbucks' ability to reach millions of people in the market every day and connect them to the land and to the people that grow coffee is critical. Through this partnership, Starbucks is stepping up to support the well-being of farmers, protect ecosystems, and educate consumers to become part of the climate change solution—triple benefits.

By the end of 2009, I then announced, with a bag of whole-bean coffee in my hands, it was our intent that all Starbucks espresso beans and espresso-based products would qualify for a new marking we had designed to articulate our practices: "Responsibly Grown. Ethically Traded. Proudly Served."

★ ★ ★

With my right hand, I reached into the breast pocket of my suit jacket and pulled out a small plastic card. "The next consumer initiative is going to be . . . a rewards program." There was a rupture of applause that seemed to say, "It's about time!" They were right. It was about time Starbucks acknowledged our most loyal customers. Other than our Starbucks Card—on which someone put, say, 25 bucks for themselves or someone else—Starbucks had nothing.

But one of the most important pieces of advice I'd heard upon my return came from a dear Seattle friend and one of the country's best retail executives, Jim Sinegal, the cofounder and CEO of Costco Wholesale Corporation. "Protect and preserve your core customers," he told our marketing team when I invited him to speak to us. "The cost of losing your core customers and trying to get them back during a down economy will be much greater than the cost of investing in them and trying to keep them."

When our business began softening in 2007, our marketing team, led by Michelle Gass and Terry Davenport, started studying customer behavior and discovered something surprising. People did not just wake up one morning and decide not to go to Starbucks anymore. They were still coming, just less frequently. For example, the mom who once came in for a latte during her early morning walk and came back in the afternoon for a pick-me-up mocha had stopped returning for that second visit.

This was a big insight: Our customers hadn't abandon were just coming by less often.

Market research, and common sense, told us something else. A good portion of our drinkers had a favorite beverage they customized in ways I, personally, could never have imagined when I began the company. "I'd like an iced grande latte with nonfat milk to the bottom line only, ice to the top with super-stiff foam with a dome lid." That's the drink Diane ordered almost religiously at our Coal Creek store in Washington. Brett in Bellevue was committed to two double-cupped venti breve, extra-hot, bone-dry cappuccinos.

Customization was not only part of the Starbucks Experience, but also presented a fantastic opportunity to incentivize and reward our biggest fans.

Beginning in April 2008, I told our shareholders, you and other Starbucks customers may use the Rewards Card to receive several benefits. A free beverage with every pound of coffee beans purchased. Free refills on brewed coffee. And Starbucks would customize beverages for free, picking up the added costs for extras like soy milk and flavored syrups.

The Card recognized our most loyal customers while addressing an emerging need for value as the economy pinched consumers' wallets. It was a way to bring a little relief to those who weren't coming into our stores as often or who were swapping their customized beverages for brewed coffee because it was less expensive.

Assuming we marketed the Rewards Card effectively, its unique power for us would be its rapid rate of adoption. The biggest hurdle in launching a successful consumer rewards program is getting the cards into people's purses and wallets. But we realized that more than five million people already had Starbucks Cards in hand! All they had to do was register them online—which for our digitally savvy customers was not a big deal—and their Starbucks Cards instantly turned into Rewards Cards. This, as Terry liked to say, was the Trojan horse that would allow Starbucks to very quickly benefit from its first-ever loyalty program.

"Starbucks' reward program, beginning in mid-April," I said to our shareholders, slipping the card back into my pocket. "And this is just the beginning."

* * *

Four more partners joined me onstage that day to announce initiatives.

Chris Bruzzo walked shareholders through our new website, MyStarbucksIdea.com. Then he officially launched the site onstage and online. Behind the curtains, Alexandra Wheeler sat at a laptop uploading ideas that had been verbally collected from shareholders that morning as they entered the auditorium. Back at the office, some of our moderators sat ready to respond. Within minutes after going live, more ideas came streaming in—"give customers a free coffee on their birthdays," "free Wi-Fi for all"—from people listening to the meeting's broadcast or reading the rolling blog posts. In the next 24 hours, 7,000 ideas were posted to MyStarbucksIdea.com. Seven thousand! The implications for Starbucks would be huge.

Andrew Linnemann, donning a green apron and standing with his colleague Leslie Wolford behind a table set for a coffee tasting, introduced Pike Place Roast, and together we announced that Starbucks would once again grind whole beans in our stores. To my surprise, Andrew also introduced a short video that had captured the reactions of shareholders as they sampled Pike Place Roast before entering McCaw Hall that day. Their spontaneous feedback—"smooth," "well balanced," "lighter," "it doesn't bite"—was music to my ears, exactly what we'd hoped to achieve with the new brew.

Finally, Clover. "What if a company could create a commercial way to replicate the benefits of the French press?" I asked the audience before Zander Nosler humbly described to the largest group he had ever spoken to how the machine that his company had invented made such a fantastic cup of coffee, which he brewed on camera for everyone to see on the huge overhead screens.

That was it. Six transformation initiatives.

The Mastrena.

Conservation International.

The Rewards Card.

MyStarbucksIdea.com.

Pike Place Roast.

Clover.

"I hope that you can see that we are deeply, deeply committed to the work at hand," I said, looking out into the auditorium.

Yet even as I spoke, the company's situation was getting bleaker. Our stock price, which had begun the day at $18.34, closed at $17.50. Day by day, sales would continue to decline. And so would the United States' economic indicators—consumer confidence, unemployment, housing starts. The only things going up seemed to be labor costs and prices for commodities like dairy products, further eroding our margins. A storm was brewing as the world's financial systems teetered on the brink, and while I believed the situation would get worse before it got better, no one, not the smartest economists or the federal government, could know just how bad it might become.

But going forward with fear would not allow our company to thrive. Some corporations are built, or rebuilt, on data-driven business plans and hired guns with formulaic strategies. They may succeed, but they lack soul. Starbucks is, by its founding nature, different. There was no doubt that the company had to mature, conducting its global operations with more rigor and discipline, hiring new talent, and consulting with outside experts. But for this organization, transformation was not only about tightening nuts and bolts. If we did not also *feel*, if we did not have conviction in our values and believe that we really were in the business of human connection—on our farms, in our offices, in our stores, in our communities—then the company was doomed.

We had to preserve our humanity.

To get the company to forge ahead and win, I had been trying to rekindle in our partners the love and pride that had fueled Starbucks for so many years. That's why the last 11 weeks had been so important: Discussing The Beatles at our first brainstorming summit. The first-ever retreat for Starbucks' top 200 leaders. Open forums. My memos. Crafting the Transformation Agenda and launching a new mission statement. The annual meeting. All of these were engaging tools that were helping us navigate our way through and share in this unpredictable journey, one milestone at a time.

"I hope you can see that what we wanted to do today is celebrate our company. Celebrate the passion we have for our customers. Celebrate our coffee and our people and bring it to life. . . . The celebration of our company, I think, needs to be done." McCaw Hall filled with applause.

It had been a good morning. A shot of confidence that Starbucks' partners and I had been hungering for.

Yet it had been only one morning.

The initiatives we introduced each heralded a return to our core— coffee, customers, innovation, values—but they would not be enough to bring Starbucks home again. The time had come for all of us to get in the mud and get our hands very, very dirty.

Part 3: Pain

Chapter 17

Whirlwind

Starbucks was entering a tremendously chaotic period.

In the first half of 2008, as we pushed new products and programs into the marketplace, we were making many decisions with little or imperfect information, in large part trusting instinct. There was a lot the company could try to control, but so much— the economy, competition, our critics— that we could not.

Everyone was so very anxious to see the needle move, but behind closed doors our people worried whether we'd gotten carried away about just how quickly we might be able to make a real difference for our customers and to the business. Was it too much? Had we overextended ourselves? Bombarded our baristas? Would it all work? Would any of it?

Rarely did I sleep more than four hours a night as I tried to predict what onslaught of opportunities, successes, and dilemmas the next day might bring.

* * *

I had just flown to Bologna and was driving with a small team to a northern Italian town. Just a few days earlier, a friend had called me from Italy singing the praises of a sweet, smooth, cold Italian-made beverage that was not ice cream or sorbet or a smoothie but—whether mixed with fruit, milk, or yogurt—tasted absolutely delicious and like nothing else available in the United States. I had been intrigued, but with so much unfolding in Seattle I was hesitant to fly abroad, so I had sent a colleague in my place. "Howard, you should get over here," he insisted after tasting the drink for himself. "We may have found the next Frappuccino."

I flew to Italy to taste it for myself at the sprawling headquarters of the company that made the product. Its offices were chic, its factory and research facility technically advanced, and our hosts could not have been more welcoming.

Cliff and Michelle were among those in the tasting room with me trying one cold, creamy blend of the drink after another. *Absolutely fantastic*, I thought. Everyone agreed. It really was unique. During the trip we ran some back-of-the-envelope numbers, and the product's potential profit margin was hard to ignore. Given the simple ingredients and easy preparation we'd witnessed, the margin could be as high as 70 percent if the product was priced right. Serious logistics had to be considered—we'd have to airfreight the base ingredient from Italy and find a US company to manufacture the machines that mix all the ingredients—but once we'd figured out the gritty details, the product had the potential to be very successful.

The taste and potential profit coupled with the urgency I was feeling to spark sales and rejuvenate the brand with innovation culminated in our decision that Starbucks would bring the drink to the United States by that summer.

I fast-tracked the Italian beverage's development and rollout. Rather than quietly testing it in a few stores to work out production kinks and polling our partners about the product's viability, we would launch it with promotional punch in more than 300 stores in Los Angeles and Orange County, California, ideal markets for jump-starting a trend for America's next refreshing drinkable treat. We named it Sorbetto, and I had high hopes that it was going to be a big success.

* * *

In April 2008, after the glow of the annual meeting, the partners in our home office had gone back to work to deliver on our promises. We'd set big goals for ourselves—I'd told *USA Today* that Starbucks would bring more innovation to the market in the next 18 months than the company had brought in the past five years—and set some incredibly tight deadlines.

Public reaction to the six initiatives we'd announced at the annual meeting was mixed, and to my annoyance, but less and less to my surprise, a vein of cynicism ran through much of the coverage in the traditional media and online.

Investment bloggers were particularly harsh, yet not completely off base. "It hardly seems that a new coffee blend and an automated beverage machine will be the cure-all for your economic woes," wrote Sarah Gilbert of BloggingStocks.com, calling us "desperate." "Rather than a return to what they do best," wrote Todd Sullivan on SeekingAlpha.com, "Starbucks seems intent . . . on running around in more directions." *The Wall Street Journal* quoted an investor who estimated that her own shares' value had lost $80,000: "I should have sold."

"They have to stop taking themselves so seriously. Let's face it—it's still coffee, not brain surgery," a corporate consultant told *USA Today* in an article sidebar doling out advice from a smattering of industry experts. Except for a few items, the list read like a page from our existing playbook: Smell good again. Embrace wired youth. Reward loyalty. Get healthier. Drop food that doesn't jibe with java. Cut the clutter. Revive "coffee theater." Open fewer stores. Sell combo meals. And give coffee away. Applying such improvements to our business may not have been "brain surgery," but outsiders failed to appreciate the nuances of invigorating a service-based business, especially a brand as emotionally charged as ours. Starbucks is not a coffee company that serves people. It is a *people* company that serves *coffee*, and human behavior is much more challenging to change than any muffin recipe or marketing strategy. Many of the decisions I was making confounded others because they did not grasp the intangible value of preserving the company's culture.

Elsewhere, Clover took a PR hit when several independent coffee shops declared, after hearing about the acquisition, that they would sell their machines, complaining that they did not want to pay Starbucks for parts and maintenance.

Opinions about our first online community, MyStarbucksIdea.com, also varied from enthusiasm to doubt. "My initial grumpy skepticism was brutally arrested when I visited the site," wrote Toby Ward of IntranetBlog.com. "The site is clean, easy to navigate and digest." Less web-savvy folks remarked that Starbucks was taking a big risk by sanctioning a suggestion box it could not control—an emotional hurdle we'd had to overcome ourselves.

Time would tell if they were right, but from our perspective, MyStarbucksIdea.com had already exceeded our initial expectations. Salesforce.com's customized technology, as well as our moderators, held up to the wave of participation. After one week online, 100,000 people voted. And in the first two months, 41,000 ideas flooded in. "Turn down the music." "Free drinks for frequent buyers." Chris Bruzzo's team shared the community's input with our product teams and research and development, public affairs, and marketing departments, as well as with me and the leadership team. Among the themes that began to emerge were, one, an increasing desire for value—people wanted more for their money—and two, loyal customers wanted to be rewarded for their frequent purchases. These findings bolstered our optimism about the potential success of the rewards program, which would launch on the heels of our new brew, Pike Place Roast.

* * *

On a bitterly cold morning under a bright blue Manhattan sky, a perfect day for a hot cup of coffee, Starbucks officially launched its new "everyday" brew: Pike Place Roast. The huge national campaign was billed as the Nation's Largest Coast-to-Coast Coffee Tasting.

I'd flown to New York City for the April 8 event and arrived with Cliff as well as my wife, Sheri, at Bryant Park, the tree-lined oasis behind the main branch of New York's public library. In the middle of the park stood a life-size replica of the original Starbucks store. I loved it! Amy Kavanaugh and her team at Edelman, our long-standing public relations agency that worked with Starbucks to orchestrate the national launch, had brought Seattle to the East Coast. We even flew in the store's former manager, Janeen Simmons, to run the mock store that day.

All around us, smiling baristas pushed coffee carts and offered passersby steaming samples of coffee. At the same time, in 7,100 US stores from California to Maine, free coffee tastings were being hosted by partners wearing black T-shirts imprinted with the word "bold," "fresh," or "smooth." In another brilliant attention to detail, our coffee cups' green siren logo had been replaced with Starbucks' original all brown, and slightly sexier, one.

The Pike Place Roast launch was by far the largest, loudest marketing event Starbucks had ever executed. Because the company never budgeted much money for national advertising, we paid for it by scraping together funds earmarked for sporadic marketing activities around the country—and still we had a shoestring budget compared to what other national retailers typically spend. Pulling off something so grand so fast required logistical and creative heroics, and a lot of anxiety had preceded this day. I'd pushed our people, as had Michelle, Terry, Cliff, and Wanda, but every department had delivered, meeting once-unthinkable deadlines and acting as if we were one store with one goal.

Standing in Bryant Park, both Cliff and I sensed that something had gone very right. It had been awhile since Starbucks' partners had galvanized around a mission other than growth, and the promotion did not feel like some hollow PR stunt, but rather an authentic celebration because it invoked Starbucks' heritage, focused on our coffee, and involved our people.

Escalating Pike Place Roast to a reinvention of brewed coffee gave all of us something meaningful to rally around, which was vitally important to the transformation journey.

The windchill was unforgiving, and all I had on was a suit and tie as I stood in front of television cameras for interviews; at one point Cliff even insisted I put on his coat, which was a size or two too big for me. Wrapped in his oversized parka, I checked e-mail and received reports that our store partners around the country were having fun sharing coffee samples and interacting with their customers. Also good news, customers liked Pike Place's taste and were pleased when they learned it would be served consistently. Brewed coffee sales were brisk that day, and Starbucks dominated the media; the newspaper and TV coverage alone was worth millions of dollars in advertising.

That afternoon we flew back to Seattle to attend another Pike Place event at the original store. On the five-hour flight we took time to consider why Pike Place Roast seemed to be working so well so we could apply what we learned to future projects. We eventually concluded that the product as well as the way we had brought it to market met three critical criteria for success at Starbucks:

It was right for and engaged our partners.

It was right for and met the needs of our customers.

And it was right for the business.

Unfortunately, I did not realize that not everything the company was trying to do that season met those three very important standards.

* * *

At the end of April 2008, we faced Starbucks' second-quarter earnings. The numbers told a dispiriting story.

Compared to a year earlier, global operating income for the quarter had sunk an unbelievable 26 percent, to $178 million. Earnings were down 28 percent, to $109 million, as our operating margins shrank from 10.7 percent to 7.1 percent of net revenues. Most frightening of all, the company's total comps were negative for the first time in Starbucks' history. In the United States alone, customer transactions were down 5 percent and ticket sales, how much each customer spent per visit, had gone up a mere 1 percent! It's hard to overstate just how much these numbers shocked many of us at Starbucks. After almost 16 years of 5 percent or higher comps, such poor performance was so unfamiliar, even unthinkable, that it quite literally took our breath away. Although Wall Street no longer knew our comps because we'd stopped reporting them, the numbers, which were printed in red on our financial spreadsheets, were branded on my brain.

Faced with these results, it was requiring more and more faith for Starbucks' senior leaders to believe that we could actually transform the company. I had complete confidence that Michelle, who had worked closely with me to finalize the Transformation Agenda, and

Cliff shared my vision, but not all of the people on the team believed in or had the discipline to execute the strategy I was putting in place. I recalled what another second-time CEO had told me when I regained control of the company: "Most of your top leaders will be gone or new within a year."

His prediction was coming true. In addition to bringing in Cliff to head our US business, appointing Michelle chief of global strategy, and naming Chris Bruzzo interim cto and Chet Kuchinad head of partner resources, I'd recently convinced one of Starbucks' most talented former leaders and a wonderful architect, Arthur Rubinfeld, to rejoin Starbucks as president of global development to manage our real estate portfolio, new store designs, and creative concepts. His most pressing assignment was to review the quality of our current retail portfolio, a task whose outcome—closing stores—had the potential to cause enormous pain to a lot of people inside and outside the company.

Again, it was a chaotic period. Leading Starbucks continued to be a delicate balancing act as I authorized investments to improve the customer experience and boost sales while simultaneously insisting that we cut costs and closely manage expenses, especially in areas not directly related to our core business.

On the second-quarter earnings call, I felt a bit schizophrenic. On one hand I was promising revival. On the other I was reporting what felt like a slow death.

"There are no sacred cows," I told the financial community prior to explaining another significant decision the company had announced earlier that week, one that for many people had come out of the blue.

Starbucks was overhauling its entertainment strategy.

Cutting this cord was particularly rough for me, especially since as chairman I'd been bullish on entertainment from the start, first seeing it as a natural extension of the brand and later championing deals with record labels, getting behind movies, and sanctioning a rash of non-coffee-related products. By now it was clear to most of us that the entertainment group, as it was currently structured, had devolved into a bloated distraction incompatible with our new mission and economic realities. Its president, who has a truly creative mind and much success in his wake, left the company, as did a number of other talented people.

My intent was not to abandon the role Starbucks had established as a cultural arbiter of sorts—music and books would remain part of the

Starbucks Experience—we just had to embrace the role in a redefined, more cost-effective manner while capitalizing on our existing relationships with AT&T for Wi-Fi, Apple for in-store technology, Concord Records for CDs, and the William Morris Agency for books. I asked Chris Bruzzo to oversee the entertainment division, which we agreed would refocus on digital strategy, CD compilations, and literature.

The second quarter did have some bright spots. Sales in our consumer packaged goods (CPG) business—primarily the coffee and Tazo teas sold in grocery stores—were up, and so was CPG's operating income. Since the launch of Pike Place Roast three weeks earlier, brewed coffee sales also had notably increased, especially in the Northeast, the biggest market for brewed. Pike Place Roast was already our number-one whole-bean coffee.

As for competitors, our internal research showed no indication that we were losing business to any one company, such as McDonald's. This was good news, yet we also had to fight public perception as well as the fast-food giant's aggressive marketing budget.

Our research also revealed that our declining sales were not primarily the result of our self-induced problems. "The economy is the top box why people are not coming as often or not coming in for a treat," I told Jeffrey Bernstein, an analyst with Lehman Brothers, when he pressed me about the sputtering economy's effect on consumer spending in our stores.

An irony did not escape me during the call. Lehman Brothers, the fourth-biggest investment house in the United States, was in the midst of its own crisis as the market raised serious questions about its financial stability and continued to devalue its stock. And Lehman wasn't alone. Other stalwart financial institutions like AIG and Bear Stearns were crumbling, and their risky investments were the source of the credit and cash crunches that had the entire country reeling! Wall Street was on its own course to crash, taking the rest of us with it.

So why did I feel like Starbucks was a punching bag?

The "$4 latte"—that untrue catchphrase that cast Starbucks as a symbol of excess in frugal times—was hardly the consumers' enemy during this period of economic turmoil. But it sure was an easy target.

I refused to give in to increasing external pressures and focused on anything that would keep the company moving forward, even if at times it felt like we were going the wrong way in a wind tunnel.

Chapter 18

A Lethal Combination

Each Starbucks store has its own fingerprint.

At first blush, they appear and sound alike—the music, the hues, the menu— and the Starbucks you visit on vacation may feel as familiar as the Starbucks in your hometown. But it's also true that, like any local café, every Starbucks is a little bit different. The reason is simple. The people.

On both sides of the counter, the people who frequent and work at Starbucks are undeniably unique.

In 2008, even as our traffic and sales slowed, Starbucks was still serving tens of millions of customers around the world each week. And wherever they were, whoever they were, customers could order their coffees and espressos in more than 80,000 different combinations. During their morning commute or a midday coffee break. On a blind date or with friends. While studying for exams, reading the Sunday paper, or writing a book.

Variety—to accommodate the habits, whims, and desires of human behavior—has always been a Starbucks staple.

Our retail partners are as diverse as the people they serve and the beverages they customize. People wearing our green aprons represent almost every race and religion. We employ twentysomethings and grandparents, single moms in need of health-care coverage, and artists in need of rent. For some, Starbucks is a stopgap gig between jobs, while others hope to build a career with the company. Whether part-timers or full-timers, Starbucks partners include high school kids saving for college, college kids in pursuit of degrees, recent grads, many in search of themselves, former executives, and people who vowed never to work in an office.

"Behind every barista is a story," reads a poster hanging in the lobby of our Seattle support center. It's true.

Amidst all the variety in each store, one individual is responsible for finding common ground. One person is in a position to nurture a welcoming environment where everyone will feel comfortable and can connect.

The store manager.

Starbucks' best store managers are coaches, bosses, marketers, entrepreneurs, accountants, community ambassadors, and merchants all at once. They are optimistic problem solvers who run their stores creatively yet analytically, calling upon passion and intelligence to drive customer traffic, partner loyalty, and profit. The best managers take their jobs personally, treating the store as if it is their very own.

Managing a store is nonetheless a challenging juggling act, and during our transformation I was aware of the stress our people were under. And even as I preached about how we all needed to put ourselves back in the shoes of the customer, I also tried to put myself in the shoes of our store partners and be empathetic to their feelings amidst the turmoil at the company and in the marketplace.

Many of us considered store managers our most influential people when it came to crafting the Starbucks Experience. Yet we were not empowering them to be the best they could be.

* * *

Cliff was growing increasingly concerned as he traveled the United States in the summer of 2008, visiting Starbucks stores and meeting with district and store managers. The more thoughtfully he observed and the more questions he asked, the more he realized that Starbucks' field operations were inadequate.

"There's no emotional shortcoming," Cliff told me at one point. "Our partners are passionate and want to do the right thing, especially from a values standpoint."

But what many of our people had in spirit they lacked in business acumen and tools. It was not uncommon, for example, for a manager to report that his or her store was doing exceptionally well when in reality it was missing revenue opportunities, barely breaking even, or even losing money. Inventory was haphazard. Floors and tables were often dirty. Food displays lost freshness as the day went on.

We also observed too much waste. An inordinate amount of coffee was being thrown out. Pastries were often out of stock or overstocked, resulting in lost sales or more discarded product. Weekly labor scheduling—coordinating baristas' availability with store traffic patterns—took managers hours, yet still stores were often understaffed or partners underutilized.

Something subtler was also being wasted: our people's time and energy. When Cliff walked into stores, he consistently witnessed partners working hard. Always, there was a great deal of hustle and bustle and running around—as well as laughter and banter and smiles—but somehow, the line of customers and the line of empty cups waiting to be filled seemed too long given the effort our people were putting out. There was a disconnect between effort and result.

Speed of service is a large part of Starbucks' value proposition—even if a customer plans to stay and sit for a while—and on this front Cliff believed we could do better, that we had to do better. Potential customers were literally walking out of our stores when faced with too long a wait.

The fault did not lie with our people in our stores. They were doing the jobs they had been asked to do with the resources and training they'd been given. For all of the brand's marketing success, Starbucks needed a more disciplined operations system to maximize our earnings potential.

* * *

The more rocks we turned over, the more problems we discovered.

One of the most glaring was our outdated technology.

In was 2008 and, as a company, we were not yet providing our district managers—who were constantly traveling and needed to stay in close touch with stores—with the same technology tools and collaborative software that most professionals around the world were using to conduct their business. It could even be tough for them to access the Internet from the road, and many used their personal e-mail accounts or lugged around heavy computers.

In the back room inside each store sat a big box of a machine so old that the screen had no modern graphics or multimedia capability. Just a constant black background. I'm sure some of our younger partners did not even recognize it as a computer! Amazingly, even in 2008, it could not access the Internet or use basic software such as spreadsheets and word processing and PowerPoint, let alone sophisticated data analysis programs to help our partners better run their businesses. Store managers could not easily e-mail people outside the company, and it could be very difficult to send and receive attachments. Watching videos, such as the one made for Espresso Excellence training, was not even an option on our stores' computers (which was why we'd had to ship each store its own DVD player).

In short, a Starbucks store was essentially the equivalent of a $1 million-a-year business, yet an iPhone had more business application power than our stores' technology.

In the front of the store, our point of sale (POS) system, a.k.a. the electronic cash register, operated on an old Microsoft-DOS platform that even Microsoft had stopped supporting in the mid-1990s. We'd upgraded our applications over the years, but the system had become so complicated that it could take six weeks to learn. It was also inflexible. If a barista did not input a beverage's ingredients in a particular order—size, drink name, then additions like an extra shot or soy milk—he or she had to void the order and ring it up again. And because customers rarely stated their beverage preferences in that order, confusion at the register was all too common.

Any moderately tech-savvy person applying for a job or working at a Starbucks—or for that matter just about anyone under age 30—was no doubt surprised by the old-school tools he or she was given to succeed. Worse, our partners were asking for help but we were not listening. It was both costly and embarrassing.

Starbucks may have started a coffee revolution, but when it came to the technology revolution, we missed the boat.

How did a $10 billion global company get to this point? It was not as if Starbucks had never invested in its skeletal backbone. Quite the opposite. In the early days, the company's leadership proactively invested in our people, processes, and facilities ahead of our growth by making such moves as building new roasting plants before they were absolutely necessary, a significant factor in our success. But some things, like the stores' technology, had clearly fallen through the cracks. And while the situation was by no means dire, discovering it posed both problem and opportunity. We now had a chance to make the experience of being in our stores easier and more enjoyable for both partners and customers.

Cliff realized very quickly that if Starbucks was going to transform the customer experience, we had to be as bold in our stores as we were being in Seattle, and he embarked on the long process of reshaping our organizational structure in the field and improving store operations.

For me, the status quo could not stand. We had to elevate backroom and customer-facing technology to a more strategic, proactive level, a shift that had to begin at the top of the organization. Historically, our chief information officer had reported to the chief financial officer, but the time had come to seat technology at the executive table as part of the senior leadership team. On top of everything else, I also began the hunt for an IT leader with the chops, vision, and values to bring Starbucks into the 21st century.

I did, however, see a silver lining in our operational shortcomings. Actually, I saw two. First, our store managers had been amazingly successful in spite of their challenges, and second, once they received the right tools and knowledge, I believed that significant performance improvements were possible.

Unfortunately, not all stores could be fixed. And while I knew we might have to close some, I had no idea just how many.

* * *

I sat transfixed at the head of the conference table as Arthur Rubinfeld and Mike Malanga, our senior vice president for US store development and one of the company's most seasoned retail real estate veterans, recommended to Starbucks' board of directors that the company close about 200 company-operated US stores.

"Are you sure that's enough?" a member of the board asked.

Arthur and Mike looked at each other and at me. We already knew that this number was huge for a retail organization that had never shuttered more than a handful of stores in its entire existence. In addition to taking an estimated $50 million write-off for that fiscal year, the move was destined to affect every department and would cause individual pain, rile the financial markets, boost our competitors, and make noise online.

Prior to the board meeting, Arthur and Mike had come to me with the same recommendation. It was as serious a conversation as I'd ever had at Starbucks, emotional for all of us. Other retailers were suffering from sales slumps as consumer confidence hit a 16-year low, but none had announced such drastic steps—at least not yet. What's more, we'd already pulled the plug on 348 planned store openings, a very tough decision in its own right. But this felt different. More than a correction, closing so many stores felt like a defeat, even if it was the right thing to ensure the company's health. I wanted to understand how Starbucks, as a company, had arrived at this point.

"If what you're proposing is true," I'd said as we sat behind my office's closed door, "explain the filters to me so that I understand what is driving the decision."

Arthur and Mike walked me through the analysis, which they had done in conjunction with our operations and finance departments, first telling me what I already knew:

Starbucks' ability to build and operate profitable stores had succeeded for years because we had adhered to a simple yet ambitious economic model: a sales-to-investment ratio of two to one. During a Starbucks store's first year in business, it needed to bring in $2 for every $1 invested to build it. If the company spent $400,000 to lease and design a store, for example, we expected and almost always got at least

$800,000 in revenue during the first 12 months of operation. Historically, the average Starbucks store in the United States had brought in about $1 million annually. These so-called unit, or store, economics were widely known to be best in class because few, if any, retailers could achieve what Starbucks had accomplished year after year.

But in 2008, Arthur and Mike informed me, Starbucks was, for the first time in its history, missing that ratio at hundreds of stores. There were longer stretches of time during the day when a store did not have enough sales to justify the labor costs. We knew some of the reasons why from our research. People were not coming in for their afternoon treats. Others were not spending as much. In some cases, one store's sales were being cannibalized by another Starbucks, or maybe the store was in a lousy location. Adding insult to injury, many of our underperforming stores had been opened in the last two years, revealing a lack of discipline in real estate decisions that was, in my opinion, an example of the hubris that had taken hold.

I took another deep breath. From where I sat as ceo, the pieces of our rapid decline were coming together in my mind. Growth had been a carcinogen. When it became our primary operating principle, it diverted attention from revenue and cost-saving opportunities, and we did not effectively manage expenses such as rising construction costs and additional monies spent on new equipment, such as warming ovens. Then, as consumers cut their spending, we faced a lethal combination—rising costs and sinking sales—which meant that Starbucks' economic model was no longer viable.

These factors, together with the others that were bearing down on the company and every single store, caught us in a perfect storm of external pressures and self-induced imperfections that left us fighting for our life on so many fronts.

The scope of our situation washed over me like a sudden storm.

* * *

Back in the boardroom, Mike Ullman spoke up after hearing Arthur and Mike's plan. "Are you sure you looked at the number of store closures as aggressively as possible?" Jamie Shennan agreed with the sentiment.

The room fell quiet. Mike Ullman had not made this suggestion lightly. Now was the time to make the most drastic changes to the business. If Starbucks Coffee Company had to close stores, if we had to lay off hundreds of partners, if we had to take a multimillion-dollar write-off and suffer the hits to partner morale and the brand's reputation in the marketplace, we did not want to do it twice.

The board asked us to go back and take another, harder look at the number of stores that we should close to help support the overall business, and someone posed a hypothetical question: "If people who were not as emotionally attached to the stores ran the company, people who were not as concerned about how their actions would affect others, only the bottom line, how many stores would *they* close?"

I understood the reasoning, but it would be impossible for me or Arthur or Mike to take emotion out of the equation. These were not just doors we would be closing. We would be disrupting lives, on both sides of the counter.

For all the flak about Starbucks' ubiquity, almost every store maintained a devoted following inside and out. A soul. With each closing, we would be erasing a fingerprint, and that was a reality I could not possibly ignore.

Chapter 19

Reverence

Building a great, enduring company requires thoughtfulness and, at times, the courage to make very difficult decisions. For Starbucks, July 2008 was a moment when I had to make choices that I never, in my 26 years at the company, had imagined I would be faced with.

Six hundred.

That was how many US stores we ultimately decided to close, three times more than had first been suggested to the board. All told, it represented 8 percent of our US company-owned and -operated retail portfolio. Most distressing: approximately 12,000 positions, or 7 percent of our global workforce, would be eliminated.

The evening before we publicly announced the news, on June 30, I considered the repercussions of other Starbucks events—the leaked memo, my return as ceo, closing 7,100 stores for Espresso Training, the six initiatives we announced at the annual meeting. All paled in comparison to the potential fallout, gossip, and, most significantly, the individual upheaval that 600 permanent store closings and the consequent layoffs would induce.

Again and again I looked over the list of stores slated to shut: In Wichita, Kansas, a drive-thru that had been open barely one month. In Federal Way, Washington, a store that had served customers for 18 years. We would close 57 stores in Texas. Thirty-nine in New York. Twenty-seven in Minnesota. Arkansas would lose eight, Mississippi and Nebraska seven each, and North Dakota four. Two-hundred and thirty-four drive-thrus. Seventy-two stores in malls. Fourteen percent of the stores to be shuttered were in California and 10 percent in Florida—not coincidentally, both regions were hubs of the subprime housing bubble and bust. Almost every major city would lose at least one Starbucks. Seven stores were located in our own backyard.

The choice about which stores to shutter was financially based. If we calculated that it would never provide acceptable returns even once we improved operations and the economy got back on track—which we knew it would, one day—then we most likely chose to close it.

In addition, Starbucks would take $340 million in expected pretax charges, including $200 million in asset write-offs and another $130 million associated with terminating the stores' leases. These were all necessary costs to fix the US business.

One particular statistic, however, raised my ire: 70 percent of all stores slated for closure had been opened in the past three years, during the aggressive growth period when we opened 2,300 locations. It was staggering. We were closing almost 20 percent of our newest stores! *We thought all we had to do was show up to be successful,* I thought to myself. As I stared at the list of 600, a lesson resonated: Success is not sustainable if it's defined by how big you become. Large numbers that once captivated me—40,000 stores!—are not what matter. The only number that matters is "one." One cup. One customer. One partner. One experience at a time. We had to get back to what mattered most.

I shook my head before trying to get an hour or two of sleep. I was not proud of our past behavior, but I deeply wanted to be proud of how all of us, as a company, acted from this point forward.

* * *

Starbucks Increases Number of U.S. Company-Operated Store Closures as Part of Transformation Strategy
Approximately 600 Underperforming Stores Will Be Closed; Company Takes Significant Step Toward Improving Long-Term Profitable Growth

At exactly 1:05 p.m. PST on Tuesday, July 1, five minutes after the stock markets closed on the East Coast, our press release hit the wires.

By 1:15 p.m., the phones in our media affairs and investor relations offices were ringing, but Starbucks was in the mandated quiet period of the fiscal quarter for another month. I was not allowed to conduct follow-up interviews with journalists or analysts, nor could anyone from the company comment other than to clarify our official statement or refer people to the Form 8-K we had filed with the Securities and Exchange Commission.

Our unavoidable silence provided a lot of room for interpretation, and the risks were huge. How could we maintain the integrity of our brand and the culture of humanity I espoused when we were disrupting so many people's lives? We were committed to transferring as many displaced partners as possible into new roles. This was paramount to our plan and something the leadership team and I had insisted upon. And we took solace in the fact that as many as 70 percent of those field and store partners could likely remain with the company. Second, we would give at least 30 days' notice to our people whose positions would be lost once a store closed, an unheard-of runway for mass layoffs, especially in retail. We also made employee assistance professionals available to address people's more personal issues.

At 1:17 p.m., my memo to Starbucks' partners was e-mailed companywide. I had striven for honesty, trusting our people to honor the realities of the situation Starbucks was in.

Throughout the history of the company, we have always aspired to put our people first. This makes our decision to close stores more difficult. . . . At the same time, we recognize that we must make decisions that will strengthen the US store portfolio and enable us to enter fiscal 2009 focused on enhancing operating efficiency, improved customer satisfaction and ensuring long-term shareholder value for our partners and customers.

By far, this is the most angst-ridden decision we have made in my more than 25 years with Starbucks, but we realize that part of transforming a company is our ability to look forward, while pursuing innovation and reflecting, in many cases with 20/20 hindsight, on the decisions we made in the past, both good and bad.

By 1:45 p.m., Starbucksgossip.com was buzzing with rumors and anonymous opinions.

At 2:30 p.m., Cliff hosted an internal conference call with regional directors and district managers while our chief financial officer led the analyst conference call.

Then, at 3 p.m., I began an open forum on the ninth floor. I took the podium in the tense hall knowing that one of our biggest challenges was not tactical, but emotional.

Outside the company, investor sentiment was unfolding and the public dialogue was taking shape. Tomorrow's coverage would be widespread as negative momentum fueled itself.

Starbucks' closures could be cast as progress toward the company's commitment to transformation, but it was likely that some would frame them as a nail in our coffin.

* * *

Six days after the announcement, on July 7, 2008, our stock fell to a 52-week low of $14.95 a share. Wall Street wanted to see much more from Starbucks than just store closings.

"Short-term investors may rally behind the restructuring theme 'feel' of this announcement," read a research note from Goldman Sachs. "However, longer-term investors may need to see further clarity on current business trends."

"The first step is admitting you have a problem," wrote Morgan Stanley's John Glass. "The rationalization is welcomed, but does not negate near-term fundamental challenges. While we believe the brand is and will remain relevant to the U.S. consumer, there is no quick fix to turn around this company."

The coverage by almost every major newspaper, business website, and national broadcast news outlet confirmed our predictions about the media's focus and tone.

"Starbucks Goes from Venti to Grande," wrote Time.com in one of the more neutral headlines.

"Is the Global Domination of Starbucks Finally on the Wane?" asked an opinion piece that first appeared in the United Kingdom and was reprinted in the *Seattle Post-Intelligencer.*

At Forbes.com: "Starbucks' Dark Side."

In *Fortune*: "Starbucks Has a Bitter Plan."

A Motley Fool syndicated newspaper column claimed that a "tag-team of doughnut shops, fast-food joints, and quick-service diners" was crowding us out of the market, while the *San Francisco Chronicle* argued that our 600 store closures was proof that the US economy was in a recession. "Americans have decided to give up their $4 lattes," it read. "In 2008, a better definition of 'recession' may not exist."

Then this from the *Christian Science Monitor*: "Why Starbucks Lost Its Mojo." The piece hypothesized that Starbucks got into trouble because we created a sense of "cool" for customers by "giving middle-class Americans exactly what they thought they wanted," a way to generate envy or status. Narrow viewpoints like the *Monitor*'s aggravated me because they overlooked or perhaps begrudged Starbucks' mission and very real social contribution: human connection. Yes, this raises cynics' eyebrows, and yes, for some customers Starbucks is an aspirational brand or even a token of pride, but the latter is an unintended effect of what we originally set out to do.

Starbucks never set out to be cool. We set out to be relevant!

And few things were more necessary, were more relevant, than human connection, especially as the world was going through such upheaval and uncertainty.

Starbucks never encouraged our baristas to be cool, but rather to be friendly and knowledgeable about our coffee and to engage with, laugh with, and reach out to their customers. The company does not make investments in health coverage and ethically source our coffee because these things are "cool." They are the right ways to conduct business.

The company's hard times could not be reduced to one cause or the death of some pop-culture trend. As I was learning every day, the story of our trials and tribulations was just not that simple.

★ ★ ★

On July 9, 2008, *The Wall Street Journal* picked up on a national phenomenon that we were dealing with back in Seattle: "Not knowing whether their local Starbucks will stay open is making customers and employees jumpy," began the article.

In Starbucks stores around the country, not only were our baristas worried about their own store's fate, but our regular customers also feared their daily routine was about to be disrupted, and they came at baristas with a barrage of questions our people could not answer: "Will you close?" "When?" "What will *you* do?" "Where will *I* go?" A blog speculating which stores might get the ax sprang up, and as anxiety grew, Starbucks was widely criticized for not publicizing the complete list of closures.

Clearly we'd underestimated the anxiety that would result from not identifying which stores were scheduled to close. Out of respect we had wanted to inform our partners in person before their stores' fate went public, as well as prevent an employee exodus or lax customer service in the months before a store actually ceased operating. Originally we had planned to reveal the first 50 closures by mid-July and the balance over many months. But once we recognized the degree of public angst, we very quickly changed course and released the full store list on July 17.

Then, in an ironic twist, something unusual occurred. After referring to Starbucks as a pricey extravagance, public discussion shifted as our customers and communities around the country pleaded "Save Our Starbucks." Their calls came in many forms. E-mails. Letters. Even petitions piled on Cliff's desk. On one independent website— Saveourstarbucks.com—the posts rang with emotion.

"Starbucks is more that just a coffeehouse," wrote a woman vying to save a store in Chino Hills, California.

You go to Starbucks to meet friends; bring the kids for some cold drinks on a hot, sunny day; study; work on the computer; read, or just enjoy some quiet time in a comfortable armchair. This Starbucks has really become a part of our little community and we want to do what we can to help.

From a gentleman in Niles, Ohio: *Please don't close our North Common Starbucks. My wife and I go there every day for our drinks. We know the staff and they know us. They have become our friends.*

From an Indiana resident: *PLEASE PLEASE PLEASE DO NOT close the Starbucks here in Portage, Indiana, on Rt. 6!!!! This is the BEST Starbucks we have EVER been to. Not only is it clean and the staff, ALL the staff, is always friendly but they seem to take pride in the store. . . . We ALWAYS go to this location. . . . We love everyone who works there. They really go the extra mile to make everyone happy. . . . PLEASE reconsider!!!!!!!*

A few lines from a woman in Minnesota summed up so much of what we were hearing: "I can't believe that 'my' Starbucks is closing. You never know how important a place is until you are about to lose it."

My personal mail was filled with more of the same, and I noticed a theme:

Dear Mr. Schultz,

For the past two years I have been coming to the Starbucks on Phillips Avenue in Jacksonville, Fl. The staff here has been wonderful. This particular team has been genuinely warm and personable day in and day out. So from my viewpoint, I would certainly consider this store to be a winner for you.

There were more like this. Most notably, the spontaneous flow spoke to our role in communities and the high quality of our store managers and baristas who provided the Starbucks Experience every day. From where I sat, I saw our customers' sentiments as proof that our store partners were succeeding and that I was not the sole or even the most important ambassador of the brand.

Back in Seattle, Cliff, Arthur, and Mike were spending an inordinate amount of time reading more heartfelt e-mails, some including passionate promises that their favorite store would bring in more business. Our people held conference calls with mayors, at least one governor, and city officials from around the country and also talked one-on-one with partners at "safe" stores who were standing up for fellow partners at closing stores.

One day Mike, who had been through mass store shutdowns at other retailers over the course of his career, turned to Cliff. "You know, this kind of outpouring would not happen at other companies."

It was challenging for everyone to keep emotion out of the work that needed to be done, and for every single store we received a letter about—every single one—Mike's team conducted another financial review. But rarely, if ever, did the numbers justify reversing a decision.

It wasn't easy for them to stick to their guns, but Mike and his team kept the bigger goal in mind: Rightsizing Starbucks' retail portfolio as quickly as possible would, in the long term, secure the health of the company's future and of the 6,500 US stores that would remain open.

* * *

For months Mike and his six-person team of real estate experts, with backup from lawyers and outside consultants, camped out in a conference room, perpetually on the phone with any one of hundreds of landlords, unwinding our legal obligations and leases. It was difficult, detailed work.

For more than 20 years, Starbucks had been a desirable tenant, and a traffic-generating magnet for other tenants. Because of the financial strength of our company, developers often felt more secure signing a lease with Starbucks than with other retailers. Now our landlords, many of whom Starbucks' partners had established relationships with, were seeing another side of the company, and their reactions ranged from calm cooperation to intractable rage. Each developer or management company faced its own economic challenges. Huge public real estate developers, real estate investment trusts, had to answer to their own shareholders. For the independent landowner, a single vacancy at a strip mall might mean not being able to pay the bills or delaying retirement. We tried our best to strike fair deals and spent millions of dollars to make the best of a bad situation for all. Trying to put ourselves in the shoes of the landlord and act accordingly expedited the process.

When a member of Mike's team got off a particularly harsh negotiation call, Mike reminded him that the typical retail tenant who breaks a lease rarely goes as far as Starbucks was. "Most just walk in, throw the keys on the desk, and walk out."

Yet there was only so much our company could do to ease the inevitable sting, and some outraged individuals took their cases to local newspapers, claiming that Starbucks was unfair and not living up to its own standards. Some went as far as suing the company. My personal e-mail account received its fair share of stormy sentiment. The backlash hurt, but our partners and landlords were hurting more.

Again, I saw a silver lining. The push-back from our customers, our people—even the reaction from landlords—affirmed that Starbucks was a positive force, a mainstay, in many communities. Never before had so many people inside and outside the company stood up and so passionately, so spontaneously, championed our existence.

"Would people go this berserk if the local Dunkin' Donuts closed?" wrote Daniel Henninger, deputy editor of *The Wall Street Journal's* editorial page in an op-ed piece. "What is going on here? It can't be about the coffee." Henninger's op-ed really captured the nuance and delicate balance at the heart of every Starbucks store:

> *A friend said that the Starbucks stores' bitter-enders reminded her of the protests against the closing of the neighborhood Catholic churches. True. The stores are like secular chapels. No sign on the wall says you must be quiet, polite or contemplative, but people are. Ritual abounds. So too with the refusal to walk two blocks to a nearby Starbucks. Back in the glory days, when cities had a church every 10 blocks, no one would go to a church blocks away with the same service. They wanted their church. But they'd drop into a Catholic or a Presbyterian Church anywhere in America, knowing the feeling would always be the same. . . . I don't go to Starbucks that much. I don't go to the Baptist church either. But I'm glad that we've got one just about everywhere.*

I took some solace in Henninger's analogy, pleased that there were some outside the company who recognized the unique value Starbucks brought to communities. And I was reminded of our value when I read every letter and when I visited dozens of stores during the coming months on a listening tour, holding town hall meetings with partners and customers.

One day, at a store in Lakewood Towne Center near Tacoma, Washington, an older woman wearing a purple turtleneck raised her hand. "I have a couple of comments," she said. "First and foremost, I have a 16½-year-old granddaughter in Madison, Mississippi, and when she knew I was going to be seeing you tonight she said, 'Grandma, get down on your knees and beg, don't let him close the Madison store!'" Then the woman stood up and, to a background of applause and supportive laughter from other customers, she got down on one knee in front of me. What could I say? I smiled and vowed to look into the Mississippi store. And we did. But tragically, like so many others, it too could not sustain itself.

My heart was heavy, but my belief that Starbucks was about so much more than coffee had never been stronger.

Chapter 20

No Silver Bullets

"We've been searching for some time for a cold beverage concept that will create the type of taste, proprietary nature, and customer excitement that our Frappuccino blended beverages did 10 years ago," I had said during our second-quarter earnings call in 2008, not yet identifying the new Italian treat by its name, Sorbetto.

The delicious product that I had urged to market that spring would launch in the summer. "We found something, finally, that took us back to our heritage." As I described Sorbetto's smooth frozen texture, I emanated sincere, confident optimism about the indulgent, drinkable treat's potential to drive traffic.

Intuitively, I understood that there was no silver bullet that would save the company. Costco's Jim Sinegal and The Limited's founder and CEO, Les Wexner, both trusted friends, also reminded me of that fact whenever we talked during the transformation. In my mind, I got this point. But in my heart I was anxious, and I could not help but hope that there just might be *one thing* that would miraculously solve all of our problems. By summer 2008, I was pinning that hope on Sorbetto.

* * *

In our quest to create demand, Sorbetto was not the only promotion hitting Starbucks stores that season. While it was the first really fresh, innovative product platform that Starbucks had brought to market in a long while, our marketing calendar was, true to our history, packed with one seasonal drink and promotion after another, and sometimes overlapping. Starbucks' promotions were not always strategically synchronized, and customers as well as baristas often felt bombarded as, for example, a blended coffee, a new Tazo tea, and a new food vied for attention. It could be challenging for a singular product to get traction.

That summer, however, in addition to Sorbetto, two things in particular held tremendous potential to create incremental demand, despite early missteps: Starbucks' first-ever loyalty program and an emerging health and wellness platform.

The rewards program I'd announced to applause at the annual meeting had fallen flat its first time out in April because we had launched it in stores at the same time as Pike Place Roast, and it took a promotional backseat to the new brew. As much as our loyal customers clamored for value, without our baristas actively and knowledgeably promoting the card, it simply got lost.

But when we relaunched the program in June 2008, solo and with more partner training and the customer incentive of getting a free beverage with online registration, its popularity exploded. By July 2008, one million people had signed up, reloading $150 million onto their Starbucks Cards.

The rewards program may not have had the visceral romance of a new beverage from Italy, but it was nonetheless the beginning of something very big and very powerful for Starbucks. With one in seven customers now using a card, we intended to take the program—and related value promotions—to a higher level. And if we could crack the code on loyalty and value, we would achieve multiple goals.

• See an uptick in sales

• Reward our core customers

• Provide the value people seek in tough economic times without cheapening the brand

• Save money by reducing the number of credit card transactions, and thus some of the millions of dollars we paid in associated fees

• Strengthen the bond with customers inexpensively in combination with our evolving online presence

We didn't have to wait long for feedback on our card and other value promotions, thanks to MyStarbucksIdea.com. Our customers had not been shy about using the online community to tell us where we had missed the mark and what they liked, and one value promotion that we offered that summer in a few cities that generated positive buzz was our Treat Receipt. Customers who bought anything in the morning could return after 2 p.m. and get any grande cold beverage for $2. Requests posted at MyStarbucksIdea.com prompted us to launch Treat Receipt nationally, which helped us make up for the afternoon slowdown.

While the Starbucks Card and Treat Receipt successfully catered to our customers' calls for value and rewards, a second initiative addressed another burgeoning consumer preference.

* * *

Around the world, people, myself included, were beginning to live healthier lifestyles, exercising more often and seeking out low-fat, low-sugar, and natural foods. For Starbucks, catering to this movement, which is as much socially as it is medically driven, is not only wise marketing, but also in sync with our values and our mission.

As a consumer brand trusted for quality, Starbucks is in a unique position to step into the lucrative health and wellness market and play. Back in January 2008, we'd quietly recommitted to health-related innovation as well as improving the nutritional value of our existing product offerings. Already we'd made progress by reducing the calorie and fat content of our core beverages and baked goods. But I thought we could take it further, and I'd been harboring a vision of how Starbucks might permeate, perhaps even own, this category.

In the short term, our first breakout health and wellness product would launch in the United States, the United Kingdom, and Canada in mid-July: Vivanno Nourishing Blends.

Vivanno is Starbucks' version of a smoothie. The thick, cold drink is prepared with one whole banana, a proprietary whey and protein powder, dairy or soy milk, and ice. The drink had actually been in development for eight months, and the two flavors we launched, Orange Mango Banana and Banana Chocolate, provided a serving of fruit, 15 grams of protein, and 5 grams of fiber at no more than 270 calories—with no artificial colors or sweeteners or high fructose corn syrup.

Vivanno faced two hurdles in its attempt to take hold with customers. First, we launched it at the exact same time that we introduced Sorbetto in California. So just as the rewards program had been overshadowed by Pike Place Roast, Vivanno risked getting lost in the attention that we lavished on our new Italian treat. Next, and more complex, was that the bananas that went into Vivanno marked the first time that perishable fruit had to be shipped, kept fresh, and discarded in our stores, posing a distribution and logistical dilemma.

The new health and wellness platform and the loyalty program both held tremendous potential to drive business in a way that was relevant to both the consumer and the Starbucks brand.

That said, I was still betting on Sorbetto.

* * *

It was just two weeks before Sorbetto's scheduled launch, and Cliff was shocked. "Where has the margin gone?" he wanted to know.

On July 15, 2008, three flavors—a yogurt-based Tangy Sorbetto, a slushy Citrus Ice Sorbetto, and a mix of the two, Tangy Citrus Ice

Sorbetto—would be available in more than 300 stores in Southern California. The base product had been shipped from Italy to our warehouses. Partners were being trained to prepare the drinks, and the in-store merchandising was bright and bold.

But we had yet to price the product, and Cliff was disturbed by the options he was hearing and what they meant for returns. A proposal to sell a 10-ounce Sorbetto, slightly larger than a tall cup of coffee, for $1.95 would drop the profit margin down to 16 percent. If priced at $2.25, the margin was 24 percent, nowhere near the 70 percent margin I'd elatedly embraced on our trip back from Italy.

The margin, it turned out, had been whittled down by higher than anticipated costs of goods and unforeseen complications. Although we planned to manufacture the base ingredient in the United States, for now we were buying and airfreighting it across the Atlantic at great expense, and the weakening value of the dollar against the euro was jacking up the already high costs. What's more, because of the consistency of the beverage, the company had to purchase hundreds of new machines to mix just the dairy-based Sorbetto drink, an investment we could not have predicted back in Italy.

It was too late to turn back, and hundreds of California stores were decked out in promotional pink decor. Brightly colored oversized "splat" spots had been stuck on store windows and floors. A 10-ounce Sorbetto, in a custom-designed container, was sold for $2.95 (we'd found our margin), and in the first few weeks it delivered a respectable sales pop, selling as many as 40 units a day per store.

Very quickly, however, problems emerged.

First, a tremendous amount of Sorbetto was being poured out instead of being served to customers.

Second, the new machines we'd procured to mix the yogurt-based Sorbetto required up to one and a half hours to clean at the end of each day, doubling our projected labor and sapping barista enthusiasm for the product. Our store partners liked Sorbetto's taste, but not the disciplined cleanup, even after we got it down to 45 minutes. And as we'd learned with Pike Place Roast, barista buy-in is essential to a new product's success in stores.

And third, Sorbetto contained a lot of sugar, making it a sweet treat that did not satisfy consumers' cravings for nutritious products or complement our emerging emphasis on health and wellness.

As summer rolled on, Sorbetto's lower-than-expected numbers

rolled in, and we had to accept that it was not generating enough incremental sales to compensate for its complexity and the high cost of goods.

Disappointed, and feeling somewhat responsible, I agreed with Cliff that we should abandon it.

At another time and in another environment, or perhaps if we had launched Sorbetto on a smaller scale, we might have been able to tweak the product. It was, after all, delicious in its own right. Instead, we opted to cut our losses because bigger issues required our attention, and we allowed Sorbetto to fade away.

What happened? I asked myself. Had my thirst for innovation blinded me? Starbucks had once been so good at creating products that right out of the gate transformed consumer behavior. Sorbetto's potential had played into that line of thinking.

I'd brashly embraced Sorbetto as a silver bullet.

But there is no such thing.

Not growing our store count. Not new coffee blends. Not loyalty or value programs. Not healthier foods and drinks.

Yes, opportunities to transform Starbucks for profitable, sustainable growth existed everywhere, but no single move, no product, no promotion, and no individual would save the company. Our success would only be won by many. Transforming Starbucks was a complex puzzle we were trying to piece together, where everything we did contributed to the whole. We just had to focus on the right, relevant things for our partners, for our customers, for our shareholders, and for our brand.

Chapter 21

I Know This to Be True

"I am sorry."

I spoke more slowly than usual to more than 1,000 Starbucks partners gathered in front of me. "And I apologize if anyone in this room feels that we have fractured the culture and values of the company with what has happened over the last few weeks, and specifically yesterday."

The ninth floor of the support center was packed with partners standing shoulder to shoulder. The crowd overflowed onto the exposed staircase and eighth floor common area, where people sat on the floor or stood, arms crossed, gazing up at the podium from where I spoke.

"It was a decision that we had to make," I explained. "And we made it with compassion."

The day before, on Tuesday, July 29, Starbucks Coffee Company had eliminated 1,000 nonstore positions, asking 550 people from throughout the organization to leave. One hundred and eighty of those people were in the greater Seattle area, the majority at the support center.

As much as possible we tried to conduct each separation meeting face-to-face, and throughout the day managers in every department, together with our partner resources professionals, held some of the toughest conversations of their careers, gently informing fellow partners and friends that they would no longer be working for Starbucks. Separated partners had a few hours to return to their desks, collect their things, download whatever information they needed from their computers, and say good-bye. If they chose to, they could come back over the weekend to collect their items instead. We let our people manage their own exits, without hovering security guards, and provided outplacement assistance, an off-site place to go to learn about their benefit options and how to move forward, a new e-mail account, as well as access to our employee assistance program. Severance packages and benefits were given to all who separated from the company, and they were fair, based on the person's position and length of employment. But still.

I'd held private conversations in my office with several partners who were leaving, and afterward I walked around the building. People were in tears, hugging coworkers good-bye.

"This is not personal," we'd told our displaced partners.

But of course being laid off *is* personal, for everyone. It was personal for the people who made the decisions and those who delivered the news. It was personal for the people who had spent years helping build our brand and for those who had only recently joined the company. It was personal for the hundreds of families who would undoubtedly be affected. For parents with mortgages, bills, and kids' birthdays coming up; for couples buying a house or just buying groceries; for men and women supporting themselves, paying off loans, assisting extended family members, and saving for retirement. And it was personal for people who had counted on Starbucks for health insurance or child care, or whose dreams were fueled by their 401(k) accounts and company stock.

> *I cannot put myself in their shoes. I can only tell you that I am sitting with this enormous responsibility to try and navigate through the most difficult economic conditions that Starbucks has ever faced, an economic situation that has deteriorated every month since January when I returned.*

Across the United States, wages were flat, consumer debt remained high, the cost of gas was climbing, and job losses were mounting. In June 2008, US unemployment had climbed to 5.5 percent, the highest it had been since October 2004. Starbucks was hardly the only organization restructuring, but all this was little comfort as people packed belongings and handed in ID cards before waiting at the bank of elevators for the last time. Few things in life are more personal than arriving home in the middle of a workday to contemplate an uncertain future.

The layoffs were also devastating for the partners who remained behind and stood before me today. I was not nervous as I spoke, but mindful of trying to honor a very tough and sad situation while being realistic about the company's pressing challenges. Our people needed confidence to move on. We had to turn this page.

> *This is a defining moment like no other for Starbucks Coffee Company, and moments like this are quite difficult and emotional so let me specifically address yesterday. I never anticipated, nor was I emotionally prepared for, the decisions that led to asking passionate, talented, deserving partners to leave our company. . . . I know people are angry and grieving and I know people are mad. But I had to make the difficult choice [and consider] the long-term sustainability of the company. Our revenue and profits have got to be linked to a lower cost structure or else we are going to find ourselves in a much worse situation. We have less customers in our stores this month than we did last month, and less last month than the month before. We are not seeing new customers come into the stores.*
>
> *The question is, How are we going to respond?*

* * *

In addition to the many initiatives under way to create customer demand and reverse the negative flow of traffic, we had to get the company's costs under control. Closing stores and fixing inefficiencies in the field was a start, but we needed to cut deeper.

Unlike the phalanx of global financial institutions that considered themselves too *big* to fail, Starbucks has never been an irresponsible spender. But perhaps because we viewed our company as too *good* to fail, we did not work or operate the business as wisely as we should have. Rarely did we make the effort or take the time to step back and question whether we made the most of our resources.

The situation in Seattle was akin to what Cliff was witnessing in stores. Our leaders and teams were always incredibly busy, putting in long hours under increasing stress, but their workloads—like empty cups waiting to be filled—kept stacking up. In our stores, rather than reconsider *how* our baristas poured coffee or made drinks, we often added people to absorb the load or in some cases tolerated less-than-perfect beverages. Similarly, in our offices—to keep pace with new store openings—we staffed up for short-term relief. More specifically, with each new store opening, our supply chain organization (SCO) was under intense pressure to deliver materials and equipment. Because SCO was moving so fast, it did not have time to figure out the most cost-effective, timely ways to work with suppliers or deliver goods. SCO was not at fault, and it was not alone. Most of our business units were striving to meet their objectives with the best of intentions. But not always with the best of practices.

During Jim Donald's two years as ceo, he did recognize Starbucks' lack of cost-management muscle and urged the company to, as he put it, "develop a new skill set" and tighten spending. But significant cuts never fully materialized, in part because there existed no acute need to run a tighter ship. Until now. The company's rapidly receding sales—comps in July were just shy of negative 7 percent—revealed a rocky foundation of operational inefficiencies, thinning our margins as never before. The leadership team and I agreed that Starbucks had no choice but to decisively pull tens of millions of dollars of permanent costs out of the business. And that meant reducing our workforce.

In a tense daylong meeting earlier that month, the leadership team, despite some resistance, had made the difficult decision that each business unit would reduce a percentage of its costs. No one prescribed to anyone else who or how many people should be let go. To absorb the pain, I think I convinced myself that we were saving the company by sacrificing a very small percentage of people to preserve the large percentage who would stay. If I were going to enhance the long-term value of the company, I had to make this difficult choice. Ultimately, it rested with me.

In the days that followed, our business unit leaders collaborated behind closed doors and—it was no secret to their staffs—went through the process of assessing who could stay and who would go. When I was handed lists of individuals who would be laid off, I looked at every name, never allowing a number on a page to replace a human being. I wanted to know the name and position of every person being asked to leave. I wanted to know who they were and how many years they'd been with the company. In many cases, a partner had been a solid performer with a strong track record, but we simply could no longer afford him or her. In certain instances I stepped in to make sure no politicizing or hidden agendas affected a decision, asking questions about why this person was being asked to leave or asked to stay.

I recognized, and so did the leadership team, that slimming down the company would be brutal. Absolutely brutal. And even as we did so as compassionately as possible, our actions still seemed unfair.

But the tragedy of doing nothing would have been far worse.

* * *

"Why don't you just sell the company?" someone outside Starbucks asked me rhetorically, suggesting that a larger organization could leverage things that we could not, given our size, and stop the bloodletting.

Unbeknownst to most of our partners, as ceo, pressure to dramatically slash costs came at me from all fronts as the chatter in the press and online insisted that Starbucks' best days were behind us. Investors wanted Starbucks to undo our company-owned and -operated store model and franchise the system, letting other people own and operate our stores and pay Starbucks royalties. On its face, it made economic sense. Franchising would have given us a war chest of cash and significantly increased our return on capital. But if Starbucks ceded ownership of stores to hundreds of individuals, it would be harder for us to maintain the fundamental trust our store partners had in the company, which, in turn, fueled the trust and connection they established with customers. Franchising worked well for other companies, but would, I believed, create a very different organization by diluting our unique culture.

"How much coffee do you roast?" someone else wanted to know.

"Four hundred million pounds a year."

"Well, if you reduce the quality just 5 percent, no one would know, and that's a few million dollars right there!" This was seriously suggested as an option. But Starbucks would never sacrifice quality for the sake of saving costs.

Others insisted I cancel our upcoming leadership conference, when we would bring almost 10,000 of our store, district, and regional managers together in one place at great expense, but for, I believed, great purpose. We desperately needed to reconnect with our own people, in person.

At these recommendations and others, I did not blink. Every brand has inherent nuances that, if compromised, will eat away at its equity regardless of short-term returns. As Starbucks navigated, we had to stay true to our values, reinvesting in and recommitting to the things that had brought us success, not quick fixes. We had to believe in our hearts that, if we were authentic and if we were true and stayed the course, this transformation would work.

"If I had a shadow of a doubt—*a shadow of a doubt*," I told the person who suggested we put Starbucks on the block, "that we would not return the glory of our company, the equity of the brand, the experience in our stores, and the pride of partners, then I would be the first one to say, 'Let's sell the company.'"

I needed to communicate this same confidence to our people at the open forum following the layoffs, to ask them to stay strong and focused, which was no easy request given the circumstances.

I can see the light, I know what we have to do. We have to show up. We have to do the work. And doing the work means we have to find answers to tough problems. We have to be highly focused on the things that matter and stop wasting time and money on things that are irrelevant.

What matters is that we push for answers for the problems in front of us and are curious about the things we do not see, and look for ways to get better, smarter, more efficient, and push for reinvention and innovation.

> *This is a true test of the company and a true test of the individu-*
> *als who are assembled here. The reason we are going to succeed is the*
> *same reason we have succeeded in the past. Not the stock price or the*
> *press. We succeeded because of what we believe in and what we*
> *stand for.*
>
> *I believe in the future of our company because I believe in all of you.*

Not everyone, of course, believed in me, and many people inside and outside the company were questioning my leadership, whether I could get us out of the deepening hole. In fact, during the past 24 hours I'd received a lot of e-mails from the people who were let go, thanking me for the opportunity to be part of Starbucks and thanking the company for dealing with them in a compassionate way. But I also got e-mails from partners who felt betrayed and questioned whether we were honoring our guiding principles. Read one curt note: "To provide an *uplifting* experience that enriches people's lives every day. Do you remember when that used to mean something? I do."

Given the frustration, it was imperative that I stand in front of our people and give them a chance to vent. Publicly. They were complaining among themselves anyway, but talking to me reinforced, I hoped, the very values people felt I had tarnished. Being transparent is my natural response, but it is also a symbol of the honesty I want everyone inside the company to embrace.

When I opened the forum floor to comments and questions, several people stepped up to the microphones stationed around the room. A few read prepared written comments. Others spoke spontaneously. When Sean Shanahan, a manager in risk management, spoke, his voice was edgy after the day of letting members of his team go. From across the room, he looked me in the eye. "We took part of the hit for you yesterday in having those conversations," he said. "And I don't want to do that again." He gathered his thoughts. "I need to know that you hear that. We are not prepared to go through this again. So, we will be looking to you for things that we may have never asked you for before. . . . Are you and the people around you prepared to be held accountable by us?"

"I think you have that right," I replied. "Thank you for saying that." Sean was right. Starbucks' leaders had to be accountable in ways we had not been in the past.

* * *

Decisiveness during this time of uncertainty was critical, especially when choosing who would lead Starbucks alongside me, and I continued to refine and realign Starbucks' leadership team, shifting people's roles, saying a respectful good-bye to others, and welcoming new talent.

The board, specifically Craig Weatherup, was impressing upon me the need to add seasoned executives from outside Starbucks to the management mix, people with rich brand-building and operational track records at larger organizations. I'd always believed that, to move forward, we needed to embrace new perspectives and approaches, and Starbucks had always attracted leaders with skill bases beyond the size and scale of the company.

Our challenge was finding individuals whose accomplishments were matched by their values and an innate sense for Starbucks' culture. This is a very fragile balance to strike, because the wrong match can pollute the integrity of the company. Political agendas. Managing upward, but not downward. An inability to earn respect or to be a trusted team player. These traits are poison. Yet when it comes to hiring, I have antennae about people's characters, a sixth sense that I often follow even if my choices raise others' eyebrows. More than once I have promoted internal leaders to positions that would be a stretch from their previous roles because their core skills, determination, and passion for what Starbucks stands for would, I wholeheartedly believed, yield success.

With the company in such dire straits, each leadership decision I made was more critical than ever. If I put or kept the wrong people in the wrong roles, the company would drift further off course.

By the end of July, along with the layoffs, I had made several significant leadership changes, including a few surprises.

I'd found our new chief information officer in Stephen Gillett, a 32-year-old from outside the retail industry. It appeared that Stephen would be the youngest CIO of a Fortune 500 company, which made some question whether he could handle the immense job of overhauling our ancient technological infrastructure. But Stephen brought a rich combination of technical acumen, valuable digital media knowledge, and insatiable curiosity to the table, all of which he'd honed at the digital media company Corbis, as well as at Yahoo! and CNET. I was also impressed by Stephen's dynamic thought process, and I sensed a good heart behind his wide grin.

To oversee our supply chain organization, I appointed Peter Gibbons, our soft-spoken yet tough-minded head of manufacturing who had come to Starbucks in 2007 from a huge chemical company, bringing discipline and pride to his work. Peter recognized, perhaps more than anyone else at Starbucks, just how broken our distribution and logistics systems were, and when I tapped him to be executive vice president of our global supply chain, the area of the business I knew the least about, I had confidence that Peter would act with informed decisiveness and professionalism.

And in September 2008, Vivek Varma joined Starbucks to lead public affairs after 12 years at Microsoft. I'd known Vivek and had asked his counsel on several complex issues that Starbucks had faced on several fronts. I found his perspective informed, confident, straightforward. And while we did not always agree, Vivek approached issues through a strategic and socially conscious lens that I believed would add sophisticated, sensitive guidance when it came to telling our story.

Cliff continued the good but hard work as president of our teetering US business. And after having worked side by side with Michelle Gass to articulate the company's direction with the Transformation Agenda, I needed her back in an operational role. She assumed the position of head of marketing and category, overseeing the teams that lead marketing, creative, beverages, coffee innovation, and food. Paula Boggs, who had come to Starbucks from Dell, remained our knowledgeable and multifaceted executive vice president of law and corporate affairs, and Chet Kuchinad was in charge of partner resources. Arthur Rubinfeld was back at the leadership table as president of global development. Arthur had stepped into the job with conviction and creativity, and in addition to tackling our real estate challenges, his design team was already looking forward, envisioning the future look and feel of Starbucks stores. Beyond these positions on the leadership team, I knew a few more changes remained.

I could not save Starbucks on my own. Being able to do so was never my intention or my belief when I returned as chief. I was no silver bullet and, like any leader, I needed to surround myself with strong talent who would bring new ideas and, with courage, challenge the old as well as challenge me. This meant watching some people leave the organization, which was never easy whether or not it was my decision.

* * *

Inside Starbucks, July 29, 2008, was dubbed Black Tuesday. It definitely was a dark time. In addition to the layoffs, some of our people were questioning what we stood for. Our sales growth was hitting new lows, especially on the weekends. Our cost structure was not sustainable.

And tomorrow I knew there would be headlines all over the world proclaiming that Starbucks had lost money for the first time in its history, because we had reported a net loss of $6.7 million for the third quarter. No matter that it was the one-time costs associated with the transformation that had taken us into negative territory—we'd actually made money before accounting for those charges, albeit not as much as the year before. A loss was still a loss. When I thought about our thicket of challenges both known and unknown, the word that came to mind was familiar and apt: "Onward." More than just a rallying cry or an attitude, "onward" seemed to connote the dual nature of how Starbucks had to do battle and do business in these increasingly complex, uncertain times.

"Onward" implied optimism with eyes wide open, a never-ending journey that honored the past while reinventing the future.

"Onward" meant fighting with not just heart and hope, but also intelligence and operational rigor, constantly striving to balance benevolence with accountability.

"Onward" was about forging ahead with steadfast belief in ourselves while putting customers' needs first and respecting the power of competition.

Yes, everyone at Starbucks could indulge his or her passion—be it for coffee, the environment, marketing, or design—but only if we did not lose sight of the need for profits.

"Onward" was about getting dirty but coming out clean; balancing our responsibility to shareholders with social conscience; juggling research and finances with instinct and humanity.

And "onward" described the fragile act of balancing by which Starbucks would survive our crucible and thrive beyond it. With heads held high but feet firmly planted in reality. This was how we would win.

I knew this to be true.

Thankfully, I was not alone in my conviction. The following

e-mail from Cindy Gange-Harris, a district manager in Edmonton, Canada, whom I had never met, arrived just before midnight on July 31, 2008.

Howard,

From the tone of your voice mail, the assorted press reports and blogs it sounds like you have many people voicing their concerns and disappointment to you around the business decisions that have been made.

I want you to know that you still have many partners who believe. I have been with Starbucks almost 11 years and know that to aspire and maintain greatness, difficult decisions must be made and sacrifices taken. I trust in the decisions that are being made to keep us on the right path. We will need to work harder than ever, with great diligence and attention to the operation of our business to keep us moving forward.

During my visits to stores I make it a point to connect with all of the partners in my stores, not just the manager, and talk to them about their training, their experience and ask for their feedback. I talk about what we are experiencing as a company and assure them that although we are facing challenges we have not faced in the past, I have seen countless examples of Starbucks facing adversity and how we work hard to "do the right thing" and make decisions based on our mission statement.

Thank you for all you are doing and creating a company that has given me my dream job. Even when some of the days are tough, they are overshadowed by all of the people that I have made a difference for and who have made a difference for me.

We ARE a different company, one of the best to work for in the industry, and I have absolute faith that fantastic things are ahead.

Part 4: Hope

Chapter 22

Truth in Crisis

On September 15, 2008, the economy spun into a free fall.

Lehman Brothers Holdings, the investment bank founded in 1844 as a general goods store, declared the largest bankruptcy in US history despite last-ditch efforts by the US Federal Reserve and competitors to prop up the failing institution. Between prep sessions for a board meeting in Los Angeles later that week, I watched on the television in my office as stunned Lehman employees filtered out of office buildings carrying boxes of belongings.

That same day, stalwart brokerage house Merrill Lynch and Company agreed to be taken over by Bank of America, essentially saving itself from Lehman's fate. Global insurer AIG was almost out of cash and teetered on the brink of collapse, a condition whose devastating consequences would ripple through dozens of countries.

And in Seattle, Washington Mutual, the Northwest's homegrown bank that had proudly flourished to become the nation's largest savings and loan institution, was under siege from its own massive portfolio of troubled mortgage-backed assets.

Few people understood, myself included, the degree to which the complex, risky investments made by the world's biggest banks were dangerously intertwined, but by the end of the day we would all have an idea. Wall Street fell more than 500 points on September 15, its biggest one-day point drop since the days following the September 11, 2001 terrorist attacks. While Starbucks' stock, which had been hovering at around $15 a share, did not take a big hit that day, hundreds of billions of dollars of personal wealth vanished, affecting millions of people, including our partners and their families.

Wrote Andrew Ross Sorkin that day in *The New York Times*:

> The humbling moves, which reshape the landscape of American finance, mark the latest chapter in a tumultuous year in which once-proud financial institutions have been brought to their knees as a result of hundreds of billions of dollars in losses because of bad mortgage finance and real estate investments. . . . "My goodness. I've been in the business 35 years, and these are the most extraordinary events I've ever seen," said Peter G. Peterson, co-founder of the private equity firm the Blackstone Group. . . . It remains to be seen whether the sale of Merrill, which was worth more than $100 billion during the last year, and the controlled demise of Lehman will be enough to finally turn the tide in the yearlong financial crisis that has crippled Wall Street and threatened the broader economy . . . which has been weakening steadily as the financial crisis has deepened over the last year, with unemployment increasing as the nation's growth rate has slowed.

So many respected companies had fallen so far so fast, to the shock of so many.

For the financial system and economy—as well as for Starbucks—it was taking a crisis to reveal fatal flaws. On one hand, Starbucks' problems as well as our mistakes paled in comparison to the financial devastation caused by the banks' mismanagement. On the other hand, our missteps could, like the banks', be our undoing, and thus it was more important than ever that Starbucks Coffee Company fix all that ailed us. We had so much at stake. Our thousands of partners needed their jobs, and our shareholders did not deserve to have their investments and trust in us disappear, too. We were better than that and had to keep accepting where we had gone wrong and fight to get it right.

This was especially true when it came to back-of-the-house operations. The escalating economic turmoil posed a further threat to our top-line sales and profit margins as already cautious consumers would no doubt cut back further on discretionary spending. And that meant, among other things, fewer trips to Starbucks. The financial crisis and the punditry, which painted Starbucks as a poster child for excess, were having a real psychological effect on our customers, making some people feel that by carrying around a cup of Starbucks coffee, they were not appearing frugal enough.

To make up for lost sales, we would have to strip hundreds of millions of dollars of permanent costs out of the business. In September 2008, cutting the fat out of Starbucks' operations took on a new urgency.

* * *

"The wheels have come off the bus," read the e-mail.

It was a Saturday morning, two weeks before the September 15 financial collapse, and Jim McDermet, Starbucks' senior vice president for the northeast Atlantic division, was e-mailing Peter Gibbons about a spate of recent problems with store deliveries. Peter was just weeks into his new job as head of Starbucks' supply chain organization and already recognized that SCO—the 1,300-partner business unit responsible for procuring, roasting, packaging, warehousing, and transporting Starbucks coffee, beverage ingredients, baked goods, merchandise, and other supplies to stores—was a bureaucratic monster.

Wrote Jim, "Across the division—and I would daresay the country— we are causing our district managers, store managers, and store partners real pain."

In Manhattan, upwards of 100 stores a day had been running out of food and other basics, like toppings for oatmeal, the popular breakfast item we'd added to the menu as part of the health and wellness platform. In store after store, delivery after delivery failed to show up on time or at all. Some stores even ran out of cups! Resourceful store managers and baristas were scrambling to make up for the shortfalls, which distracted them from customers. While the New York City problem was partly due to problems that our suppliers were experiencing, the performance was still unacceptable. It also was not an anomaly. In pockets throughout the Northeast, stores' sales and morale were suffering from a logistics breakdown.

Starbucks' supply chain operations had always been uniquely challenging. Every week, around the world, we made 83,000 deliveries of perishable and nonperishable items from our four coffee warehouses, five regional coffee-roasting plants, 50 distribution centers, and multiple suppliers. Every year in the United States and Canada, 608 million pastries were delivered to our company-owned stores. So were 103 million gallons of milk and 242 million pounds of coffee. Most of our stores received at least one delivery every single day. And depending on changes in weather conditions, orders varied. A humid day in Chicago meant stores could run out of nonfat milk by midday. A rainy week equaled inventory overstock.

If a store receives only *some* of the merchandise it orders, customer requests go unfulfilled and the store and company lose not only sales, but also customer goodwill. That's exactly what was happening. In 2008 the chance of a store getting everything it asked for on time and intact was about 35 percent, and it was highly likely that every day, thousands of stores were out of something. Tougher to measure were customer and partner disappointment. Every time a barista had to tell a customer, "Sorry, we're out of vanilla syrup" or "We didn't receive our banana shipment so I can't make your Vivanno," the fragile trust between Starbucks and our partners and between Starbucks and our customers fractured.

As part of the company's transformation, SCO was under intense pressure from the US business to improve service to stores and, simultaneously, under pressure from our cfo to drive down soaring costs.

The company had not been completely oblivious to SCO's problems, and prior to Peter's leadership there had been a reorganization— but it was widely thought to have only complicated matters and further confused our people and suppliers. As Jim McDermet had stated, our continued lack of discipline in this area was becoming painfully obvious.

At 5 a.m. on Wednesday, September 3, 2008, four days after Jim's SOS e-mail to Peter, a longtime partner and district manager in St. Louis, Tina Serrano, sent an e-mail to the distribution manager of her region about the shortage of bottled water in her stores.

I have heard of about a dozen or so stores that were zeroed out of Ethos. Some stores have been out for close to a week. Can you help? We have a major fair coming to town this weekend and no water.

Six hours later, having done more due diligence, Tina shot off another e-mail.

FYI—We are out EVERYWHERE!!

Throughout the day Tina's e-mails were forwarded from one person to another and worked their way up the organization. Finally, the next day, at 6:36 a.m., an "Out of Ethos" e-mail was sent to Rich Nelsen, regional vice president, who e-mailed Craig Russell, senior vice president of store services, who immediately e-mailed Peter Gibbons.

Peter,
    I wanted to ensure you had visibility to the Ethos supply issues impacting SE Plains. The teams are responding but the problem seems well beyond that team's scope of control.

When news of the problem somehow reached me, I walked up to the ninth floor and into Peter's office and slumped back on a chair in front of his desk as he briefed me about the situation. Dozens of Starbucks stores were running out of Ethos water, or their supplies had already hit bottom, and many warehouses did not have any Ethos in stock to replenish it. I was incredulous.

"How could this happen?" The fact that a portion of Ethos sales was donated added to my frustration.

"Don't worry," Peter calmly assured me. "This is all going to be fixed."

"But *how could it happen?*"

Instead of dancing around my question, Peter answered me straight up. "SCO is so confused with all the changes that have taken place that no one knew who was supposed to order the water." *Unbelievable.* "We'll get it straightened out. It won't happen again."

I'd known for years that the overall cost-effectiveness and efficiency of our manufacturing and supply operations was not on a par with the quality of our coffee. I'd heard the complaints, but for years SCO was so busy keeping up with the company's explosive growth—"Just get products to stores" was the mandate—that it did not have the time to properly invest in the discipline and competency that building a world-class supply chain requires. Nor was there a reason for the company's senior leaders to insist that we invest in SCO. The financial success of our stores more than made up for, or rather covered up, logistics and distribution inefficiencies. Nonetheless, we still incurred hundreds of thousands of dollars in unnecessary expenses each year, such as paying to ship US-sourced supplies overseas to our European stores rather than sourcing them locally. Or doing business with so many local bakeries that our food tasted inconsistent and prevented the cost savings that come from purchasing large quantities of, say, blueberry muffins from one or two suppliers.

Like our information technology systems, Starbucks' supply chain operations had not matured as the organization they supported grew in size and complexity.

Another source of the problem, to the board's point, was our lack of deep supply chain expertise. Fault didn't lie with SCO's current leaders or managers, but rather with our culture. Starbucks had a pattern of promoting talented people into new roles to stretch and develop them, even if they did not always seem to have the obvious credentials. For years that worked fine, and our people loved the opportunities, but our supply chain operations in particular had become too sophisticated to simply allow well-meaning, hardworking people to learn on the job, even if they were committed to success. SCO desperately needed specialists, not generalists.

I accepted part of the blame. Starbucks' supply chain was not, historically, an area I focused on as chairman or as chief executive. Quite frankly, my attention went to the engine of the company: driving revenue by building the Starbucks brand, creating the Starbucks Experience, and inspiring our partners. These were my priorities and passions, as well as my skills, and like many people I gravitated to my strengths.

But debacles such as the Ethos shortage, while not necessarily life threatening to the business, enlightened me to my own shortcomings as a leader: I hadn't delved far enough into the areas of the business that I was not comfortable with or had little innate interest in. I should have looked under the hood more often. Now I had an opportunity to self-correct and become as well versed in the company's back-end operations as I was in my own core competencies—which had been one of my intentions when I eliminated the coo role.

Still, SCO had needed its own leader who could come in and, with decisive authority, identify what was broken and adapt proven solutions. I put tremendous trust in Peter, who had joined Starbucks as head of manufacturing even though it was a step down from his previous responsibilities. Peter had been steeped in back-end operations since age 18, when he worked in a vinyl-floor factory in Scotland, and more than once in his two-decade career he'd driven radical supply chain changes through larger organizations with more locations and product variations than Starbucks. Plus, Peter is a natural leader. His confidence and straight-talking yet personal communication style belie his technical training, and he quickly earned the respect of partners who, as he sensed after hosting his first SCO open forum, were hungry to be led by someone with a back-to-basics clarity.

"At the end of the day," Peter would repeat over and over, "someone places an order, someone fulfills that order in a warehouse, it gets loaded on a truck and is delivered to a store. That's what we do."

His strategy to transform SCO was all of three words: "Service. Cost. People." Under Peter, SCO would have three goals: Deliver great service to all who placed an order, be they our stores or hotels that served our coffee. Second, lower our costs. And third, develop internal talent and recruit specialists in transportation, logistics, engineering, and quality control.

"I won't take up your time with a lot of words or promises," Peter had written in an e-mail to Cliff and about one dozen regional vice presidents about SCO's poor service record. "I just want you to know that the service levels that are being provided to you are not acceptable and will not be allowed to continue."

Not only did Peter have to overhaul the current system—rebuilding it to accommodate the company for years to come—but he also had to do so while preserving our coffee's quality and not further alienating our vendors.

What's more, every new product the company was launching presented SCO with another piece to add to the puzzle. On September 10, 2008, it was my turn to receive an e-mail bemoaning our supply chain, albeit indirectly. The complaint came from a customer.

> *Dear Sir,*
>
> *It sure is difficult to find stores with the ingredients in stock to make orange mango banana Vivannos. I have to drive all over. Some run out of bananas and others run out of the juice. Hope this will improve. Honestly, it's every day, and they taste soooo good, if you can get them and get them right.*

I forwarded the e-mail to Peter without explanation. The original e-mail's subject—"Vivannos Missing In Action"—would tell him all he needed to know.

Five days later, the collapse of Lehman's sparked an economic crisis that would soon sweep the world.

★ ★ ★

In September 2008, the debate about what the fall of Wall Street meant for Main Street was in full swing, and I left Seattle to do a scheduled tour of Starbucks stores in Los Angeles as part of a board meeting. Cliff and two of our directors were visiting stores with me. At a Starbucks in downtown LA, after visiting with the baristas, Clara Rolan, the store's manager—who began at Starbucks as a barista in 2003—took us in the back office for a private conversation to discuss her store's performance. I wanted to know what was selling, what was not. And what she was witnessing with consumers.

"With the economy so bad," I asked Clara. "How do you keep customers coming back?" Clara paused for a moment before answering.

"I think it would be better if one of our regular customers answers that question," Clara said. I was unsure whether having a customer in the back office was a good idea, but I deferred to Clara, who walked out of the room and walked back in with a man in a suit. I could not help but notice he had a gun on his hip. "Don't worry," he said, noticing me noticing his pistol. "I'm a police officer." It turned out he was a detective for the Los Angeles Police Department who frequented Clara's store two or three times a day.

I asked him directly why he came to Starbucks so often.

"I could just as easily go to a 7-Eleven," he said matter-of-factly. Then he shared a conversation that he and his wife had had at their kitchen table that past weekend as they reviewed their family's budget, just as millions of other families had been doing of late. "My wife asked whether I could give up my daily Starbucks." Standing there in the back room, he recounted his reply. "Let me tell you why I cannot give it up. Because it's not about a cup of coffee. I have a tough job. I see things on a daily basis that no one should see and experience. But the one good thing I can count on every single day is how the people in that store make me feel." Then he addressed me directly. "I want to tell you about your employees. They know my kids' names. They know where I go on vacation. They write notes on my coffee cup. I could be seventh in line and they start making my drink." The baristas knew he took his grande nonfat latte with two Splendas, extra hot with no foam.

He added that, as a police officer, he understood the importance of treating every person he came in contact with in his job with respect. "You never know what's going on in people's lives when you serve them," he paused. "For all you know, it could be someone's last day on earth." Coming from a detective who had seen his share of trauma, this was not a statement made in jest. "This is my little escape," he said he had finally told his wife. "You just have to allow me that." And with that, Officer Kevin Coffey—I swear that was his name, Kevin Coffey—thanked us for our time, hugged Clara, and walked out.

It is one thing for me to espouse the importance of human connection. But hearing it from a customer was just the boost I needed before meeting with the board.

Chapter 23

A Galvanizing Moment

One month after Wall Street's September 2008 meltdown and a few weeks before Starbucks would announce shockingly reduced profits for the fourth quarter, I was being pressured to cancel Starbucks' leadership conference, a once biennial meeting the company holds for all North American district, regional, and store managers—about 10,000 people. But I refused. From the moment I came back as ceo I was steadfast in my decision to hold this event.

As local leaders, Starbucks' store managers were keys to the company's transformation. All the cost cuts and innovation meant nothing unless our baristas understood their personal responsibility to connect with customers and unless our store managers felt personally accountable for operating profitable stores. The in-store experiences our partners created would carry the brand—wherever we decided to take it—and as our sales and our stock and the economy fell, I needed an unfiltered venue for expressing my empathy about all that we were asking our partners to do and telling them plainly what was at stake.

Some former attempts to bring our managers together had been canceled, one because it fell on the heels of the September 11 terrorist attacks and another because it was deemed an unnecessary expense. Now, in the fall of 2008, there was no question, at least for me. Starbucks was in dire need of an event that would educate our partners and reinstill confidence in the company's purpose.

Almost every major US city wanted to host us. The food and lodging revenue alone—a significant piece of the conference's $30 million price tag—would be a windfall for any local economy.

But we chose New Orleans.

To some people this seemed absurd. We had never held the conference outside Seattle, and coordinating travel and lodging and meals and programs for tens of thousands of people in a hard-to-reach city that was still recovering from 2005's devastating Hurricane Katrina would be a logistical nightmare. But the reasons against going to New Orleans—that spicy southern city known for jazz and Mardi Gras and hospitality—were the very reasons we had to go. After our July layoffs and store closings (none, however, in New Orleans), Starbucks was losing not just money but also partners' trust. Unless we rallied our store managers around our new mission and taught them how to more profitably operate their stores, our company would drown. I was sure of it.

But reigniting people's hearts and minds had to be done in person. For all the promise of digital media to bring people together, I still believe that the most sincere, lasting powers of human connection come from looking directly into someone else's eyes, with no screen in between. And at this tenuous juncture, our partners needed to connect with me, with other Starbucks leaders, and with one another not online, but in New Orleans.

At that time, no other US city's experience seemed like such a natural extension of our values as well as our crucible. Historically, there is a coffee connection. New Orleans straddles the Mississippi River before it pours into the Gulf of Mexico and was the first port to bring coffee into the United States. But more relevant was that we identified with New Orleans because of the city's ongoing uphill battle to recover. The massive storm was one of the five most deadly hurricanes in US history, and when it hit land the powerful floods from failed levees destroyed thousands of homes, schools, possessions, and livelihoods; almost 2,000 people were killed, and thousands more were rendered homeless. At one point, 80 percent of New Orleans was underwater. The city lost well over 100,000 trees, and when the storm was over, the physical destruction it left amounted to *37 years worth of garbage*, all generated in one day.

Most appalling, however, had been the slow emergency response and recovery assistance and the utter lack of attention from government agencies that New Orleans received. Like other organizations and individuals around the country, Starbucks, in part through the company's foundation, pledged $5 million to the city right after the hurricane. And Sheri and I donated another $1 million. But three years later, the city was still struggling, and when Craig Russell and Sherry Cromett, the leadership conference's organizers, met with city leaders to plan the event, a captain from the New Orleans police department broke down describing how his family had suffered through Katrina. The manager of one national hotel chain teared up at the thought that Starbucks would bring its business to his city.

When I walked the streets of the Ninth Ward with Cliff a month prior to the conference, I too was stunned. We saw neighborhoods still in tatters and homes barely standing, like wood skeletons rotting in the sun. Parks, playgrounds, schools were all still broken. Empty. Entire neighborhoods were flattened and emanated the numbing atmosphere of a cemetery. It was unimaginably tragic. After the storm, many citizens left New Orleans to live elsewhere, but those who stayed were determined to rebuild. They loved their city. In some respects, their attitude reminded me of villages in Rwanda that exuded a palpable combination of desperation and fortitude and hope and self-reliance as they tried to recover from the 1994 genocide. I knew that when Starbucks' almost 8,000 store managers, 900 district managers, 120 regional directors, 250 international partners, dozens of senior leaders, and support staff converged on the city for a week in October, we would do much more than help ourselves. We would help the community.

If done right—and it had to be done right—a leadership conference in New Orleans would be a galvanizing event, raising our company's level of passion and performance where we needed it most: in front of our customers.

But if the week felt like a rah-rah, feel-good corporate party, it would fail.

If it was a self-indulgent trade show, a tense lecture, or a boring training seminar led by talking heads, it would fail.

It had to be visceral. Interactive. Genuine. Emotional. Intelligent.

Our week in New Orleans could not feel like a shallow extravagance during a time of cutbacks, but an investment in the company's people and our transformation, a sincere reminder of what Starbucks stands for and a transfer of tools and knowledge so each manager would be excited and incentivized to return to his or her store and run a better business.

If done right, a week in New Orleans would be an invaluable, reinvigorating deposit in the evaporating reservoir of trust between our people and the company.

A lot had to happen in New Orleans.

* * *

On Sunday, October 26, 2008, I left Seattle and traveled with Michelle, Vivek, Wanda, and Valerie to the conference. At the same time, thousands of partners were leaving their homes and their stores, boarding planes, and racing to make connecting flights to meet us there. None of us could predict exactly how the week would pan out, including Craig's small team of seven, who had been planning the conference for months.

The degree of logistical coordination required to house, feed, teach, and inspire almost 10,000 people—in a manner that was both safe for our partners and respectful to our hosting city—was staggering. We would fill 38 hotels. Serve 33,000 meals each day, make dinner reservations at 32 restaurants and banquet halls, and usher everyone through breakfasts and lunches at the city's massive convention center, where the staff was not big enough to serve all our needs. We wound up recruiting folks from local homeless shelters to help us out.

We had to prepare about 10,000 welcome bags and almost 10,000 different agendas since every partner followed a unique schedule for the week. They included participation in five major activities:

- **Informational sessions,** roundtables, panels, and educational electives

- **Four huge interactive galleries** designed to bring Starbucks' mission, values, operations, and store-management skills to life

- **Community volunteer events** rebuilding and refurbishing some of the city's most devastated public spaces and neighborhoods

- **A closing general session,** the one time all of us would gather together for the same presentation, during which we would make two surprise announcements that, I knew, would bring our people to their feet

- **A four-block street fair** organized for Starbucks' partners and featuring hundreds of local restaurants, artists, musicians, and entertainers

I had been involved in the planning and yet still was hard-pressed to imagine exactly what the conference's look and feel would actually be. I knew what we needed to achieve, but the costs had added up, even beyond what I had estimated, and as the plane began its descent, my nervousness heightened. The New Orleans leadership conference was possibly Starbucks' riskiest move since January, more costly and questioned than Pike Place Roast and Clover and Sorbetto. I was feeling pressure to deliver on the investment even though we would never be able to formally measure the return.

Immediately upon landing at Louis Armstrong New Orleans International Airport, I felt the energy. A marching band was on hand to meet our partners, and the drive to our hotel took us down streets where, hanging from streetlamps, large blue and green banners declared "BELIEVE." Michelle explained that Starbucks had sent hundreds of these banners and posters to the New Orleans Chamber of Commerce, which had distributed them throughout welcome mats for our partners. Amazing. We also drove vastated Ninth Ward, where some families were still vernment-provided trailers because their homes were e. The level of poverty and despair was beyond my n.

I was so proud of the reasons we had come to New Orleans, but those reasons also made my stomach churn.

Arriving at the hotel, my mood shifted yet again. I could not check in fast enough! I felt like a kid going to Disneyland for the first time, propelled by insatiable curiosity and anticipation. I paced in the hotel lobby waiting for Michelle and Vivek. "Let's go, let's go," I clapped with a smile. I was anxious to get to the convention center and view the galleries. SYPartners, the strategy and design firm that had come to know our company so intimately since our very first Beatles session in Seattle earlier in the year, had conceptualized the four different galleries based on specific takeaways that Cliff and Michelle wanted our store managers to absorb. Touch Worldwide, a design and production company, brought SYPartners' ideas to life. In the car, Michelle described what I had only seen in drawings: Each of the four 100,000-square-foot galleries had a different theme—coffee, customers, partners, and stores. I wanted to walk through and experience each just as our partners would.

We pulled up to the massive Ernest M. Morial Convention Center, entered through a wall of glass doors, and quickly made our way to the exhibition hall that featured the coffee gallery. Inside, I stopped abruptly, awestruck by the scene sprawled out before me. The at least two-story-high pavilion looked like nothing you'd see at a typical trade show, but rather a stage set with dramatic scenes from a play about coffee's journey from soil to cup. There were nearly 1,000 actual coffee trees representing our coffee beans' countries of origin. There was a mock drying patio like coffee farms have, where anyone could run his or her hands through a bushel of green coffee beans or grab a rake to churn thousands of beans strewn across the floor as if to dry in the sun. A huge coffee roaster had been assembled so several of our roast masters could take store managers on a virtual tour of a roasting plant. Oversized posters and photos and videos illustrated what it means to source coffee ethically, how Starbucks works with farmers, as well as the enormity and untapped potential of the global coffee market. The gallery culminated with the beans' "last 10 feet," where ground coffee is put in the hands of the barista for brewing and, finally, is poured into a customer's cup. Dub Hay, among our most-esteemed coffee aficionados, would end this gallery's tour with a coffee tasting.

It was unbelievable.

In another pavilion, this one housing the customer gallery, every set was designed to put our partners in our customers' shoes. At one towering display I could pick up a coffee cup, hold it up to my ear (like the old-fashioned children's game "telephone"), and listen to actual recordings of people who had called in to our support center with praise or critiques of their store experiences.

A hilarious video reminded our people to treat every customer with the same level of respect and attention, from the überloyalist who knows every barista's name (we affectionately called this composite customer "Bob") to the first-time Starbucks visitor who doesn't know the difference between a grande and a venti (known internally as "not Bob").

In a quieter exhibit, partners could walk among a three-dimensional photomontage of candid shots of people in our stores. Each photo and its caption was a reminder that every Starbucks location is a rare place where people who increasingly live their lives in front of screens and behind steering wheels can physically interact with others. The pictures reinforced how much a barista's job matters given that he or she quite possibly might serve up the only human connection in a customer's day.

The partner and store galleries—also 100,000 square feet each and divided into thematic sections—were equally as grand and powerful. Almost every item used in the galleries as a prop was recyclable, reusable, or something we could take back home with us to avoid leaving a big footprint at the convention center. I was amazed by the resourcefulness, the creativity, and the nonverbal cues of the entire experience. Each gallery was interactive. It was emotional. It was multisensory. It was storytelling!

Ultimately the galleries created an immersive experience that had the power to positively change our partners' behavior. When people can see things, feel things, interact with things, that is when their minds actually begin to shift. I believed that our store managers would, as we had intended, walk away from the conference with new skills for managing their teams, treating customers, and running their stores—even for the way they understood and talked about coffee. I simply could not wait for them to experience each gallery.

Standing near a doorway, taking in the magnitude of what had been created for our people, a sense of calm washed over me. I spoke just above a whisper. "Okay," I said, more to myself but loud enough for Michelle to overhear. "We're going to be okay."

* * *

"How many people are you bringing?"

"Ten thousand." Even through the phone, Craig Russell could see people's stunned expressions. Months before we arrived in New Orleans, Craig's team had contacted several nonprofit community and nongovernmental organizations—NGOs—to let them know Starbucks' leadership conference was coming to their city and that our people wanted to help. Although the groups were grateful, it quickly became clear that they simply had no precedent for hosting thousands of volunteers all at once. The NGOs did not have enough supervisors. There were not enough shovels! So, in addition to bodies, we bought our own shovels and hammers and other supplies, $1 million worth, enough to fill two rental trucks.

Each day of the conference, from Monday through Thursday, about 2,000 partners joined one of six organizations for five hours to do whatever needed doing in New Orleans. In City Park—a 1,300-acre public sanctuary that had suffered millions of dollars in landscaping damages from Katrina and had to reduce its 260-person staff to just more than 30—our partners planted 6,500 plugs of coastal grasses, installed 10 picnic tables, and laid four dump truck loads of mulch. At Tad Gormley Stadium, a popular venue for high school football games, partners scraped and painted 1,296 steps, 12 entrance ramps, hundreds of yards of railing, and a half-mile-long fence. In the Gentilly neighborhood, two playgrounds were constructed. In Broadmoor, 22 city blocks of street and storm drains were cleaned. In Hollygrove, partners did construction and leveled dirt for New Orleans' first urban farm. We collaborated with the Crescent City Art Project to paint, in one day, 1,350 murals at 25 public school grounds, and with Hike for KaTREEna, we planted 1,040 trees.

The NGOs were astonished at our productivity. Most had never hosted a group of our size and were used to volunteers coming in and swinging a hammer for an hour or so. But when our teams of partners showed up—aggressive, athletic, passionate—they could finish a project in two and a half hours even when they were scheduled for four. "Give us more!" we cried, and more we got.

I spent my volunteer hours helping more than a dozen store managers whom I'd never met paint a house, one of the 86 homes our volunteers repaired that week so families could move back in after three years of displacement. While there was laughter and a sense of camaraderie as we climbed ladders, painted front stoops, and caulked and raked and planted and dug and drilled and sawed and hammered and fixed doors and laid down floors, there was also a heartwrenching pang. Many of us spent time talking with the men and women who had lived through Katrina, and we heard stories of not only individual sacrifice and loss, but also of neighbors taking care of neighbors. The power of community was so evident in New Orleans, and when people's appreciation of our efforts was tough for them to put into words or a smile was not enough, they expressed themselves with quiet tears or a hug. Incredibly emotional.

"When you give up," said a slim older man whose home we rebuilt, "you might as well lay down and die." It was obvious that we weren't just giving people back their homes, but also restoring a sense of dignity. No doubt, our community contribution reinforced what it meant to work for Starbucks, and I knew that the experience would be difficult to adequately describe to people who were unable to attend.

Throughout the week, our volunteers' presence could be seen en masse. We arrived at work sites by the busload, almost everyone clad in jeans and the same white T-shirt or navy sweatshirt. The name "Starbucks" did not appear on our clothing. Instead, "Onward" was printed across the chest. I'd been surprised to see the shirt design when I'd pulled it from my own welcome bag in my hotel room. Incorporating "Onward" had not been my idea, and as far as I could recall this was the first time my signature sign-off had been lifted from my memos. It was somewhat surreal, but I could not have imagined a more appropriate time or place to give that word more life.

All told, Starbucks' partners volunteered approximately 50,000 hours of time in New Orleans. It was unprecedented, and I was beyond proud. Our partners were as well. Proud of the impact we were able to make during our visit to New Orleans, as well as even a little bit prouder of the company that we had come here to rebuild.

"In times of adversity and change, we really discover who we are and what we're made of," I would later hear one partner say as he reflected on the week. "To be a part of this organization as it moves through transformation, that is really exciting."

New Orleans was serving its purpose in helping us rediscover ours. And the week had only just begun.

★ ★ ★

Whenever I see someone carrying a cup of coffee from a Starbucks competitor, whether it's an independent coffee shop or a fast-food chain, I take their decision not to come to Starbucks personally. I wonder what I, as Starbucks' chairman and ceo, might have done to keep them away and what I might do to encourage them to come back or to try us for the first time. I ask myself what I can do today to win someone's business and earn his or her loyalty. If we were going to really transform the company, Starbucks' store managers needed to take their jobs just as personally as I take mine—to act in their stores just as they were acting here in New Orleans, where every tree planted or house painted mattered. We'd come here not as bystanders, but as participants, and on Wednesday, as the conference neared its close, it was time to turn our attention inward and accept that, as a company, we were in the midst of our own crisis and could not afford to stand back and hope for the best. We each had a responsibility to help ourselves and recognize that every little act matters: A store manager's job is not to oversee millions of customer transactions a week, but one transaction millions of times a week.

The general session would give me one shot to help our partners fall back in love with Starbucks and ensure that they understood their roles.

Inside the New Orleans Arena, the home of the NBA's Hornets basketball team, my intent was to share with the audience of almost 10,000 my thoughts on what had gone wrong at Starbucks and how we needed to self-correct, an endeavor that was as much about attitude as it was about business tools, tactics, and resources. I had no script, but knew I wanted to strike a balance between harsh realism and belief in our future. The massive arena was dark except for the lit stage. Every seat was filled. When I walked in front of a huge lime green screen that read "Onward," the arena settled down into serious quiet.

We are here for a reason. We are here to celebrate our heritage and traditions and also to have an honest and direct conversation about what we are responsible to do as leaders. . . . We are not a perfect company. We make mistakes every single day. We put our heart and our conscience first, but we have lots of issues that we are trying to balance. Expectations are high from every constituent and we are trying our best, especially during this downturn and in this economy, to do the right thing. . . .

Now, we can point to many things that perhaps are causing the issues that we have faced this year. Like many other companies, we are facing perhaps the most difficult economic situation since the Great Depression. It's real. It is serious. People do not have as much money as they once did, and Starbucks more often than not is a discretionary purchase. So we have the economy. And we also have something else. Something new. We have competitors small and large who think we are vulnerable and not as good as we used to be. Not as passionate. And they are trying to take our customers away. Which is why one of the themes of this conference has been to make it personal.

But what does that mean?

What does it mean when approximately 50 customers a day are not coming into our stores versus last year? What does it mean when at eight o'clock in the morning the line is out the door and a customer peels off and leaves? What does it mean when you see a customer you recognize with a cup of coffee that is not ours? What does it mean when you know for a fact that the beverage you just handed over to the customer was not made to the standard of Espresso Excellence? These are serious questions, and what they mean, I have always believed strongly, is that we have to take accountability and responsibility for the things that we observe. The things that we experience. And the things that we learn.

I spoke for more than half an hour, and it was actually difficult for me to wrap up; I had the attention of the people with the power to turn Starbucks around. I did not want to let them go, and I took every last second of my time to reach them. "I will do everything humanly possible to represent you the way that I ask you to represent the company. Passionately. Honestly. With great sincerity and humility and doing everything I can to exceed your expectations to make sure our future is as great as our past."

The next few hours of the general session took a page from our annual meeting, using that platform as an opportunity to blend substance with inspiration, to inform as well as rally. Gospel choirs sang. Other leaders spoke. And backstage we had two surprises that I knew would electrify our partners. I just wasn't sure which would get the bigger response.

★ ★ ★

"I was going to jump out of a cranberry scone, but maybe not."

Bono, lead singer for U2, global activist, and someone I consider a friend, had joined me onstage to everyone's shock, and now he leaned into a speaker's podium and, in a black shirt and his signature red-tinted sunglasses, spoke candidly. I had come to know Bono through our mutual interest in and support of African countries, and I was grateful that he had been able to make it to New Orleans, not to wow us with celebrity, but to educate and motivate store managers about a new multiyear partnership between Starbucks and his organization.

My conversations about partnering with (RED) had begun a year before with Tom Freston, the cofounder and former CEO of MTV Networks, back when we both were sitting on the DreamWorks board. Thanks to Michelle's diligence, my initial dialogue with Tom had finally come to fruition, and during the 2008 holiday season Starbucks would designate its three holiday drinks (RED) and give a nickel for each one sold in the United States and Canada to the Global Fund, which finances programs to fight AIDS, tuberculosis, and malaria. Like all monies collected through purchases of (RED) products at Gap, Apple, Converse, and Dell, our contributions would go directly to the Global Fund for AIDS programs in Africa. The announcement thrilled many of our partners who had been disappointed that Starbucks had not "gone (RED)" sooner, given the natural synergy of our organizations' values.

"These are interesting times," Bono began.

Howard has brought me to talk to you in interesting, strange, unsettling times. For Starbucks. For America generally. Times of crisis. Times of chaos. Times of opportunity. . . . The sight of your stores closing— well, a sign of the times. Historically, though, it is times like these, times of disruption, where America seems to discover its greatness.

Bono spoke not just about Starbucks and the United States but also, more importantly, about his travels to Africa, a continent where 4,000 lives were being lost every day to preventable, treatable diseases, and where 12 million children had been orphaned because of HIV. It had sparked in Bono a rage that ultimately drove him to create (PRODUCT) RED. He moved us by speaking in our own language about the absolute necessity of companies to do well by doing good.

Some people say, "Come on, markets are not about morals, they are about profits." I say that is old thinking. That's a false choice. The great companies will be the ones that find a way to have and hold on to their values while chasing their profits, and brand value will converge to create a new business model that unites commerce and compassion. The heart and the wallet. . . . The great companies of this century will be sharp to success and at the same time sensitive to the idea that you can't measure the true success of a company on a spreadsheet—

He paused for a second and smiled wryly. "I can't believe I just said the word 'spreadsheet.' Please do not tell the band I said the word 'spreadsheet.'"

We laughed, but most everyone in the arena also believed, especially after the week we'd just had, that Bono was right: People want to do business with companies they respect and trust, especially in the current climate, when they are being more discerning and are scrutinizing their purchases.

Ever since we'd expanded our relationship with Conservation International back in March, Starbucks had taken more steps to do the right thing as well as to earn consumers' respect, including putting a stake in the ground and setting some significant goals for how we would approach business in the future. We called this effort Starbucks Shared Planet, and it represents our commitment to doing business in a manner that is good for people as well as the earth. Starbucks Shared Planet is not just a philosophy, but also a set of tangible, ambitious, forward-looking goals that, for the first time, Starbucks committed to publicly.

The goals address how we design and build stores, the environmental footprint of our cups, how we give back to neighborhoods, and, of course, how we source Starbucks' coffee. We reaffirmed our commitment to ethical sourcing by, first, announcing there would be more farmer support centers, this time in East Africa, and vowing to ethically source 100 percent of Starbucks' coffee by 2015, 45 percent more than we were currently procuring.

We also committed to double our annual purchase of Fairtrade certified coffee to 40 million pounds in 2009, making us the largest purchaser, roaster, and retailer of Fairtrade coffee in the world that year. The move would affect thousands of farmers, including many who only harvested two or three acres of land.

Putting ourselves out there in this way at such a tenuous time in our business affirmed for many of our partners—who held the company to high standards in this regard—that, despite financial challenges, Starbucks was not abandoning its values. In fact, we doubled-down.

At the end of Bono's talk, Michelle walked onstage and put a red barista apron on him. Our partners exploded into applause. I thought nothing else could match their joy at Starbucks' long overdue participation in (RED), our Shared Planet commitments, or the image of Bono as a barista. But I was wrong.

★ ★ ★

Bono was upstaged. By Cliff.

The head of Starbucks' US business walked onstage holding a mysterious metal briefcase, the contents of which he had just gotten the go-ahead to publicly announce. In fact, Cliff had been in his hotel room the night before when he received an e-mail from our chief information officer, Stephen Gillett. Since Stephen had stepped into that role, he'd initiated sweeping IT reforms, among them negotiating to acquire 10,000 Hewlett-Packard laptops to supplement our stores' outdated computer systems. Stephen couldn't make it to New Orleans because his wife was due to have their fourth child, and his back-and-forth discussions with HP were still going on when he arrived at the hospital. Finally, from just outside the delivery room, Stephen e-mailed an anxious Cliff: "Go ahead and tell the partners. I just closed the deal." And with that, a relieved Stephen clicked off his cell and returned to his wife's side.

Before opening the silver case onstage, Cliff first reviewed the various new support tools coming to stores: a new, easier-to-use point-of-sale system (essentially, the automated cash registers) would be ready to pilot in 2009. Labor scheduling software would empower managers to better control staffing and expenses. A "retail dashboard" would provide data and a common language to improve business acumen. Each announcement was followed by cheers from a stadium filled with store managers fed up with Starbucks' antiquated technologies.

"Okay, you've been wondering what's in this briefcase." Cliff picked it up and placed the case on the podium. He flipped open the top and removed a black laptop computer. A roar of applause. There were whistles. High fives. Hoots. Cliff received a standing ovation that rivaled Bono's. "The tools you need to do your job are on the way," said Cliff above the din, announcing that every store would soon be getting its own laptop. The volume and duration of our part-ners' jubilation exceeded anything we had heard or seen that day, providing proof of just how desperately our managers needed better resources and how hungry they were to do a better job.

I spoke for the last time.

The power of this company is you. We need to recognize as leaders that, unlike any other time in our history, this is a seminal moment. This is a test. A crucible. A challenge for how we are going to respond. And my primary message is to share with you the pride that I have in being your partner. The faith that I have in you. People talk about the power of the Starbucks brand, but the power of the Starbucks brand is not some external force. It is you and the people you represent. You are going to restore it. People are going to be writing history books about the business of Starbucks, and the busi-ness of Starbucks is going to once again demonstrate that you can build a company with a conscience.

Please remember what you have experienced here. Remember how you felt. And when you get back, please do not be a bystander. Change and refine behavior when you see it is inconsistent with the standards that we all have observed here this week. We made this investment in you because we believe in you. And all we ask is that you take all this back. Do not allow the pressures of the day to in any way erode the emotion, the feeling, and the power of 10,000 that you have each experienced in the last few days.

The conference ended. Our partners packed their bags. They headed home. The city seemed empty.

Craig Russell, his assignment over, was exhausted from a week of 16-hour days spent orchestrating events with his team, and before heading back to Seattle he stayed in the city on Friday to relax. Later, he told me this story: As he walked through New Orleans' famed French Quarter, he stopped at the booth of a young street vendor to admire the art.

"Where you from?" the artist asked.

"Seattle," responded Craig.

"Did you have anything to do with Starbucks being here?" When Craig answered yes, the young man got choked up. "You paid my mortgage this month."

That's when it hit Craig. The New Orleans conference had been an unequivocal success.

* * *

Opportunities to authentically galvanize people are few and far between. These moments cannot be invented. They must be real and above reproach and exist on their own merits. Like Craig, I had a gut feeling that New Orleans had met this test, and as with so many other touchstone moments in Starbucks' history, the only proof I needed was the direct feedback from our partners. Hundreds e-mailed me in the days and weeks following the leadership conference, including eight-year partner Gina Hurstak, a regional director of operations:

> *Howard,*
> *I can't begin to tell you how proud I am to be a partner . . . working with amazing people who want to and will transform this company one cup at a time! These four days have been life changing for many. . . . The highlight was definitely rebuilding New Orleans. I appreciate your passion and belief in all of us. . . . We won't let you, the coffee, our partners, customers, farmers or shareholders down. The troubled economy and competition are challenging our business. Our partners are looking for leadership. And our customers expect more. . . . We will deliver! Thank you for having a vision, sharing it, and allowing us to carry it on.*

As I did my own reflecting on the power of the week, a word I'd not consciously thought of for what seemed a long while came to mind. "Love." I've always loved this company. Love is why I had come back as ceo and why I feel so personally responsible for its failure and success. Yet somewhere along our journey, the love our people had for Starbucks had blurred. New Orleans had brought it back into focus, and once again our values stood in stark relief. I felt confident that thousands of others also loved what we had built, and because of everything we experienced in New Orleans, it was apparent to all of us what it meant to love something—and the responsibility that goes with it.

Chapter 24

Nimble

Someone tapped Terry Davenport on the shoulder before plopping a MacBook on his lap.

"Watch this," said David Lubars, the chief creative officer of our advertising agency, BBDO.

Terry was sitting in the front of one of the buses that was taking Starbucks' partners from the conference's general session back to their hotels. David stood in the aisle of the moving bus and pushed "play" on the computer. Terry waited. First he heard delicate, almost primitive piano music. Then on the screen, against a subdued burlap background, dark green words in clean capital letters popped up one at a time to form a question, then another. There was no talking in the video. Just piano music and two questions:

WHAT IF WE ALL CARED ENOUGH TO VOTE?
NOT JUST 54% OF US,
BUT 100% OF US?

It was less than one week before the 2008 presidential election in the United States, and the race had been historic. Former first lady and senator Hillary Rodham Clinton had narrowly lost the Democratic primary to the first African-American presidential candidate, a senator from the state of Illinois, Barack Obama. And in five days, on November 4, 2008, Americans would go to the polls and vote for either Senator Obama and his running mate, Senator Joe Biden, or for Republican presidential candidate Senator John McCain and his unexpected running mate, the governor from the state of Alaska, Sarah Palin. Yet despite the importance of this election, only slightly more than half—54 percent—of Americans were expected to show up at the polls to vote.

As the bus rolled down the streets of New Orleans, Terry watched the commercial, intrigued as more green words and questions danced on the screen, sometimes pushing each other aside, to the dramatic piano notes that seemed to crescendo with each silent question:

WHAT IF WE CARED AS MUCH ON NOV. 5TH
AS WE CARE ON NOV. 4TH?
WHAT IF WE CARED ALL OF THE TIME
THE WAY WE CARE SOME OF THE TIME?
WHAT IF WE CARED WHEN IT WAS INCONVENIENT
AS MUCH AS WE CARE WHEN IT'S CONVENIENT?
WOULD YOUR COMMUNITY BE A BETTER PLACE?
WOULD OUR COUNTRY BE A BETTER PLACE?
WOULD OUR WORLD BE A BETTER PLACE?

WE THINK SO, TOO.
IF YOU CARE ENOUGH TO VOTE,
WE CARE ENOUGH TO GIVE YOU
A FREE CUP OF COFFEE.
COME INTO STARBUCKS ON NOV. 4TH
TELL US YOU VOTED,
AND WE'LL PROUDLY GIVE YOU
A TALL CUP OF BREWED COFFEE ON US.

With David hovering over his shoulder, Terry watched the last words crop up on the screen:

YOU & STARBUCKS.
IT'S BIGGER THAN COFFEE.

The 60-second ad was, Terry knew immediately, brilliant.

Simple. Quiet. Smart. Emotional. The spot was unlike anything he'd seen on television, at least recently given that the airwaves seemed dominated by political pundits screaming over each other. Yet it was relevant to this particular moment in time. The ad worked because it was not about Starbucks, but rather about what Starbucks is about, especially just coming out of New Orleans: community and personal responsibility.

"We have to do this," said Terry.

BBDO was barely two weeks into its role as Starbucks' new advertising agency of record, and half a dozen of the firm's people were in New Orleans with us, including Jeff Mordos, BBDO's wise and personable chief operating officer. No one at Starbucks was expecting the agency to deliver anything yet, just to watch and listen. But the idea for an election-themed ad had struck David before coming to New Orleans, and after being incredibly moved by what he witnessed, he had asked his creative team to pull something together. Quickly.

When I first saw the spot, I agreed that Starbucks had to run it. The ad felt pitch-perfect, and I also thought it would make our store partners proud. I shared the ad with Norman Lear, the revered television writer and producer who is also a good friend and had joined me in New Orleans. Norman, whose taste I trust implicitly, also thought it was dead-on.

If we could pull this off, the commercial would be only the second time Starbucks advertised on television.

If.

If our marketing and public relations teams could rally instead of resting once we all returned to Seattle after a successful but exhausting week.

If we could secure the right commercial time slots and maximize its exposure.

If we could afford it.

If we could get the word out to customers and coordinate our store partners.

And *if* we had enough coffee to handle traffic overflow.

We had four days to figure it all out.

* * *

I have never embraced traditional advertising for Starbucks. Unlike most consumer brands that are built with hundreds of millions of dollars spent on marketing, our success had been won with millions of daily interactions. Starbucks is the quintessential experiential brand—what happens between our customers and partners inside our stores—and that had defined us for three decades. But it was no longer enough.

I've known David Lubars for a very long time, and he understood, perhaps better than other marketing professionals, my avoidance of traditional advertising. We'd last worked together in Starbucks' earlier days, and David had taken the top job at BBDO in 2004 and was being hailed as one of the most out-of-the-box thinkers on Madison Avenue. He'd been the conceptual mind behind the groundbreaking minifilms for BMW as well as innovative campaigns for Apple, HBO, and FedEx. In September 2008, Starbucks had parted ways, somewhat painfully, with our primary advertising agency of four years, Portland, Oregon-based Wieden+Kennedy. I have great respect for Dan Wieden, who coined the Nike tagline "Just Do It" as well as developing other iconic campaigns. Dan is undoubtedly one of advertising's greatest professionals, and I was sorry to see the relationship end. In the following months, several other agencies, including BBDO, pitched to win our business, and in October I reunited with David for a spontaneous meeting in San Francisco. Jeff Mordos also joined us.

Over coffee, I discussed my change of heart about the role advertising could play for Starbucks, expanding on what our marketing team had already told BBDO. For the first time in Starbucks' history, out-side forces were defining us. That very fall a McDonald's billboard campaign had declared, "Four bucks is dumb" on a sign not far from our Seattle support center. Yet we were silent. It infuriated me. "We have got to get on the offensive," I said. "Not on the attack. But pro-actively define ourselves, find our voice, and express the personality of the company."

While I was ready to talk seriously about how Starbucks should use advertising, I was not interested in a traditional client-agency relation-ship. Instead of looking to an agency for answers, Starbucks needed a partner open to creative debate and tension, with whom we could have an ongoing dialogue, free of time-consuming formalities, to help us problem solve.

"We're being squeezed from the bottom by fast-food brands like McDonald's and Dunkin' Donuts, and from the top by high-end independent coffee shops," I explained. "We have to make certain that we don't get caught in the middle."

If Starbucks were to establish such a relationship with BBDO, we wanted to avoid the type of bureaucratic agency-client dynamics that can suck creativity out of the process. After we selected BBDO, I insisted that David be closely involved with Starbucks, especially dur-ing the transformation, because I so highly valued his sensibilities. David vowed to make us a top priority.

Before our conversation in San Francisco ended, I changed the subject, telling David and Jeff about a highly secretive project that, if BBDO joined our team, they would work on come 2009. I slid my hand into my bag and pulled out a skinny little foil sleeve about the length and size of an index finger whose contents, I told them, would reinvent the coffee category as well as propel Starbucks' growth. But that was a discussion for another day.

After Terry awarded BBDO our business, he and I invited David, Jeff, and their team to the New Orleans leadership conference, the ideal venue for absorbing our culture and values. BBDO's ability to come up with such a fresh, brand-relevant idea so quickly and share it with us so freely—followed up with their enthusiasm to do what-ever was necessary to polish the spot in short order—was further proof that BBDO was the right partner for Starbucks at this transi-tional time.

I was also taken by my own team's gut enthusiasm. After seeing the ad, we could have gotten bogged down in details and multiple opinions and potential roadblocks. Instead, we went for it. We acted nimbly, a telling sign that we had effectively dusted off our entrepreneurial spirit.

* * *

"We don't want to invite the country to a party and run out of coffee," cautioned Terry early Friday morning back in Seattle. He had just shown the spot to Michelle, and they were strategizing our next move.

They had already reached out to Peter in SCO as well as the coffee team, asking them to run scenarios and see whether our US stores would have enough coffee and supplies for a free-coffee campaign. Meanwhile, Cliff was calling his direct reports in the field to survey if they thought our thousands of stores could pull it off. To their credit, our regional managers supported the idea, agreeing to do their best to make it happen. Once we felt comfortable that our company-operated stores would have enough coffee on hand—our licensed stores would not participate—we gave BBDO the go-ahead to produce the television spot.

Perhaps the first and biggest coup was securing prime television time. For that, the stars aligned. The general consensus was that we should pack a punch and run the ad only once before Election Day, during a high-profile TV program. We targeted *Saturday Night Live*. That season, the late-night sketch comedy show was garnering record numbers of viewers thanks to its political satire, primarily comedian Tina Fey's popular impersonation of Governor Palin. *SNL*'s skits were generating significant watercooler chatter, and the talk-currency extended itself to ads that ran during the 90-minute show, especially during the first half. The weekend before the national election, *SNL*'s audience was sure to be huge, and while our ad's neutral election theme seemed a natural fit with what *SNL* was calling its "Election Bash" show, securing coveted commercial space could be tricky at such a late date.

To help us, Norman Lear and Phil Griffin, the newly named president of business-news network MSNBC, graciously reached out to their contacts while BBDO's media partner, PHD, began to orchestrate a buy with NBC for a price that, while it was more money than Starbucks had ever spent on a single ad placement, was not astronomical. Not until Saturday evening would we know exactly when during *SNL* our election ad would appear.

Again, the stars aligned. Just after 11:30 p.m. eastern time, after a hilarious opening sketch featuring Tina Fey as Sarah Palin and the real Senator McCain hawking election memorabilia on the home-shopping network QVC, our ad's now-familiar piano music played and the Starbucks commercial that had been brought to life on a bus in New Orleans four days earlier was the very first commercial to air.

WHAT IF WE CARED ALL OF THE TIME THE WAY WE CARE SOME OF THE TIME?

Watching it at home with Sheri was almost surreal.

★ ★ ★

SNL was the highest rated of all the late-night and prime-time programs that evening, and the show got the second-highest household rating it had received in nearly 11 years.

Starbucks, however, was not done, and immediately after the ad aired, our digital team put into play a plan they'd been working on nonstop for the last 36 hours.

A torrent of digital and social media activity would amplify the 60-second spot, which ran only one time on television. We updated our home page (which could not yet host videos) to direct people to YouTube, where, right after the *SNL* spot aired, we posted the commercial so it could be watched endlessly by anyone. Next, we e-mailed information about Tuesday's free-coffee event to all Starbucks registered cardholders, whose e-mail addresses we had in our database. We also tapped Twitter. In August, our digital team had begun using Twitter as another channel to authentically connect with customers, and with little fanfare or cumbersome strategizing, a former barista turned product manager, Brad Nelson, began tweeting on behalf of Starbucks. Now, he was alerting thousands of his followers that they may want to visit YouTube, vote on Tuesday, and get their free cup of coffee.

The election campaign's main engine, however, was Facebook, the number-one social networking site. Several Starbucks fans had already established their own Starbucks pages, but our company had only recently established its own official presence. The election campaign was our opportunity to elevate it. Despite the time challenge, we jumped on it. Working with Facebook, we created a Starbucks page and negotiated an ad buy: For the next few days, one of two Starbucks ads would be among the first five ads anyone logging on to Facebook would see. One ad was the actual election commercial. The other online ad invited people to come to a Starbucks after they voted and asked them (in a first for Facebook) to RSVP by clicking "yes," "maybe," or "no."

Every time someone clicked a response or watched the actual video, the action triggered a message to his or her Facebook news feed. For example, some of Chris Bruzzo's Facebook friends were notified that he'd RSVP'd "yes" to Starbucks' free coffee day, exposing his entire network to Starbucks' election campaign. This second-hand or "viral" exposure added 14 million more individual impressions on top of the 75 million original impressions Facebook yielded, meaning that, all told, 89 million people were exposed to the election campaign in some way. Starbucks placed additional, more traditional ads on other media websites, but Facebook fueled the widespread exposure.

After months of watching others promulgate negative buzz about Starbucks online, it was empowering to finally be the source of so much positive buzz.

Now all Starbucks had to do was deliver in the stores.

* * *

Truly, we did not know what would happen on Election Day.

Our store operations teams did everything they could under the circumstances to increase coffee stock and prepare our partners. After I voted that morning, I visited various stores. They were bustling, a hint of esprit de corps definitely prevailed, and throughout the day I got word that volunteers at polling places around the country were actually reminding voters to get their free coffee after casting their ballots.

The confluence of the beautifully conceived and executed commercial, the *SNL* spot, the digital marketing, and the resulting news coverage sparked conversation and store traffic. On that seminal day, Starbucks was so much more than a source of great, free coffee. We were a communal gathering place, which was, after all, what we'd set out to be.

Of course we hit inevitable bumps. Some stores ran out of pastries. The increased traffic put an additional burden on our already hard-working baristas. And while many of our partners felt proud and had fun with the spirit of the campaign, the sudden, intense influx of customers in some stores strained our staff.

Controversy also found us. According to rumors, the election campaign was Starbucks' attempt to influence how people voted. Then claims surfaced that our free-coffee promotion violated federal and some state election laws because it promised an incentive in return for voting. To avoid any legal tussles, we again turned on a dime and extended the free-coffee offer to any customer who requested it. Unfortunately, word of the shift often got to customers before our partners, and at times confusion reigned.

But overall the election campaign succeeded on several levels. Starbucks' US stores served more than two million cups of coffee that day, at least two and a half times more than on a typical weekday. More significantly, beyond the traffic and additional pastry sales, a sense of community enveloped the stores. For partners, pride in the company's intentions trumped pockets of inconvenience and chaos.

Operationally, the harried experience reminded us that Starbucks could act nimbly and not be grounded by our size or leashed to bad habits. I think we were all stunned, given the relatively low cost of the entire campaign, at the sheer magnitude of the audience we reached. On YouTube, the ad was viewed 419,000 times, making it the fourth-most-viewed video on Election Day. On Facebook, 405,000 people replied "yes" or "maybe" to our invitation. On Twitter, someone, not just Brad, was tweeting about Starbucks every eight seconds. We also reaped 70 million impressions via traditional print, broadcast, and online news outlets that covered the Starbucks campaign in some form.

The election campaign was a turning point, with Starbucks discovering powerful ways to drive traffic and positively engage with customers at a low cost that was still in keeping with the brand. With BBDO, we even coined a term for our election ad–inspired marketing approach: brand sparks. These subtle, surprising, and rare marketing events—usually linked to cultural or humanitarian issues and devoid of a self-serving sales pitch—would characterize how we went to market.

Whether or not someone walked into a Starbucks on November 4, the election campaign no doubt generated goodwill among several ⸱ᵃˢ, placing a halo above our somewhat battered brand. ito winter, Starbucks needed all the goodwill we

Chapter 25

Plan B

Starbucks' mission from the beginning was to build a different kind of company, one that would achieve a healthy balance between profit and social conscience. Never had the earnings side of the equation been in more jeopardy than during the fall of 2008.

For Starbucks' fourth quarter ending in September, profits plunged 97 percent to $5.4 million. For the year, earnings were down 53 percent, to $316 million. While the drops included $105 million in one-time charges associated with the restructuring and transformation, without those charges the company still came in four cents a share below earnings estimates.

Our outlook was also bleak. We publicly predicted that, in 2009, sales would be slow to rebound if costs of staples like gas and food continued to rise and home values and credit continued to contract. As the crisis spread to Europe and Asia, we were also pulling back on plans to open as many new stores overseas as previously announced. Our comps were trending at negative 8 percent, dangerously close to the double-digit declines plaguing other retailers.

Because no one inside or outside the company knew just how bad the economic situation might get, Starbucks' board of directors had steered us to prepare for the worst and, in an unprecedented request, had asked the leadership team to financially model what would happen if our comparative store sales dipped to negative 15 percent or even *negative 20 percent*. It was a chilling request. The exercise alone spoke to our dire straits, and once we ran the numbers it was immediately apparent that, should sales fall to those levels, Starbucks Coffee Company would be in very, very big trouble. Put simply, our earnings would decline even faster than the rate of our sales decline.

Beyond modeling death-defying comps, the board also urged us to cut costs far beyond what we'd done to date. "Go deep" was the directive.

We'd already retrenched once, back in April 2008, when the leadership team had agreed to reduce spending by more than $150 million, a decision that led in part to the July store closings and layoffs. Actions already taken would save us approximately $205 million in fiscal 2009. But that was not enough, and in the weeks prior to a scheduled November board meeting every department revisited its budget and, starting from zero spending, hunkered down and justified every line item.

Working furiously, we looked for ways to reduce our cost structure. The challenge was as much emotional as it was financial, as we asked ourselves how to eliminate spending in ways that were not consumer facing and wouldn't subtly fracture the culture and values of the company. Finding a balance between Starbucks' fiscal responsibilities and our responsibilities to live up to our partners' expectations was more art than science, an ongoing struggle that prompted debate almost every time we sat down to talk about specific cuts.

When it came to our back-end infrastructure, however, although Starbucks had never been a lavish operation, just relatively undisciplined, we quickly identified low-hanging fruit that we had never gone after in a lasting or meaningful way. In SCO, Peter's due diligence revealed that operating costs—the day-to-day expenses incurred in running supply chain operations—were exploding by $100 million each year, a runaway expense he subsequently referred to as a "supertanker" that he insisted be stopped in its tracks by January 2009. Peter further committed to reducing manufacturing and logistics costs by $25 million and finding another $75 million in procurement savings.

As Cliff and his US team examined the unit economics of our stores, they committed to reducing the cost of waste—the food, coffee, and milk that aren't sold—by $25 million. Another $75 million would be cut from labor costs, not by cutting jobs but by holistically reshaping how and when work got done within the four walls of our stores. More specifically, Cliff and his team were already applying Lean techniques to simplify and streamline the work of our baristas, finding efficiencies by optimizing their time and energy while improving the speed of service during busy morning hours and, in the afternoons, reducing labor hours to reflect traffic slowdowns. District managers who once focused on opening new stores would now attend to improving existing stores.

Such deep cost analysis was a very healthy process for the company and its management. We could not control the economy, but we could exert greater control over how we operated in it—not just by reducing or freezing new spending, but also by designing a less costly operating model. Even once we revived the Starbucks Experience, brought back the theater and quality and partner engagement, even when our customer-facing initiatives panned out, we would need to operate differently over the long term if we were to survive financially.

Eventually the leadership team felt confident that we could take out $400 million in permanent costs.

This, we told the board in November, was Plan B.

No, the board responded, it should be your new Plan A.

* * *

Boards of directors do not exist to manage companies, but rather to make sure companies are managed well.

Boards are at their best, I believe, when directors have complete transparency so they can provide informed guidance, offering an outsider's experienced perspective to push a company's management further than they might otherwise go. In the spring of 2008, for example, as we created the final Transformation Agenda, Starbucks' board had been instrumental in helping Michelle and me more clearly articulate our overall goals and milestones.

When it comes to working with their boards, chief executives are at their best when they frequently communicate the good news as well as the bad, and when they listen to the experience and advice of board members. A CEO does not need to do everything a board suggests, but unless we open our ears to directors' perspectives, we miss opportunities to self-correct.

In 2008, Starbucks' board was a group diverse in experience as well as background.

- **Barbara Bass,** a Starbucks director since January 1996, was the president of the Gerson Bakar Foundation and former president and chief executive officer of the Emporium Weinstock Division of Carter Hawley Hale Stores.

- **Bill Bradley,** a managing director of Allen and Company, had served in the US Senate from 1979 until 1997 and for 10 years had played professional basketball for the New York Knicks. He joined our board in June 2003.

- **Mellody Hobson** had served as a director since February 2005. The president as well as a director of Ariel Investments, an investment management firm, she was also sitting on the boards of DreamWorks Animation SKG and the Estée Lauder Companies.

- **Olden Lee,** a Starbucks director since June 2003, had worked for 28 years at PepsiCo, some of it as senior vice president of human resources of its Taco Bell division and senior vice president and chief personnel officer of KFC; he was also on the board of TLC Vision Corporation.

- **Jamie Shennan** had been a general partner at Trinity Ventures, a venture capital organization, from 1989 to 2005, when he became a general partner emeritus. He was also a director of P.F. Chang's China Bistro. He had been one of Starbucks' original investors and had served on the board since 1990.

- **Javier Teruel** had been the vice chairman of Colgate-Palmolive Company before retiring after a 36-year career with the company. Javier was also on the boards of the Pepsi Bottling Group and JCPenney Company.

- **Myron "Mike" Ullman,** our lead director, was the chairman of the board and chief executive officer of JCPenney Company. Prior to that, he had served as group managing director of LVMH Moët Hennessy–Louis Vuitton, chairman and CEO of DFS Group Limited, and CEO of R.H. Macy and Company. Mike became a Starbucks director in January 2003.

- **Craig Weatherup,** a nine-year board member, had served as the CEO of PepsiCo's worldwide Pepsi-Cola business, as president of PepsiCo, and as chairman and CEO of the Pepsi Bottling Group. He was also on the board of Macy's and had been on the board of Starbucks since February 1999.

Jamie Shennan had a creative yet simple way of articulating important ideas, and he once observed that the more critical the times, the more important it is for a board and CEO to work together in a non-political, unemotional, fact-focused way. Throughout 2008, I made it a point to stay in frequent contact with Starbucks' directors, and by fall there had been many times when I—and ultimately Starbucks—had benefitted from our one-on-one dealings.

Mike Ullman had been especially instrumental in assisting me with my transition back as ceo, and he continued to be a mentor. More recently, over dinner in Seattle with Craig Weatherup, I had listened intently as he recounted his own tumultuous times at PepsiCo. Just hearing how someone I deeply respected forged ahead to overcome significant business challenges helped ease some of my own pressures.

Perhaps most significantly, Olden Lee, a six-year Starbucks director, was having a profound effect on my own maturation as a business leader. A former PepsiCo executive, Olden had stepped in as our temporary head of partner resources when Chet left Starbucks to address family issues. Olden was consistently measured in his communication style, nailing the heart of an issue with a few well-chosen words. His balanced perspective was enormously respected. We did not know each other well at the time he somewhat grudgingly accepted the temporary HR post—it's uncommon for a director to assume a management role, and for a CEO to be comfortable with such a move—but Starbucks and I needed Olden's wisdom, and he selflessly provided it.

The two of us began to meet regularly, and our discussions increasingly went beyond HR issues to my own leadership style. Olden sat in on leadership meetings, and afterward, behind closed doors, he often shared his observations of my approach, suggesting alternate ways I might have, for example, led a discussion or handled a particular situation. In Olden I had the benefit of a coach.

But I also needed friends, and during this period, maintaining relationships with my peers outside the company was extremely helpful. I was grateful for the support of a cadre of individuals who routinely checked in or listened when I needed an ear: Todd Morgan, Steve and Patty Fleischmann, Richard Yarmuth, Dan Levitan, Nicole David, Dave Wirtschafter, Jonathan and Stacey Levine, Lauren Hostek, Matt McCutchen, Doron and Kai Linz, Jeff Brotman, Jim Sinegal, Norman Lear, Robert Fisher, Panos Marinopoulos, Mohammed Alshaya, Alberto Torrado, Robert Stilin, Pete McCormick, and Jeffrey Katzenberg. These were my behind-the-scenes supports.

Although I never stopped believing that Starbucks would emerge from the darkness, I was nonetheless experiencing an emotional roller coaster daily. I tried, admittedly not always successfully, to keep my feelings in check when interacting with our partners. I was acutely aware of my mood's domino effect, and first and foremost our people needed reassurance of my own confidence. That's why the freedom I felt to be candid with Olden and trusted friends proved as psychologically beneficial as it was educational. Quite simply, I am human and needed an outlet. Some CEOs may have felt uncomfortable having a board member so close, but I trusted Olden. After all, he and I—and for that matter the entire board—all had the same goal: the success of Starbucks.

* * *

The board's push to enact Plan B was dead-on.

Redesigning the company's cost structure was vital to our maturity as an organization, but also a significant headline when our leadership team went to New York City to host Starbucks' biennial analyst conference, a meeting that would put us face-to-face with institutions that sought to buy or sell Starbucks shares and the analysts who upgraded and downgraded our stock. The conference was an opportunity to regain credibility and trust on the Street by telling our story in more detail than we could on an earnings call.

But what, exactly, was our story? What, for that matter, was any company's story as 2008 spun out of control? There was no blueprint, no historical textbook that told us all what to do. Weren't most of us just fighting for our lives in uncharted waters, in what former Federal Reserve chairman Alan Greenspan had recently characterized as a "once-in-a-lifetime credit tsunami"? In fact, the day Starbucks announced earnings, the largest US electronics retailer, Circuit City, filed for bankruptcy. At $2.92, General Motors' stock hit its lowest level since World War II, and its competitor, the once venerable Ford Motor Company, was trading at $1.80. When I phoned other CEOs to learn what they were doing to combat uncertainty, they wanted to know what I was doing! No one had a real handle on this unprecedented moment. Anyone who insisted he or she did was lying.

Much more than just the global economic landscape was changing. More than stock prices and housing values were in flux. The cultural zeitgeist was shifting beneath our feet. Habits. Priorities. Trust. Expectations. The crisis was forcing people all along the economic spectrum to come to terms with new realities and redefine how they lived in the world. Starbucks and I were hardly alone in our transformation. During this period, the most important steps business leaders could take were to put our feet in the shoes of our customers, listen to our advisors as well as our own intuition, and refuse to surrender our core values. And, when necessary, agree to enact Plan B.

Chapter 26

Stay the Course

It was hardly an ideal time for us to present to Wall Street.

Throughout November 2008, as the leadership team and I worked diligently to restructure budgets and operations, an analyst conference loomed. Months earlier, this biennial event for investors and Wall Street analysts had been scheduled for December 4 in New York City, and it would mark the first time since the March annual meeting that I stood in front of shareholders when the company was not performing well. Attendees would expect, and rightly so, a comprehensive picture of Starbucks Coffee Company. But because the team and I were in the thick of such significant structural changes, and because many of our initiatives during the past year had yet to have a material impact on our financial performance, preparing for the conference was like trying to put on a show while still writing the script.

Rescheduling was not an option. The implications would be too dangerous. We had to go to New York.

Then, just weeks prior, Starbucks' cfo resigned. He'd been with Starbucks less than a year and was leaving to join a technology organization. I was stunned by the poor timing, but it took me about five minutes to identify the best person, perhaps a better person, to step into the role.

I asked Troy Alstead to come to my office. Troy was senior vice president of global finance, had already been working closely with our cfo, and had been with Starbucks for 16 years. He is incredibly intelligent and an articulate communicator, especially when it comes to finance, and had long ago won the respect and fondness of partners. A runner-up for the cfo post when Michael Casey left after 12 years, Troy had held financial roles throughout the company—in the United States and internationally, in corporate as well as in operating units—all of which gave him a detailed command of the company's strategies and operations. Troy embodied Starbucks' culture: smart, confident, genuine, and decisive when needed.

"I would like you to be Starbucks' new chief financial officer," I bluntly informed Troy.

Selecting the right people for Starbucks' leadership team was among the most critical decisions I was making during this tenuous time. I'd already brought in Peter and Cliff and was utilizing Michelle's skills where and when they were most needed. When Wanda left after her scheduled 11-month return leading Starbucks' communications, Vivek jumped in from Microsoft with ambitious plans. And like bringing Stephen on as cio amidst some skepticism about his youth, I knew a few eyebrows would rise because I did not hire an experienced cfo, but rather promoted from within. Even Troy assumed he'd have a few more years to go before stepping into a cfo position. But I always trust my antennae to recognize people whose skill, knowledge, passion, and loyalty will align to serve Starbucks well, even if the person's resume might imply otherwise.

I promoted Troy with no doubts that he would win the trust of Wall Street; internally, his ascent was also gratifying for many partners who saw one of their own being rewarded for years of hard work and exceptional performance.

The analyst conference would be Troy's debut.

★ ★ ★

It felt as if the sand in the hourglass was running out. December 2, Tuesday, two days before the analyst conference, the dining room in my Manhattan apartment was crowded and the mood tense. Cliff, Michelle, Terry, Vivek, and Troy were among the people there, along with Michael Casey, our former cfo, who had graciously hopped on a plane at my request to help us prepare for this crucial event.

This would be the first time we'd held this conference outside Seattle. We'd chosen New York City, the hub of the global financial world, in large part because the burden of proof for Starbucks' performance had shifted from the analysts to us. The company was not delivering as we had in the past and now we had to show the Street how we would rebound. Not by overpromising or making bold predictions, but by confidently reaffirming that we understood and were correcting our problems.

Sitting around the dining room table, we continued to write and rewrite the script and corresponding slides, a task we would have completed in Seattle had we not been consumed with other responsibilities. Pulling all the facts together in a cohesive, optimistic story, especially under such time pressure, was incredibly stressful. We'd accomplished a great deal during the past 11 months, but it seemed overshadowed by recent bad news. Our comps were down across the board: negative 9 percent in the United States, negative 3 percent internationally, negative 8 percent worldwide. Nine weeks into the first quarter, it was only getting worse, and we projected missing external earnings estimates of 22 cents a share.

Because I felt we needed an outsider's perspective, I'd invited one non-Starbucks person to join us. Billy Etkin runs a successful boutique merger and acquisition firm and has one of the most intelligent business minds I know, especially when it comes to communicating critical and often complicated information to Wall Street. While some were cautious about an outsider chiming in, Billy's business acumen and unfiltered, respectful opinions helped us, I think, to see the forest through the trees and articulate the company's situation. I trusted Billy and his intentions implicitly, and he showed up for no other reason than to help Starbucks.

* * *

On Wednesday, December 3, 2008, the group gathered in an empty auditorium at the TimesCenter on West 41st Street to rehearse our presentations. Sitting among rows of empty seats, my mood was spiraling to levels it had not sunk to in ages. Maybe ever. I sensed a level of insecurity, which was understandable given our lack of prep time and the challenges we were knee-deep in back home, which created a daily intensity, like hand-to-hand combat, as we fought to save the business. When members of the leadership team took the stage, I was quick to interrupt or redirect their presentations, not making it easy for anyone to muster confidence.

Finally Vivek turned to me. "Howard, I think you need to leave," he suggested respectfully. Vivek was right. Everyone knew what he or she needed to do, and in this instance my input was more obtrusive than constructive. I grabbed my coat and left the rehearsal.

Later that evening, Billy and I sat down for dinner at a small table inside Vespa, a modern little Italian restaurant on Second Avenue between 84th and 85th Streets. In summer, sunlight poured into Vespa's open garden, but this December night was dark and cold, and I felt an uncharacteristic level of angst. I even got frustrated trying to explain to our waiter that I did not want a specific dish off the menu, just grilled swordfish and pasta. Not fried or doused in spices. Just. Plain. Grilled. Swordfish. As the confused waiter walked away from the table, my head swirled with images of the dour faces of my team, the bad press about Starbucks, and the single-digit share price.

"The stock could drop to $5 tomorrow," I said aloud to Billy, deeply concerned about what might happen if it did. "We could be taken over."

This was, again, such an uncharacteristic fear for me, not to mention an unlikely scenario for the company, but my anxiety had reached a fever pitch. It had been such a long year. An endless treadmill as Starbucks planned and executed new products and events, one after the other. And we were still waiting for most to bear fruit. I had experienced such highs with the annual meeting, Pike Place Roast, and New Orleans, yet also such lows with store closures and the layoffs and Sorbetto and our sinking market capitalization. Our cfo quitting at such a crucial time had put me over the edge. As 2008 drew to a close, I was simply exhausted. Physically and emotionally.

"Howard, you have to stay the course," Billy reassured me with his steady tone and even a smile. "You have to stay true to your values and true to the company's core. Those are your rudder now. And when the seas calm and the winds shift . . . and," he went on, "the seas will calm and the winds will shift, unless you believe that the economy is never coming back. Or that all along Starbucks' value proposition and connection to its customers has been a ruse. Or that the millions of people still walking into your stores every week all over the world are kidding themselves. Now is the time to stay focused on the moves you have to make to rightsize the business, to innovate, and to return to the core. The confluence of these factors will propel Starbucks forward and will make all of today's naysayers positive about Starbucks again. I am absolutely sure of this."

Billy was not telling me anything I did not already believe.

But he was telling me things I needed to hear.

* * *

Finally, Thursday morning, December 4. The auditorium filled with some 200 influential people. Buy-side and sell-side analysts, institutional investors, a few guests, a smattering of press, and 11 of our top 30 shareholders—almost double the crowd that typically attended the conference in Seattle. Close to 1,000 more, including Starbucks partners, would tune in via a live webcast. I did not think there had ever been a more important meeting at which Starbucks needed to communicate with clarity and confidence.

Backstage in the greenroom, I waited with the rest of the Starbucks team. I would speak first, followed by Troy, Michelle, Terry, and Cliff. Then Troy again to emphasize the company's heightened rigor concerning cost management. More than 100 slides were ready to flash on the overhead screen, an impressive photo album document-ing a very full year. On one hand, we were proud. On the other, we felt intense pressure. How we discussed our business that day had to instill confidence in our ability to build long-term shareholder value. Dinner the night before had been cathartic for me, but I was still soaking up the tension of the room. Something had to break.

"Bill!" I stood up and walked over to Bill Bradley, who had quite unexpectedly entered the greenroom. I hadn't known he was going to be at the conference and was glad, if not relieved, to see one of our board members. The former US senator, Knicks player, and two-time NBA champion towered over us, smiling as if he knew some-thing we did not. And then, like a coach with the starting lineup of a team about to take the court, Bill corralled our attention and deliv-ered what must have been a 15-minute pep talk, reinforcing our strengths and, like Billy the previous evening, reminding us of what we already knew to be true. Every company was feeling pain. But Starbucks had a good story to tell. An authentic story. A story about a year in the life of one of the world's most respected brands. A year spent taking stock and taking risks. He reminded us all of how far we had come during the crisis. Bill was so confident in his belief in us, so sure that the company would prevail, that we would shine that day—it was contagious.

Like other members of Starbucks' board of directors, Bill Bradley had unique gifts to share with the company and seemed to know just when to bestow them. For all the wisdom and talent among our team, a locker-room speech was exactly what we needed, an unexpected burst of positive energy. Amazing, actually. And the wind shifted. When Bill left the greenroom, I think we all stood a little taller, ready to go onstage and get the job done, as a team, with conviction.

★ ★ ★

As I walked onto the stage, I knew I had to set the tone, to build on the faith Bill had instilled in us backstage and provide the rest of the team with a little bit of tailwind. I was also keenly aware of my responsibility not just to shareholders, but to everyone back in Seattle and all of Starbucks' partners. Representing the company was my job. It is also my life.

"Good morning. Thank you for coming. We are all obviously liv-ing in extraordinary times, and we appreciate the fact that you've come here today." I was not performing. I was just speaking honestly, and with each word my conviction in Starbucks' purpose and our potential came rushing back.

> *There are some who say, "Perhaps you should change your business model because the environment is so different." And I ask rhetorically, for all of you that are in your own business, who have built something, you have guiding principles. You have a culture and a set of values. This is not the time to change strategies so significantly that you lose your reason for being. . . . Things are going to get better. People will continue to drink coffee, and the equity of our brand and the relevancy of the sense of community in the third place and the growth opportunities for Starbucks, domestically and around the world, will be stronger than ever.*
>
> *We have assembled a very strong team. We have a common purpose. We certainly have creative debate, but we are up for this challenge. Let me share with you who they are.*

One by one, each took the stage to articulate aspects of our unfolding story.

Troy, in his first time presenting as cfo, rose to the task and did a great job of setting a somber, practical tone by outlining our cost-saving efforts and projections: $400 million in permanent cost take-outs, $200 million of which would be realized in 2009 on top of the $205 million resulting from actions we had taken earlier in the year.

"These are sustainable changes to our cost structure," he reassured the Street before ceding the floor to Michelle.

"So let's talk about what's been happening in our business," Michelle said, alluding to an overhead graph that showed the 12-month correlation between Starbucks' declining US traffic and weakening consumer confidence. "If we look at our transaction comps, they started decelerating about a year ago, which as we all know this week was reported to have been the start of the recession." It was true. A report released the day before by the National Bureau of Economic Research had pegged December 2007 as the beginning of the US recession. A statement I had made a year ago was now official.

Michelle, with her impressive command of numbers, provided an extensive overview of our past as well as our future: our more extensive customer research, our strategy to maintain our coffee authority, and the new beverage and food platforms we'd brought to market in 2008, including expanding the Tazo tea line and bringing back the infamous breakfast sandwiches.

After I'd announced the end of the breakfast sandwich on the earnings call back in January 2008, we had immediately pulled the sandwiches out of stores' display cases, although customers could still order them by request. And, as predicted, we saw an immediate decline in sales at stores that had carried the product, but we also saw impassioned customer comments posted at MyStarbucksIdea.com and got them at our customer call center. A website even sprang up: Savethebreakfastsandwich.com.

With my full knowledge but admittedly tempered enthusiasm, the food team continued to study the sandwich to address my complaints as well as customers' pleas, and they discovered that improving the quality of the ingredients—leaner bacon, higher-quality ham and cheese—helped reduce the aroma. They also learned that the tang of the English muffin was partly to blame for the sharp smell, so we adjusted the recipe with our baked goods supplier and also offered more bread options, such as ciabatta. Finally, by moving the cheese to the top of the sandwich and lowering the baking temperature to about 300°F, the cheese was less likely to burn. The result was, I had to admit, a breakfast offering that was worthy of our coffee.

With my blessing, the breakfast sandwiches had returned to the stores in June 2008 and in the last six months had done extremely well. What's more, improving the sandwiches had actually helped us move our entire food program forward. We had updated nearly all of our recipes, paring down the number of ingredients and eliminating artificial flavors, artificial dyes, trans fats, and high fructose corn syrup.

In retrospect, I realize that the ferocity of my reaction to the breakfast sandwich was likely heightened by my frustration with other shortcomings at the company. More emblematic than problematic, the sandwich turned out to be among the least of Starbucks' ills. But like so many other things we had dealt with in the past year, we had turned the sandwiches around and learned from the experience how to improve the business.

Michelle wrapped up her presentation and introduced Terry, who spoke about a critical yet nuanced marketing strategy: delivering value in a manner consistent with our brand.

* * *

In fall 2008 the retail world was on sale.

Every street I walked down had "Sale" signs displayed in windows, from Madison Avenue's high-end boutiques to Marks and Spencer's London department store. I recall seeing one sign declaring that customers could get as much as 80 percent off. There was so much pressure for every retailer and restaurant to discount prices. The unique challenge for Starbucks, however, was how to honor consumers' needs for lower prices and reward our core customers' loyalty without putting Starbucks on sale. Deep discounting is a slippery slope that can be impossible to climb back up. It would also play into McDonald's game, and that was not how I wanted to compete. Starbucks would compete as we always did. On quality and service.

Still, we had to do something for our core customers. As Costco's Jim Sinegal had advised us earlier in the year, we could not let them slip away. Giving them value at almost any cost would be much less expensive than trying to win them back.

The good news was that, by the time of the analyst conference, we were beginning to figure out how.

Three months prior, I and several other people, including Terry Davenport, had flown back to Seattle together from a meeting in Los Angeles. During the two-hour flight, we began brainstorming about how to breathe life into what was sure to be one of our worst holiday seasons on record. For inspiration we considered our Rewards Card, our loyalty program that had been chugging along nicely since its June 2008 relaunch. What could we do with a card to provide even more value than the rewards program? We played with some numbers and eventually came up with the idea for a $25 Gold Card that would give cardholders 10 percent off on anything they bought at Starbucks for one year. Excited, we called the Rewards Card team from the plane to discuss benefits and pitfalls, and by the time we landed in Seattle I had given the Starbucks Gold Card the go-ahead, assuming no major problems cropped up.

Our goal was to sell 25,000 cards in the first week. We surpassed that amount in the first *weekend*.

Starbucks' card programs—the Starbucks Card, single-product ~~~~~~~~~~ial cards, the Rewards and Gold Cards—were emerging as ny's winning way to deliver meaningful value. Cards are se and have higher redemption rates than coupons. They enhance the brand, becoming part of the Starbucks Experience via the actual customer–barista transaction and, because the card lives in wallets, part of people's lives.

The cards were also bringing us closer to customers. To receive rewards, a person registers it online by providing his or her e-mail address. As a result, Starbucks was building a rich database that we could use to better understand our customers' behaviors and reward them accordingly. The database also allowed us to reach out to customers in meaningful, cost-effective ways, like we did with the election campaign. And when Vivanno launched that summer, for example, we invited cardholders to come in and try a free drink. The 16 percent response rate was exceptional for an e-mail campaign.

"For a brand that does not spend a lot on traditional mass marketing," Terry summed up for the analysts, "the database is going to be one of the hidden assets." He was right. The card program was a truly sustainable, competitive advantage for us in the marketplace and, given the state of discretionary spending, perhaps the most relevant marketing tool that we discussed that morning.

* * *

We were rallying, individually and as a team. From my seat in the audience I sensed, despite a palpable cynicism, that our main message to Wall Street was for the most part getting through: Starbucks was focused on its foundation as well as innovation and would emerge from the crisis in a position of strength. With each presentation, my anxiety dissipated. We were staying the course. And as I quietly checked my iPhone throughout the morning, the market seemed to agree—our stock price never dipped below $8 that day.

The conference was allowing our team to take a step back from the operational details that had consumed us for the past few months and ponder what we had achieved and what lay ahead. As Cliff briefly outlined during his presentation, Starbucks also had multiple revenue opportunities beyond our company-operated US stores:

- **The consumer packaged goods business,** mainly the whole and ground beans we sold in grocery stores

- **Almost 4,000 licensed stores**

- **Twenty-five-million-plus cups of Starbucks coffee served per week** in hotels, restaurants, and other venues that fall under our food-service business

- **The at-home and single-serve coffee markets**

- **Seattle's Best Coffee,** a brand Starbucks had acquired in 2003 and whose potential had yet to be tapped

The largest potential for growth, however, was in Starbucks Coffee International, the unit that includes all Starbucks business outside the United States. It was by far the company's most exciting and largest prospect. Since opening the company's third store in Vancouver, British Columbia, our Canadian business had been a consistently strong performer, albeit too often unsung as it sat in the shadow of the United States. Outside North America, we had 5,000 stores in 48 countries, and from day one of opening our first overseas store in Tokyo in 1996, the third-place experience, that sense of community Starbucks stores offer, was embraced. The Starbucks brand was recognized worldwide.

Our international business—actually, I dislike the term "international," and "global" for that matter, because it implies that we are not a united organization—had been profitable, but not to the extent it could have been. The business model had grown complicated, becoming the equivalent of overseeing dozens of different businesses not only in different geographic regions, but also with unique financial structures and partnerships and operating under local laws and regulations. The successes we did have were in large part due to the high quality of our local business partners; in most countries, we partner with a company that operates our stores, and many are private, family-owned entities that share our values. For years we had vetted these partners very carefully under the thoughtful guidance of Jinlong Wang, who originally helped open Starbucks abroad and whom I credit with establishing Starbucks' premium position in the Asian market, and Herman Uscategui, whose congeniality came through in each of the seven languages he spoke.

Yet despite its successes, Starbucks Coffee International had much room for improvement. Unfortunately, getting our arms around each market was not something I could focus on until the floundering US business was stable. But once it was, the size of the prize waiting outside North America, especially in China, was huge.

International.

Innovation beyond our retail footprint.

Unleashing languishing business units.

All of these areas would garner more of my attention in 2009. For now, we had to fix the foundation. Again, stay the course.

During the question-and-answer session, the analysts doggedly tried to get a handle on what to expect. When one analyst pointedly asked me to elaborate on Starbucks' new growth model, I tempered my response. "This is not a time, I think, for us to make lofty statements about growth and number of stores. This is a time to have a much different lens on the business. And it's about, as we've said all morning, maximizing productivity and profitability at the store level. But," I could not resist adding, "I do believe that Starbucks will return to being a growth company." This was something I had believed throughout the transformation.

Ultimately, my worst fears were not realized that day. Overall, the conference went very well because the team had stepped up, exceeding even their own expectations and presenting a tremendous amount of information with authenticity and, again, conviction. Whatever the market's reaction, we came off the court that December day feeling as if we had won.

And comments from attendees were generally positive. For the most part, investors and analysts felt we had addressed the business's most relevant issues. Analyst notes following the event were cautious, but applauded our cost-saving initiatives and seemed to appreciate the balance Starbucks had to strike between maintaining our premium position and offering value. And despite pockets of criticism that the company was not taking competition seriously enough or advertising enough or slowing new-store growth enough, Starbucks' share price ticked up to a daily high of $9.41 and closed at $8.61, slightly higher than it began the week.

Still, the stock was a dismal 61 percent lower than it had been a year before, when it was at $22.34.

It was time for me to close the conference, and I stepped back on stage.

We are not satisfied with where shareholder value has gone. A great deal, as you heard here today, is due to the significant downturn in the economy, but we're also responsible for some of the decisions that we made in the past. But I believe very strongly that when we meet again, two years from today, we'll be talking about how the stock had improved compared to where it is today. Those people who took advantage of the opportunity will have significant returns.

There was a fine line between confidence and overpromising, and I did not think I had crossed it that day. I was just stating what I whole-heartedly believed to be true.

Part 5:
Courage

Where it all began, in 1971.

The first Starbucks store in Seattle's Pike Place Market.

Rwanda

Starbucks has been buying coffee from the African nation of Rwanda since 2004. During my third trip there in June 2008 to visit with farmers and tour their co-op, I again marveled at the country's beauty and the fortitude of the Rwandan people, whose fight to heal themselves after the country's tragic 1994 genocide is one of the most inspiring acts of rebirth in human history.

Growing high-quality coffee is a craft, requiring a unique skill set often passed down from generation to generation.

The proof is in the cup

On February 26, 2008, in an unprecedented move, Starbucks closed all of its 7,100 US company-owned stores for three hours to retrain baristas on espresso preparation so they could create the perfect beverage every time.

We're taking time to perfect our art of espresso.

Great espresso requires practice. That's why we're dedicating ourselves to honing our craft.

We will be closed Tuesday, February 26 from 5:30 p.m. to 9:00 p.m.

We're always striving for perfection and look forward to serving you a truly exceptional espresso beverage when we reopen at **5:30am** on **Wednesday**

Steve Dixon
Store Manager

Starbucks has always been about so much more than coffee. But without great coffee we have no reason to exist.

Returning to our heritage

Starbucks is at its best when we are creating enduring relationships and personal connections. This is the essence of who we are.

Ethically sourced coffee

Starbucks sources coffee beans from tens of thousands of farmers in almost thirty countries. Most of these are families who work on small farms of only a few acres. The company's effect on the global coffee industry can be measured not just in the nearly 400 million pounds of coffee beans we buy each year, but also by our high ethical-sourcing standards that strive to respect the environment and improve the quality of life for farmers and their communities.

Treating farmers with respect and dignity is at the heart of what we do.

The Starbucks Experience

For the nearly 60 million weekly visitors to Starbucks stores in fifty-four countries, we continue to recreate the coffeehouse experience with architectural features, environmentally friendly elements, and regional flavors that reflect local communities as well as balance sustainability with the comfort and essence of the "third place."

1

2

3

4

5

7

6

8

10

9

11

Each Starbucks store has its own fingerprint.

12

1. University Village, Seattle, our first redesigned store; **2.** Edinburgh, Scotland; **3.** 15th Avenue Coffee & Tea, Seattle, our first new concept store; **4.** Roy Street Coffee & Tea, Seattle, experimenting with live music, film, and local food; **5.** First and Pike, Seattle, our first new concept store receiving LEED Gold certification; **6.** Customers awaiting the opening of Starbucks in Fuzhou, China; **7.** Sanfang Qixiang, Fuzhou, China; **8.** Chenghuang Miao, Shanghai, China; **9.** Binjiang, Shanghai, China; **10.** Grand opening of Starbucks in Budapest; **11.** Plácido Arango, Howard, and Orin Smith at Paris, France's first store opening; **12.** First Starbucks in Paris.

Taking it personally

At Starbucks' 2008 global leadership conference, a four-day event held at the height of the US economic crisis, nearly ten thousand Starbucks partners convened in New Orleans, a city still reeling from the effects of Hurricane Katrina, to contribute thousands of hours of community service as well as to hear, directly from Starbucks' leaders, about changes the company needed to make and the responsibility each partner had to help secure our successful future.

If done right—and it had to be done right—the leadership conference in New Orleans would raise our company's level of personal accountability, passion, and performance.

Top: Howard in New Orleans with guest Bono, lead singer of U2 and activist, announcing the partnership between (RED) and Starbucks.

Reimagining our future

In the early stages of Starbucks' transformation, people from throughout the organization came together in large and small working groups to reconnect with our values and identify business priorities. From these sessions two key documents emerged: Starbucks' new mission statement, which articulated our guiding principals, and the Transformation Agenda, which identified our goals.

4 Expand our global presence—while making each store the heart of the local neighborhood

What does it mean to reinvent an icon?

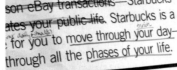

STARBUCKS
The Fourth Place:
The ultimate public good

STAR
...is the one safe, welcoming, open to all—at all hours. For dates, meetings, community organizing, ...time, rites of passage, ...son eBay transactions—Starbucks ...ates your public life. Starbucks is a ...for you to move through your day—through all the phases of your life.

Community
the ultimate safe haven—all the tools and inspiration for daily living

Coffee

Starbucks partners sign an enlarged copy of Starbucks' new mission statement, which begins, "To inspire and nurture the human spirit."

Innovation

Upon returning as Starbucks' ceo, I wanted to reawaken our entrepreneurial spirit and remind our partners of the excitement that comes from assaulting the status quo and trusting yourself and your coworkers, and above all from creating truly great products. The results—unexpected beverages, new store designs, engaging digital experiences—are reigniting the emotional connection we share with our customers.

1

2

3

4

5

6

> When I first tried Don's coffee—an instant version of Starbucks—I was stunned. I did not believe it was instant.

7

8

9

10

11

12

13

1. Introducing limited-release Starbucks Reserve coffees; **2.** Olive Way, a redesigned store in Seattle that also serves wine and beer; **3.** Starbucks Digital Network; **4.** Pike Place Roast; **5.** My Starbucks Rewards Card; **6.** In 2010, Starbucks announced the rebranding and expansion of Seattle's Best Coffee; **7.** Don Valencia and VIA Ready Brew; **8.** Howard in Tokyo with executives from ANA airlines, announcing that VIA will be served on ANA flights; **9.** Howard's dear friends, the late Hal Gaba, co-owner of Concord Music Group (left), and television producer Norman Lear (right) celebrating the album Starbucks coproduced with Concord, Ray Charles's *Genius Loves Company*, after it led the 2005 Grammy Awards with eight awards, including Album of the Year; **10.** VIA; **11.** Howard and Kris Engskov, Starbucks regional vp and former director of public policy, in Washington, DC, discussing health-care reform with members of Congress; **12.** Vivanno Nourishing Blends; **13.** Clover.

Onward...

Top: Starbucks Senior Leadership Team, Fall 2010.

Left to right (standing): Jeff Hansberry, president, Global Consumer Products and Foodservice; Vivek Varma, executive vice president, Public Affairs; Mary Egan, senior vice president, Global Corporate Strategy; Troy Alstead, chief financial officer and chief administrative officer; Michelle Gass, president, Seattle's Best Coffee; Stephen Gillett, executive vice president, chief information officer, and general manager, Digital Ventures; Dervala Hanley, vice president, Corporate Initiatives and Planning; Paula Boggs, executive vice president, general counsel, and secretary; Cliff Burrows, president, Starbucks Coffee U.S.; Annie Young-Scrivner, chief marketing officer.

Left to right (seated): John Culver, president, Starbucks Coffee International; Peter Gibbons, executive vice president, Global Supply Chain Operations; Kalen Holmes, executive vice president, Partner Resources; Arthur Rubinfeld, president, Global Development; Howard Schultz, chairman, president, and chief executive officer.

Bottom: Starbucks Board of Directors, photographed for FORTUNE magazine in 2010.

Left to right: Olden Lee, retired executive, PepsiCo, Inc.; Kevin Johnson, chief executive officer, Juniper Networks, Inc.; Javier Teruel, retired vice chairman, Colgate-Palmolive Company; Mellody Hobson, president, Ariel Investments, LLC; Bill Bradley (standing), managing director, Allen & Company LLC; Myron Ullman, chairman and chief executive, J.C. Penney Company, Inc.; Barbara Bass (above), chief executive officer, Gerson Bakar Foundation; Sheryl Sandberg, chief operating officer, Facebook, Inc.; Howard Schultz (standing), chairman, president, and chief executive officer, Starbucks; Craig Weatherup, retired chief executive officer, Pepsi-Cola Company; James Shennan, Jr., general partner emeritus, Trinity Ventures.

Chapter 27

Innovate

For more than a decade, a glass
bottle containing a thin brown liquid
had sat on my desk. What appeared
at first glance to be a stout version
of an old-fashioned soda bottle was
actually a carbonated coffee drink
that, back in the late 1990s, Starbucks
had co-invented, marketed, and then
watched fail miserably.

Mazagran.

The name was printed across the bottle in white capital letters, but the product's symbolism was also imprinted on my psyche: Celebrate, learn from, and do not hide from mistakes.

Mazagran, a cold, effervescent beverage infused with Starbucks coffee, had been my first attempt—in collaboration with board member Craig Weatherup when he was at PepsiCo—to extend Starbucks' coffee outside the walls of our stores in an unfamiliar form. This was before the company sold whole and ground coffee in grocery aisles and prior to iced coffee's popularity. I was proud of our courage to create a new beverage category, and its failure to win over consumers, while intensely disappointing, did not sour my taste for creating.

But over the years, Starbucks deviated from its once unquenchable desire to truly innovate. Not since Frappuccino had we really shocked the marketplace and created a significant product platform with a multimillion-dollar revenue stream. The company's will to risk had dimmed. Was it laziness? Fear of failure? Perhaps, but failure often leads to great things. Mazagran may not have succeeded, but its development helped lead us to Frappuccino, a product line that by 2009 would be a $2 billion business.

I have always taken pride in the fact that Starbucks chases the unexpected, and part of my role as chief executive officer is to instill in the organization the same excitement about and courage for developing new products that has gripped me since Starbucks' earliest days. It is a responsibility that I try to live up to by pushing people further than they think they can go, yet not further than I believe they are capable of going.

As I tried to reorient our people to think boldly, I was also reorienting myself, learning how to innovate the right way for the multibillion-dollar global organization that Starbucks had become since I was last in charge. Going into 2009, I was insistent that Starbucks go after big, bold, original ideas, but I also appreciated that those ideas, such as Sorbetto, could not be fueled by instinct alone. They had to be relevant to our business, scalable, thoroughly tested, integrated across business channels, and embraced by our partners in Seattle and in our stores.

In short, a new idea's execution had to be as good as the idea itself.

Taking a more cautious, calculated approach to innovation goes against my just-do-it entrepreneurial nature, which plays off my gut and pushes for speed. But I was recognizing that the company and I needed to shift the way we brought products to market, bringing to the process the same degree of mastery that we had historically applied to roasting coffee. And because I no longer wanted the company's growth to rely only on building more stores, Starbucks' future depended on its ability to innovate on several fronts, in multiple channels of global distribution.

One seemingly natural extension of the brand that I had long entertained introducing was having Starbucks become a larger player in the health and wellness market, beyond just offering healthier food and beverages in our stores. To explore this option, I asked Richard Tait—who, as the cofounder of the award-winning Cranium game and toy company, has a knack for reinventing the status quo—to apply his innovative muscle to articulating how Starbucks might succeed in the health and wellness market. Richard made a compelling case that included some exciting but risky new ideas, and Starbucks' leadership team and I would have to decide if the company had the resources to take them on at this time in our evolution.

In 2009, as we explored future options for innovative, disciplined growth, we were asking ourselves several questions.

- How could we re-create and improve the store experience, which is our heritage and the foundation of the brand's identity?

- How might we expand on our value proposition, which has always been about emotional and human connection?

- How should we strengthen our voice to better tell our story?

- And how could the company extend its coffee authority beyond the stores, as I'd once envisioned happening with Mazagran?

Personally I did not fear failure. While I did not like or want to fail, I was willing to take risks. And I did worry that the company, given its battered stock price and morale, would not be able to emotionally or financially survive a high-profile setback. Whatever we chose to do had to be done right and done well.

The risks were huge. But the way I saw it, Starbucks had no choice but to forge ahead and create. After all, innovation is in our DNA.

* * *

Back in 1989, Dave Olsen had come into my office and offered me a cup of coffee to taste.

"How do you like it?" he asked.

"It's great," I answered after taking a sip. "Is it a new arrival?"

Dave said no, of my favorite coffee, Sumatra. But it was not freshly brewed. It had been made from a powder. I was incredulous. Essentially, Dave explained, what I had just tasted and enjoyed was an instant version of Starbucks. Again, I did not believe him. How could any instant coffee—a universally sour, watery, and simply undrinkable liquid made from a combination of robusta and arabica beans—smell or taste even remotely like Starbucks' rich dark roast? Where did it come from?

Prior to Dave walking into my office, a man named Don Valencia had walked into our Pike Place store and handed a barista a small pouch containing a coffee powder that he had created. He asked the baristas to mix it with hot water and taste it. They obliged and kindly told him that what they had just sampled was okay, but definitely not as good as Starbucks' coffee. Don was in town from Sacramento to visit his wife Heather's family, and after he bought a latte for his wife, the baristas also sold him a pound of Sumatra, one of our best-selling coffees. When Don returned to Sacramento, he made another powder, this time using Starbucks' coffee, and sent a sample back to our baristas, who were impressed enough to pass it on to the coffee specialists at our support center. Not long after that, Dave brought the beverage to me and told me about Don.

I had to meet him myself, and a few days later I flew to Sacramento to hear his full story.

Don was a remarkable individual.

He was a cell biologist who specialized in autoimmune disease diagnostics—essentially, the science of determining whether people are suffering from any number of autoimmune diseases, such as lupus, in which the body attacks its own cells. At age 28, he founded a company, Immuno Concepts, to pursue an idea that others told him was a waste of time. But Don proved them wrong by successfully inventing a better way for doctors to test blood for autoimmune diseases. Similar to test kits already being used by doctors and hospitals, Don's product included cells. But unlike other tests, the cells in Don's kit had a long shelf life because Don had figured out a way to safely freeze-dry them without compromising their properties. Health-care practitioners around the world began using Don's invention.

Then he told me about the coffee. In his free time, Don was an outdoorsman, but the only kind of coffee he could carry with him when he and Heather went hiking was instant, which to Don tasted lousy. One day he decided to apply the same science that he had applied to the cells in his kits to the extract from coffee grounds.

Don turned his kitchen into a makeshift lab where, on weekends, he made a concentrated form of coffee that he then brought to his office laboratory. There, using a tall, boxy machine that freeze-dried cells, Don subjected the concentrated coffee grounds to the same delicate process he used on cells, trying to find the best way to dehydrate the concentrate but preserve the flavor and aroma. On Monday mornings, Don's colleagues would walk into a lab that smelled like coffee and sample his latest batch.

Eventually, Don nailed it. His process produced a soluble powder that, when mixed with water, delivered a much better-tasting cup of instant coffee than he'd ever had.

Until I met Don in the late 1980s, it had never occurred to me that Starbucks might go into the instant coffee business. The mere notion seemed an anomaly, incongruent with our brand and premium position. There were many reasons to dismiss it: Starbucks is a retailer, not a consumer products company, and we did not have aspirations or the resources to become one. Besides, people's bias alone would kill the idea. Mention "Starbucks" and "instant" in the same breath, and loyal Starbucks customers as well as our baristas would cringe. Instant was lowbrow. Beneath our standards.

The reason most instant coffee is so vastly inferior to high-quality brewed coffee is because its manufacturers subject poor-quality beans to intense water extraction and drying processes that strip the beans of their natural aromatic compounds and flavors. By the time the resulting powder, or "crystals," are mixed with water, any quality in the raw bean is long gone. Yet instant coffee consumers accepted this mediocrity. Their palates had adapted. And without customers demanding a better product, consumer goods companies focused on making water-soluble coffee as cost-effectively as possible. As a result, the instant coffee market had not seen any real innovation since just after World War II.

Why, most people would ask, should a small coffee company even bother to try?

It would have been easy, and understandable, for me to thank Don for sharing his experiment with us, wish him well, and return to my work. But Don Valencia and his invention intrigued me. His scientific prowess, his innate curiosity, and his deep-rooted values further impressed me. I also genuinely liked visiting with Don. He, too, was an entrepreneur motivated by impossibilities; "it can't be done" was perhaps the one statement that most motivated him. I knew he could be an asset to Starbucks.

We stayed in touch, and by 1993 Don had accepted my offer to run Starbucks' research and development operations. Of course, we did not have an R&D facility, but it didn't matter. Don had introduced me to an exciting new possibility, and because Starbucks was young and hungry and nimble enough to adopt the unexpected, I would have been shortsighted, as an entrepreneur and as Starbucks' chief executive officer, not to turn his enthusiasm and innovative work into potential value for the company. So instead of asking "Why?" I asked, in true entrepreneurial fashion, "Why not?" and asked Don—a man who had never worked in the retail or coffee industry—to build a world-class R&D team and create a water-soluble coffee that was as bold and rich as a cup of fresh-brewed Starbucks and could be mass-produced and commercialized.

To be clear, the goal was *not* to make a better cup of instant coffee. No. Our aspiration was much higher. And while I might not have specifically articulated this back then, I sensed that Starbucks had the potential to once again create a new product category so that, one day, coffee lovers who once would not have dreamed of drinking instant coffee would drink ours.

★ ★ ★

Don labeled the secret assignment JAWS, an acronym for "just add water and stir." Neither of us imagined that something sounding so simple would prove to be so very, very complex.

Don approached his research intellectually, studying the chemical properties of coffee and trying to understand why aromatic compounds got lost during the process of extraction and drying, destroying the coffee's flavor. Yet scaling the process that Don had conjured up in his lab so the powder could be produced in large batches proved incredibly difficult. Every time he experimented with a new process, the resulting powder, once in the cup and mixed with water, did not taste or smell fresh-brewed—or anything like Starbucks. But Don did not give up. Instead, he brought a handful of other talented people into the fold.

Among them was a tenacious Panamanian engineer named Urano "Uri" Robinson. Like Don, Uri did not have a coffee background—he came from the pharmaceutical world—but as Don confidently described JAWS's proposition, the daunting David-versus-Goliath challenge piqued Uri's interest. Uri was a dogged engineer and, like many others who worked for Starbucks, also desired to do work that he found meaningful. In 1997 Uri moved his family to Seattle to join Starbucks' tiny R&D department.

Over the years—and it would be years—Don and Uri and a rotating team that included product developer Hannah Su secretly toiled away on a project that no one else at Starbucks knew or cared much about. Don routinely equated the JAWS journey to hiking Mount Kilimanjaro. It demanded well-honed skills, resilience, self-confidence, and, most importantly, a passionate belief in the project's goal and purpose: Reshape the coffee industry by improving the perception and quality of instant. Once again, Starbucks could change the way people drink coffee. If we could crack the code.

* * *

In 1998, on a shoestring budget, Don, Uri, and their small cadre of engineers developed something they had not originally been after: a coffee powder that, while not of high enough quality to fulfill Don's original vision, had another useful and lucrative purpose. Known internally as BBCB, the extract became the new coffee base for Starbucks' blended Frappuccino beverages and, eventually, bottled Frappuccino, a popular product Starbucks and PepsiCo jointly produced.

Discovering this powder was no small achievement. Up until that time, our baristas had prepared every Frappuccino by blending extra-strong brewed coffee, milk, sugar, and other ingredients. The preparation was complicated and time-consuming, and as Starbucks' Frappuccino business skyrocketed, simplifying the process to keep up with demand became a priority. The new powder reduced

Frappuccino's prep time and preserved its authentic coffee taste, as well as boosted the product's profitability. In fact, BBCB's benefit to the company was so significant that, by 2000, with Starbucks stores rapidly expanding outside North America, JAWS was put on hold and the R&D team's attention turned to scaling up BBCB's production for our Frappuccino platform of products around the world. This intense, five-year focus would take Uri and others to Europe, Asia, and South America. Eventually, working with manufacturers on two continents, Starbucks produced two proprietary soluble powders that are used for a variety of our ready-to-drink beverages and brand extensions, from flavored ice creams to coffee liqueur.

When Don retired in 1999 to spend more time with Heather and his two children and engage in charitable work, I felt as if a close friend was leaving the company. While he did not achieve the original goal he had set out to, Don's innovations were nonetheless invaluable to Starbucks. And even once he left, Uri and his colleagues did not let Don's original vision die.

* * *

By 2005 Starbucks' ability to produce enough soluble powders for our global ready-to-drink and brand-extension businesses was at capacity. Not only were we seeking out additional sources of production, but also, in our quest for quality and efficiency, the R&D team was perpetually working to develop even higher-quality yet less-expensive soluble coffee powders. That year, the R&D team began a formal initiative to expand our pantry of soluble coffees.

In 2006 the team developed a three-year plan, and built into their schedule was an initiative to refine one of the soluble powder forms to such a degree that it could stand on its own when mixed and stirred with hot water. In other words, JAWS was back on our R&D radar. The work, which still needed to be conducted in secret, was renamed Stardust.

Later that year, I was preparing for my first trip to Africa. Not knowing where or if I would be able to find high-quality coffee as I traveled the continent, I asked the R&D department for a small sample of one of its soluble powders to carry with me. While it was not meant to be consumed raw, I assumed it would taste better than any instant coffee on the market and certainly better than nothing. On the trip, I was delighted to discover that it tasted much better than I expected. Hardly perfect, but the team had definitely come a long way.

"How close do you think we are?" I asked when I returned to Seattle, wondering if Don's vision might finally be attainable.

"About 60 percent," I was told. "Maybe 75."

We had the technology to get us that far but needed to work with the right manufacturing partner to take us further. Intrigued, I set up a meeting to discuss what it would take for Starbucks to finally bring its version of instant coffee to market.

* * *

The seventh-floor Bella Vista conference room was crowded. Next to me, members of Starbucks' leadership team sat across from experts from our R&D and coffee departments, including Andrew Linnemann, Uri, and Tom Jones, the current director of R&D. Tom was walking us through a timeline, explaining why a Starbucks instant coffee product would take approximately 32 more months to launch.

"Why must it take so long?" I interjected, sounding impatient. "If Apple could develop the iPod in less than a year, we can do this!"

I was frustrated by what I perceived as a lack of urgency, but at that point in time, January 2007, I was also frustrated by a variety of shortcomings at the company, many of which I would soon outline for the leadership team in the Valentine's Day memo.

Tom calmly articulated the reasons. Not only did the existing soluble powder need to be improved upon to be worthy of Starbucks' high standards—the very code Don had been trying to crack—but there also were a host of complicated activities that had to unfold in parallel, activities the company had little or no experience doing at such scale and speed. If Starbucks was going to shock the market by introducing its premium coffee in an instant form, the company had to come together as never before, across business functions, to overcome logistical as well as perceptual hurdles. Planning. Packaging. Trademarks and patents. Manufacturing. Global production and distribution. Customer research. Testing. Integrated marketing, digital and promotional campaigns. Winning partners' support. The product did not even have a name!

The elephant in the room, which no one spoke of, was that very few people inside Starbucks wanted anything to do with instant coffee. The bias against such a down-market category was considerable; even our then head of US operations (a predecessor to Cliff Burrows) wanted nothing like it in our stores. Some partners even worried that being assigned to the Stardust project might hurt their careers at the company.

But I was resolute that we had to move forward. Going against conventional wisdom is the foundation of innovation, the basis for Starbucks' own existence. Now, we once again had a rare opportunity to create a new category of beverage—this time, an instant coffee for people who did not drink instant. A chance to give everyone access to a great cup of coffee, anytime and anywhere. And while Starbucks was no longer as small as we had been back when Don had walked into my office, we could not walk away. I had confidence in the people seated across from me.

I respected Tom's position that successfully launching a product this audacious in less than a year was probably impossible, but my reaction in what would become known to some as the "iPod meeting" did cast a sense of urgency over the project.

Uri led the charge, and during the next nine months he and Andrew's respective teams worked in close partnership with a foreign supplier whose commitment to quality and innovation matched Starbucks' own. During 14-hour days and weeks away from Seattle, the engineers and coffee experts experimented, tweaked, and tasted and tweaked again, until one day they all took a sip and agreed. They had exceeded even their own expectations, improving upon one of our existing powders so much that, when added to water and stirred, it produced a cup of coffee as rich and distinctive as Starbucks' fresh-brewed. In the fall of 2007, almost 20 years after I had first met Don, Starbucks had cracked the code.

Finally, the proof was in the cup.

* * *

"Howard, I think you should go see Don," said Dave Olsen over the phone. "He's not doing well."

In 2006 Don Valencia had been diagnosed with squamous cell carcinoma that had invaded his lungs, liver, and colon. *Of all people, Don will surely beat this*, I thought. And for 15 months, he fought a valiant battle. But by October 2007, he was very sick. I was in the midst of planning my return as Starbucks' chief executive, but every other week I visited Don at home. Behind closed doors, with Don lying covered with a blanket on a couch and me sitting nearby in a big chair, we would talk for well over an hour about so much more than coffee.

The last time I saw Don was in the hospital on a Tuesday in early December. Standing at his bedside, I leaned in close. "Don, we are going to roll out Stardust," I whispered. I wanted Don to know that his vision—one of so many that he had brought to fruition during his lifetime—was also becoming reality.

Four days later, on December 8, 2007, Don Valencia passed away.

Chapter 28

Conviction

Sometimes, the earliest days of Starbucks seemed very far away.

Like straining to remember the sound of your child's voice as a toddler as he or she heads off to college, Starbucks' nascent days got more elusive as the company grew.

But then an old friend would pop a head into my office, or maybe I would walk into the original Pike Place store, and a scene or feeling from the past suddenly came alive for me, crystal clear, as if it had occurred yesterday. And in a way, it had.

Everything that had happened as Starbucks grew, from my first Il Giornale store with its black laminate countertops to our stores in far-flung places, was a part of me. And even though, as a second-time ceo in 2009, more than two decades had passed and I had learned from mistakes and matured with experience, the core of who I'd been as a young entrepreneur remained the same: When I wholeheartedly believe in something, I can be relentless in my enthusiasm, passion, and drive to bring it to life.

Without a shred of doubt, I believed that the instant coffee Don had originally shared with me—and that our partners had worked so hard and so long to perfect—would change consumer behavior. Why was I so absolute in my thinking? Because the best innovations sense and fulfill a need before others realize the need even exists, creating a new mind-set. Starbucks' natural soluble coffee powder did just that, reminding me of the way Starbucks' Italian-inspired espresso bars had shifted the way people around the world drink coffee and spend their time.

Perhaps it was ironic that bringing instant coffee to market mirrored the start of the company. With instant as with espresso bars, the intent was to reinvent a commodity, to recast something tired and stale into something magical and fresh, an ambitious goal that was not about stealing market share from existing competitors, but about establishing a new market. Starbucks instant would convert the existing instant coffee drinker and also give a non-instant customer a value-added reason to become one. In the same vein that the third place fulfills a cultural desire for community, Starbucks' "just add water" promise gave the new millennium's intensely mobile, on-the-go population of discriminating coffee drinkers a single, delicious cup of coffee anywhere, anytime. More than 20 years before, I had believed that people would pay a premium for high-quality coffee paired with an incomparable experience. Again, I knew this to be true. And just as my early dream was not to open only one or two stores, but to build an enterprise, the current dream was not limited to selling one or two flavors of Starbucks instant coffee, but rather to build a brand platform from which other products would arise.

In another irony, naysayers who bombarded me with reasons why Starbucks should avoid instant coffee also echoed the past. I remember investors whom I had approached to fund Il Giornale bluntly saying they thought I was selling a crazy idea. That I was out of my mind. Insane! "Why on earth do you think this is going to work? Americans are never going to spend a dollar and a half on coffee."

Doubters of instant coffee were just as vehement.

"It's going to be a shelf puppy!" one of Starbucks' most senior executives insisted as he stood in front of my desk, referring to products that sit idle on grocery aisles, collecting dust. Others predicted that launching something so radical before the company turned a corner, or launching it at all, would incite critics to characterize our entry into the instant market as a desperate ploy rather than a strategic growth strategy. I was warned that instant coffee would destroy the integrity of our brand. Some even doubted I was behind it. "If Howard knew we were doing this, he'd stop the project!" one partner in the field blurted out when he heard about our plans to put our name on instant coffee. The doubt that permeated Starbucks' partner population is hard to overstate. While many people shared my enthusiasm, it is fair to say there were many who also wanted no part of it.

I was willing to hear people out—the reasons behind their worries would inform how we marketed to consumers—but I refused to allow dissenters to derail my conviction.

My wise longtime friend and mentor, Warren Bennis, the well-regarded scholar of leadership, once observed that a core capacity of leadership is the ability to make right decisions while flying blind, basing them on knowledge, wisdom, and the ability to stay wedded to an overriding goal. I thought of Warren often and spoke with him many times after I returned as ceo. It occurred to me that trying to save Starbucks during the company's crisis paralleled America's simultaneous struggle to survive the global economic crisis: Both company and country were, to paraphrase Warren, improvising without a net and working within a constantly evolving context. Flying somewhat blind.

When it came to big decisions like launching instant coffee, I took heart in knowing that my belief in the product was rooted in knowledge. First and foremost, I knew the product performed. I also knew there existed a huge market for what we had created. Globally, instant coffee accounts for about 40 percent of all coffee consumption, with annual sales hovering at about $20 billion and a higher-end segment worth close to $3.4 billion. Any market that had not seen innovation for decades was ripe for renewal. If Starbucks was serious about expanding its consumer packaged goods business into more significant revenue sources, there was no bigger prize than instant coffee.

My intuition, born of my years witnessing Starbucks' winning over millions of customers, told me that doubters of Starbucks instant would eventually realize it was neither a compromise nor a ploy and, taste by taste, our partners would rally behind it with pride.

Launching Starbucks instant coffee was also, back to Warren's point, in line with the company's overriding goals. If executed well, it stayed true to the seven pillars of the Transformation Agenda:

- Be the undisputed coffee authority.

- Engage and inspire our partners.

- Ignite the emotional attachment with our customers.

- Expand our global presence.

- Be a leader in ethical sourcing and environmental impact.

- Create innovative growth platforms worthy of our coffee.

- Deliver a sustainable economic model.

If I thought Starbucks had settled for an inferior product or that our instant coffee took us off course, I would not have had the fortitude to move forward with such a big bet.

Perhaps no one understood this more than Sheri. She had been one of the only people outside Starbucks to experience Don's original creation. We had been on a trip abroad when I pulled out the package Don had given me and made Sheri a cup. She was astonished at the taste, and throughout the years, even during periods when its development took a backseat to other research, Sheri continued to urge me to have Starbucks introduce an instant product. As a coffee lover, a traveler, and an accomplished businesswoman, Sheri inherently understood the value of the product for consumers as well as for Starbucks.

As always, Sheri's behind-the-scenes conviction fueled my own, which in 2009 was no less fierce than it had been back in 1985 when I had pounded the Seattle pavement trying to convince strangers to invest in my future.

Now I had to do much more than raise money. I had to raise tens of thousands of spirits, engaging our partners in a shared purpose and then leading them toward a shared future. I recognized that many of our partners were burdened with fear. Fear of risk. Fear of public failure. And in an uncertain economy, fear for their own futures, which were tied to the future of the company. But I could not allow this fear to hold us back.

So I put a stake in the ground. Starbucks was going to be courageous. We were going to do what people said could not be done and build a billion-dollar business on instant coffee.

* * *

One person's passion cannot successfully launch any Starbucks product. Like all effective leadership, mine is linked to the organization's ability to execute.

Instant coffee would be the biggest and most complicated product introduction in Starbucks' history. We were launching an entirely new category, worldwide, that required all the company's departments and experts to solve problems and work together in a manner they had never needed to before.

To oversee the effort, we appointed Aimee Johnson, a bright, talented emerging leader who had come to Starbucks from Campbell Soup Company. Starbucks instant coffee would be unique from all of our other beverages, including bottled Frappuccino, because it could be sold in thousands of venues where Starbucks did not yet have a presence, such as at outdoor gear retailer REI. Selling a product at so many points of distribution around the globe would be impossible without Peter Gibbons' ongoing overhaul of Starbucks' supply chain; before his changes, the company could not have dreamed of successfully manufacturing, warehousing, and distributing something so ambitious.

And from a marketing perspective, every aspect of the product had to brazenly defy instant coffee's stigma.

First, we had to find the perfect name.

More art than science, naming a product is akin to going on a treasure hunt without a map. There is no guaranteed route. We hired outside experts. We sat in rooms and brainstormed. We e-mailed each other in the middle of the night. How about Sidekick? Spark? Café Cadabra? SB Kazam? Little Hero? Or why not just sub-brand it Starbucks Instant? At its peak, the list of possible names neared 500, which was whittled down based on evolving criteria. At one point, our internal creative studio added one. VIA. It made the short list of names.

Via, it turns out, is Italian for "street" or "route," and could connote "on the go" or "between places." Not only did it speak to my original Italian inspiration for Starbucks, but it also communicated the intended nature of the product. Portable. Readily available. VIA was also tight and easy to pronounce. The word itself, when printed in all capital letters, looked elegant. The marketing team's vote was almost unanimous.

"We have it," Aimee and Michelle said when they entered my office. I heard it and hesitated, taking a moment to digest it. *VIA*. Eventually it hit me:

VIA.

*Valenc*IA.

I thought of Don and smiled.

We really had discovered the perfect name.

★ ★ ★

I was extremely disappointed.

It was a Friday afternoon, just days before VIA's packaging had to be finalized, and I was not at all happy with the generic, rainbow-colored designs I was being shown. Something was missing. The boxes that held the coffee's single-serve sleeves lacked an all-important nonverbal appeal that would convince consumers that VIA was not their grandmother's instant coffee—but rather a revolutionary yet familiar drinking experience. I knew the creative team behind the designs had tried hard. And I knew it was the 11th hour as the clock ticked toward VIA's scheduled launch date. But still I shook my head. I couldn't do it. I could not approve the creative even though a redesign risked disrupting the schedule. Too many people had worked too hard and for too long, and too much was at stake, not to get every detail pitch-perfect.

While VIA's package would not in and of itself lead to the product's success, the wrong design could kill it. I knew it could be better. No compromises. So rather than sending it back for a redo and hoping for the best, I did something I would have done during Starbucks' earliest, most entrepreneurial days.

"Come to my house Sunday," I told only Aimee and Michelle. I did not invite anyone else from Starbucks or explain why until they arrived.

"This is Jack Anderson." I proudly introduced Aimee and Michelle to the cofounder of Hornall Anderson, one of Seattle's oldest strategic branding and design firms. Jack had worked with me during Starbucks' earliest years, when his firm had designed the identity for Frappuccino as well as the stores' first shopping bags and catalogs, bringing a much-needed warmth and earthiness to the brand. This was one of those times when Starbucks' transformation demanded attention from someone who inherently understood my language and the gestalt of the brand.

At my request, Jack had come with one of his most talented designers, David Bates, and the firm's vice president of strategy, Laura Jakobsen. They did not know Starbucks was about to launch an instant coffee named VIA or that I wanted them to redesign the package.

I could not have been more resolute or eager in my explanation. "This product will be so foreign to our customers and our partners that, to get people to believe in it, to try it, it must have a certain look and feel that is reminiscent of a Starbucks product but still connotes innovation." As I knew he would, Jack got it, and within the week his team and Aimee's were collaborating.

News that I'd brought in an outside firm under the radar met with some inevitable frustration. It was never my intent to undermine anyone, but there were moments throughout the transformation— and for that matter throughout Starbucks' history—when I had to make tough choices, at times deciding that the best interests of the organization were contrary to the interests of an individual or group. Sacrificing people's feelings, and more than once even a personal relationship, for the good of thousands of partners is one of the most painful elements of my job as Starbucks' chief executive.

Bringing Jack and his colleagues back into the Starbucks fold proved a wise move. In a simple yet brilliant design, the firm met the packaging challenge by transferring the quality and trust associated with beverages sold in Starbucks stores to VIA. On the front of each small box that contained VIA's narrow, single-serve foil packets was a cutout with the distinctive profile of a Starbucks coffee cup. Also on the package, on an inner panel behind the cutout, was an adaptation of the check boxes that appear on every white Starbucks hot-coffee cup; these are the squares baristas mark to indicate customers' drink preferences—decaf and shots, syrup, and milk. The visual representation of our iconic cup and the boxes were analogues of Starbucks' in-store experience, referencing the heritage of the company while simultaneously validating the new product's quality. Subtle yet straightforward. Sophisticated without being gimmicky. Utterly authentic.

Hornall Anderson also helped us better articulate VIA's unique, simple promise in a tagline: Never be without great coffee. With VIA, it was now possible for people to enjoy a high-quality cup of natural, ethically sourced coffee in places and at times when the option had not been available. A sachet of VIA in a purse, pocket, or backpack, for example, meant enjoying Starbucks coffee when hiking. On any airplane. On a job site. In a foreign country. In a dorm room, at other people's houses, or in one's own home in lieu of brewing a full pot.

The greater marketing challenge, however, was figuring out how to talk about the product so people immediately understood that VIA was not just another instant coffee, but the game changer many of us believed it to be. I never forgot another sage piece of advice I heard from Costco's Jim Sinegal, who encouraged me not to run away from the word "instant," but to embrace it. There was a lot of debate internally about this. Should we even associate VIA with instant, given its negative connotation? Was our new coffee even in the same category as instant? Eventually, our creative studio crafted a simple, elegant turn of phrase that effectively reframed the way the product was viewed. A phrase that connoted a new beverage as well as a new behavior. The line—"Starbucks coffee, in an instant"—said it all.

* * *

The positioning. The packaging. The name.

Each of these elements would help recast public opinion about what instant coffee could be. But for VIA to succeed, our partners had to view it with the same respect they had for every other Starbucks coffee. Overcoming the company's own bias was a top priority, and again I could not do it alone.

In their own efforts to build consensus, Aimee and her colleague Brady Brewer, a vice president of marketing, had discovered a solution.

If partners knew VIA was an instant coffee prior to trying it, then they brought to the experience negative assumptions that tainted their perception. So we fooled them. At one meeting, every partner received two small paper cups and was told that he or she would be tasting two different brewed Starbucks coffees. As people sipped and discussed the flavors, no one questioned the samples' authenticity. But when it was announced that both cups were Starbucks' new instant coffee, the collective evaporation of bias was almost palpable. The element of surprise had displaced suspicion.

This trick was played out again and again in our offices and conference rooms, in stores with partners, even in my own dining room at dinner parties when I secretly served VIA to guests. The surprise taste test created a snowball of acceptance.

Rather than fearing skepticism, we were using it, a tactic that would help turn the tide when we launched VIA publicly.

★ ★ ★

At first, however, our fears did come true.

On February 13, 2009, four days before the official public announcement that Starbucks would enter the instant coffee market, this headline ran on the investment website the Motley Fool: "No, Starbucks, Please Don't!"

The news *about* VIA—but not VIA itself—had been leaked to *Advertising Age*, and a rash of bloggers had responded by criticizing a product they had never tasted. The Fool column wrote about Starbucks' "plans to delve—or is the word *devolve?*—into the world of instant coffee" and blatantly asked, "Is Howard Schultz panicking, getting desperate to show that management's doing something, *anything?*" Other bloggers harped on how we were "trading down" to instant coffee despite its reputation for "poor quality and so-so taste," as one blogger put it, adding, "How many aspiring poets, musicians and philosophers will go to Starbucks to think profound thoughts and guzzle *instant* coffee?"

With the bloggers being so merciless, a small part of me was still wondering what the mainstream media would say when, on February 17, 2009, I took the stage in front of a standing-room-only press conference in New York City to announce VIA. In the audience were individuals whom we wanted to taste VIA and understand the business opportunity before they rushed to judgment and influenced public opinion when VIA was launched as a test in stores in Seattle, Chicago, and London over the next few weeks.

I looked out at these influencers quietly sipping the cups of Colombian and Italian coffee we had poured for them as part, we had said, of a routine coffee tasting, which often preceded Starbucks' meetings. Which was true. Finally, with the tempered excitement of a kid quietly unloading a great secret he'd been keeping, I revealed that both coffees were—surprise—a new long-term strategy for Starbucks. VIA Ready Brew.

"Yes, it fooled us," *The New York Times*'s Joe Nocera would write in his column.

I had gotten their attention. Now I had to convince them that instant coffee was no Hail Mary pass for Starbucks, but a homegrown innovation grounded in our coffee roots with tremendous implications for the company's future.

"This is not your mother's instant coffee," I assured the room, "and it is a big move for us, an opportunity to reinvent a category, create new rituals, and grow our customer base."

I stated the business case. Starbucks, despite its reputation for ubiquity, had only a 4 percent share of the 65 billion cups of coffee consumed annually in the United States. VIA could potentially expand the market as well as our share of it by creating new coffee-drinking occasions.

But the big prize was outside North America. Globally, the instant coffee market is worth more than $20 billion. In Japan alone, where Starbucks has 839 stores, the $2.9 billion of annual instant coffee sales account for more than half of all of Japan's coffee consumption. In the United Kingdom, where Starbucks has more than 700 stores, instant coffee is a $1.2 billion business, more than *80 percent* of all the country's coffee sales. The data were impressive—most Americans had no idea instant coffee was so popular in the rest of the world—but as we had predicted, for VIA to be taken seriously it had to perform in the cup, and after the press conference we waited for the verdicts as journalists in newsrooms around the country held their own private taste tests. Slowly their reviews poured in:

A panel of seasoned Ad Age newsroom coffee junkies surprised themselves Wednesday when they were unable to tell the difference

between Starbucks' new instant coffee and the chain's in-store brew.—
AdAge.com

*Before you start accusing the iconic retailer of desperate measures,
give Via a try. Here at Fortune, we have a machine that brews a fresh
cup from Starbucks beans in less than a minute. We compared it to the
Via and couldn't tell which cup was the instant. Both had a rich aroma
and flavor.*—Fortune

*[After trying several other instant coffees,] we all agreed the taste of
the instant products was drastically different from fresh-brewed—dominated by bitterness in many cases, and lacking in complex flavor and
aroma. So when we finally had the opportunity to sample Starbucks'
new Via instant, we were surprised: It actually tastes like coffee.*—
SmartMoney.com

As always, our coffee and our company also had their critics. Some
conceded only that VIA was better than other instant coffees, but not
equal to brewed. Others scratched their heads at our strategy. "I see it
as being a very short-term approach to a long-term brand problem,"
one coffee industry consultant was quoted as saying. "To me it looks
like a big gamble."

Wall Street also withheld its approval. The day we announced
VIA, Starbucks' stock closed at $9.65, down 48 cents from the last
market close.

Our battle was far from won. But we had advanced further than
many people thought we ever would.

★ ★ ★

I've never bought into the notion that there is a single recipe for successful leadership. But I do think effective leaders share two intertwined attributes: an unbridled level of confidence about where their
organizations are headed, and the ability to bring people along.

When it came to VIA, my conviction was already unparalleled;
winning our partners' confidence and enthusiasm was the greater
challenge. But I did not doubt that by the time VIA launched nation-
ally in the fall, and then globally, our partners in Seattle and in stores
around the world would rally behind it—not just because VIA is a

wonderful product, but because at this point in the transformation and amidst the wider economic turmoil, almost everyone was hungry for something concrete to believe in. Something to hope for.

But for Starbucks in the fall of 2008, that "something" had to be bigger than a new espresso machine or a customer loyalty program, and more consumer facing and companywide than the New Orleans leadership conference. Starbucks needed an even more seismic event that, unlike Sorbetto, was authentic to our coffee heritage but, like Frappuccino, unequivocally original. We needed something that actively involved store partners and made them proud and positioned the company to capture share of a new market.

However VIA ended up performing, it would be much more important to the company than the earnings it generated. VIA had the potential to awaken an entrepreneurial spirit and once again imprint the importance of innovation upon the organization, reminding our partners of the excitement that comes from assaulting the status quo and trusting yourself, your coworkers, and above all a truly great product. VIA could renew our courage to lead, and Starbucks is at its best when we lead, not follow, when we reinvent categories, create new rituals, and transform an industry. I had no doubt: VIA was helping us transform ourselves.

Chapter 29

Connecting Dots

Barely a few hours after the VIA press conference, I was sitting in front of a television camera on the floor of the New York Stock Exchange doing a live interview with CNBC's Maria Bartiromo. The first question Maria asked me was not about VIA or Starbucks, but about the economy.

On that same day, February 17, 2009, President Obama had signed into law an ambitious $787 billion stimulus package to try to rescue a nation reeling from an economy weaker than it had been in decades. Unemployment in the United States was on its way to a 25-year high of 8.1 percent. The country's gross domestic product, or GDP, the value of all the goods and services produced, had shrunk by 6.2 percent in the last quarter, its steepest decline in 27 years. Consumer confidence had plummeted to 25, its lowest level since 1967.

"Is [the stimulus] going to be helpful in terms of getting the consumer out of this funk?" Maria asked me above the din of the Exchange. My perspective, which I shared with her, was that its most immediate effect would be to lift consumer confidence, which was so critical for people to feel comfortable enough to spend money again. But I also said that I did not think the current climate was going to dramatically improve anytime soon, something that all companies had to accept. The deteriorating economic situation was beyond any organization's control; all any of us could do was to affect how our companies responded to it. At Starbucks, we continued the incredibly complicated, sometimes painful work of cost cutting and making our processes more efficient. Revamping the supply chain. Streamlining store operations. Overhauling our IT systems. We were even closing 300 more stores than previously planned. Most difficult was that we had just gone through another round of layoffs, although not as large. In a perfect world, our partners would not have to endure such a painful experience more than once, but since July 2008 the economic situation had grown significantly worse, greatly affecting the assumptions we had made half a year ago.

In addition to the operations of their businesses, companies, including us, also had to attend to the front end and put ourselves in our customers' shoes as the recession deepened. Our customers were hurting, and we needed to find ways to offer value without damaging the brand through price cuts.

Starbucks had been trying to do this with its Rewards and Gold Cards, the $2 beverages with the Treat Receipt, as well as offering food-and-coffee pairings for under $4. VIA, I told Maria during the interview, which cost less than $1 a cup, was another way Starbucks was able to be relevant to consumers in the current environment. A three-pack of VIA would sell for $2.95, and a 12-pack for $9.95.

"Tell me what you are seeing in terms of consumers today," she further inquired, a question I got a lot because Starbucks stores around the world often serve as barometers, even early indicators, of spending behavior.

"It has not really gotten any worse in North America since the fall," I answered. "The place that concerns us is Western Europe and especially the UK. The UK is in a spiral. . . . I think consumer confidence in the UK is very, very poor."

Five minutes later, the interview ended. I left the studio for my next appointment, and by the time I went to sleep that evening in my New York apartment I was pleased but drained—and completely unaware of how events were unfolding in the city and across the Atlantic.

★ ★ ★

The next morning, I woke up and, as usual, made myself a French press of Sumatra and immediately checked e-mail. I had an unbelievably large amount for so early in the day. I checked voice mail. I had at least three dozen messages!

I thought someone must have died.

What soon became apparent was that sometime after I had appeared on CNBC, Maria had interviewed Britain's business secretary, Lord Peter Mandelson, who was in New York to promote his country's economic stability. The very first thing she asked him to do was to respond to my dire characterization of the UK's economy. Mandelson shot back, "The UK is not spiraling, although I notice that Starbucks is in a great deal of trouble. But that may be because of their overexposure given the state of the market. So please do not project Starbucks' performance on the British economy."

According to subsequent newspaper reports that went viral on the Internet, Lord Mandelson attended a cocktail event later that day where, obviously still upset, he made disparaging comments about me personally. It was perfect front-page fodder for England's tabloids.

"Peter Mandelson Launches Fierce Attack on Starbucks Chief," hyped England's *Telegraph* newspaper the next day. "Mandelson and Starbucks Clash on UK Economy," shouted the *Guardian*'s front page. Subsequent articles and blog posts exacerbated the issue, and it spread like wildfire online! Inundated with calls, Starbucks was compelled to release a reassuring statement about the company's confidence in and commitment to the UK market.

The incident, which ended almost as quickly as it began, was significant mainly for what it represented. First, similar to the memo that had leaked two years earlier, almost to the day, in 2007, the experience signified once again just how quickly information flows—and can get out of hand, particularly in the digital age. In contrast to all the months spent preparing to tell VIA's story and business strategy, it took only a few hours for one unrelated comment to refocus the conversation about Starbucks.

Second, Starbucks is a consumer brand that people talk about and want to communicate with. Negatively and positively. Whether we make big moves or small. And as I had believed upon my return as ceo, there was an opportunity for us to interact more in the dialogue, whether or not we initiated a specific conversation.

Our presence on social networks such as Facebook and Twitter and our own MyStarbucksIdea.com were helping us listen to and connect with customers as well as improve the business. To date, 25 ideas had been adopted based on My Starbucks Idea posts; most impressively, the site inspired the first versions of our loyalty programs, the Rewards and Gold Cards. Over time, our loyalty program had evolved into one of the company's most successful and lucrative endeavors to date. On Facebook, Starbucks' number of fans was nearing one million, and 150,000 people were following Starbucks on Twitter. These audiences wanted to hear from us.

More than ever before, Starbucks was initiating conversations, engaging moment by moment with the people who were most interested in what we were doing. For us, social networks were proving to be an area where Starbucks could lead instead of using the defensive tactics the company had fallen into employing elsewhere. As long as we did not bombard our followers with coupons, as long as we conversed about issues that were important to both Starbucks and our customers—from coffee to recycling—and as long as we listened as well as talked, people would stick with us and perhaps even become more attached. More than adding a halo to the brand, Starbucks was developing a two-way digital dialogue that drove awareness of our activities, drove trust, and, ultimately, drove sales.

During the previous holiday season, for example, we had used our then nascent Facebook page to tell our Facebook friends about (STARBUCKS) RED, exposure that helped boost Starbucks' (PRODUCT) RED sales to provide the equivalent of more than 3.4 million days of antiretroviral medicine for people with HIV or AIDS in Africa. The next month, on January 20, 2009, when Barack Obama was inaugurated as the 44th president of the United States, Starbucks encouraged its online fans to come into our stores and pledge volunteer time. All told, our stores recorded 1.2 million hours of pledged service.

With the understanding that digital and social media would continue to play a role in how we engaged with customers and went to market, we invited Facebook's chief operating officer, and one of Google's first 300 employees, Sheryl Sandberg, to join our board of directors. At the same time, I was pleased to also recruit Kevin Johnson to join the board. I had gotten to know Kevin when he was with Microsoft, where he was president of the group running the Windows and online services businesses. He had recently become the chief executive of Juniper Networks; his presence on the board would give us another active CEO point of view. And both Sheryl's and Kevin's combination of technology, business, and leadership skills would add more depth to our board.

In the spring of 2009, I felt confident that few other companies were leveraging social and digital media as we would continue to do, and each day brought new possibilities.

Yet we had to tread carefully.

The wrong tone, message, or association risked diluting our brand or harming our customer relationships. We had to be incredibly selective in how and where Starbucks showed up digitally—stay open to innovative ideas, definitely, but act deliberately.

* * *

Standing in front of the leadership team in our boardroom, Starbucks' chief information officer Stephen Gillett was explaining how Starbucks could significantly increase monthly comps almost immediately.

I had asked the team to think big and then think bigger. Even with VIA on its way to market, there was never a silver bullet and we needed to continue to challenge ourselves: What else could we do to add value for our customers as well as shareholders? How could we make better use of all the assets Starbucks had? Stephen, almost one year into his role, not only was overhauling our IT systems, but also had come up with something no one else at the table could have imagined.

"How many of you know GameStop?" Stephen asked. No hands went up. GameStop, he informed us, is the world's largest retailer of new and used video games. And while the rest of the retail world was suffering, GameStop's comp sales at its 6,000-plus locations had been up 10 percent in the last quarter. Starbucks had been down 10 percent. Then Stephen posed another question. "Does anyone know the number-one–selling online game of all time?" Again, no hands.

Stephen smiled. "World of Warcraft."

The name could not have been more foreign to me. Stephen went on to explain to the equally bemused Starbucks leadership team that World of Warcraft is an online, interactive, multiplayer fantasy game where—in a make-believe world akin to that in the *Lord of the Rings* tales—human players create their own digital characters that embark on adventures and quests, acquiring points along the way. Apparently, almost 12 million people around the globe play World of Warcraft, and Stephen was not only one of them, we would soon learn, but also among the most successful and renowned players, a star within the gaming community. And that community, Stephen said, consists mostly of males ages 18 to 34, a demographic that Starbucks had yet to capture.

Stephen was suggesting that Starbucks explore the GameStop business model—clearly they were doing something right—as well as a possible relationship with World of Warcraft's parent company, Blizzard Entertainment. Maybe we could sell video games in our stores. Maybe a virtual Starbucks "pet" could become part of the Warcraft world of coveted characters. How about a Starbucks–World of Warcraft Rewards Card?

At first blush, such a relationship seemed unlikely. But the numbers Stephen had pulled together should such a relationship succeed were extremely compelling. A Starbucks partnership with Blizzard, he projected, could quite possibly usher millions of new customers into our stores around the world, leading to much-needed comp sales growth.

I sat back in my chair. I'd asked for big, out-of-the-box ideas, and Stephen, who is not a merchant but an information technology professional, had certainly delivered. Although it was obvious that "warcraft" did not fit with Starbucks' values, I resisted jumping to conclusions as people had with VIA when they had assumed without much knowledge that the idea would fail. I wanted to give Stephen the benefit of at least exploring the idea. So, in April 2009, a small group of us flew to Blizzard Entertainment's headquarters in Irvine, California.

The only sign that Blizzard is not a staid software outfit but a fantasy gaming producer is a 12-foot-tall bronze statue of an Orc warrior, one of the types of characters in World of Warcraft, riding a menacing wolf at the building's entrance. I shook my head, but Stephen was smiling from ear to ear. He was in his element. After meeting with Blizzard's executives and discussing their business model and intensely passionate customer base, I was impressed. Rarely had I seen such devotion to a product! In many respects, Blizzard's customers are a lot like ours.

I flew back to Seattle and left Stephen in Irvine to further explore options. He was joined by one of Starbucks' newest partners, Adam Brotman, who had founded the Redmond, Washington–based PlayNetwork, which provides customized music programming and systems for Starbucks stores and other retailers. Adam possesses a natural curiosity and a knack for melding business strategy, marketing, and technology, and Stephen had asked him to help Starbucks develop a new business unit, Digital Ventures.

On their flight back to Seattle, Stephen and Adam debated the pros and cons of a Starbucks-Blizzard partnership. It had undeniable potential to make Starbucks relevant to a new demographic, young adult males, and drive massive numbers of new customers into our stores, giving us an almost overnight sales boost. So very, very tempting. But by the time the plane landed, they had agreed with what Michelle and I had also concluded: World of Warcraft simply strayed too far from Starbucks' core.

Again, this was not an easy choice given the financial and competitive pressures Starbucks was under. Any company, when faced with adversity, would be tempted to go forward with an idea that promises to quickly erase pain. But in business as in life, people have to stay true to their guiding principles. To their cores. Whatever they may be. Pursuing short-term rewards is always shortsighted. So while on one level, Stephen Gillett would have loved nothing more than to be in business with Blizzard Entertainment, he—as well as Adam, Michelle, and I—had the intuitive sense to know that World of Warcraft, while a fascinating product and phenomenal employee culture, was not the right fit for Starbucks at this time.

Exploring an imperfect idea can often lead to a better one, and Stephen's original vision led us to ask some important questions about how Starbucks might connect even more deeply with customers in the digital space, especially given the unique power and incomparable reach of our in-store wireless networks. Starbucks had the largest footprint of company-owned stores with Wi-Fi in the world, and millions of customers already logged on every day.

Hovering above every third place is a virtual fourth place, and the time had come for Starbucks to use it much more deliberately as a way to offer new value to our customers.

* * *

Innovation, as I had often said, is not only about rethinking products, but also rethinking the nature of relationships. When it came to our customers, connecting with them in a store and online did not have to be mutually exclusive experiences. Figuring out exactly how the retail and virtual worlds might coexist would be a matter of connecting the dots, and just as I had with Chris Bruzzo, I had given Stephen license to be disruptive, which was exactly what he and Adam tried to be after returning from Irvine.

For the next few months, Adam hit the road, meeting with people at all kinds of companies to listen and learn about their products and business models while exploring possible relationships. Almost every company, he quickly realized, wanted to strike a deal with Starbucks to introduce its products to our customers. In a way, this was surprising. Despite the pummeling the company was taking in the press and on Wall Street, we remained a brand others wanted to be associated with. Our role as a discriminating curator of music and books could extend to other things. Obviously, Starbucks was not interested in once again cluttering store shelves with irrelevant products—we had learned that lesson—but the power of our brand's affinity was yet another under-utilized asset, a subtle but important truth.

One day, in conversation with a provider of online financial services, Adam posed a question: Would the company be willing to give its content away for free, but only to customers in Starbucks stores? The answer, he was told, was yes. Dots began to connect.

Our customers were already inviting Starbucks into their digital lives through their social networks. What if we extended that emotional connection by giving them more reason to meet us online? What if we partnered with, say, news organizations, book publishers, and music companies to offer our customers who were using the Starbucks in-store networks free access to exclusive digital content? Yes, for years we had been introducing people to new music and books in our stores, but this would be different, an even more dynamic, multifaceted way for us, as a retailer, to add another level of value to people's experiences in our stores. Someone sitting at a table using a laptop would, for instance, be able to watch an exclusive movie preview, get free access to premium services, read newspaper articles he or she otherwise might have to pay for or that others could not yet access. And, because our networks are hyperlocalized, maybe we could further connect customers to places and activities in their communities. A farmer's market. A restaurant. A play or an upcoming blood drive.

The potential was exciting. Creating a Starbucks digital network that served as a private channel for our customers could further bridge the virtual world of the Internet and the physical world of stores as well as the neighborhoods where we do business. Such an innovative tool extended the third place experience and stayed true to one of the original three pillars of the Transformation Agenda: reigniting Starbucks' emotional attachment with its customers.

★ ★ ★

Meanwhile, in April 2009, something curious was happening in our business. For the first time in almost a year, Starbucks' US comparable store sales were creeping upward. Although still distressingly deep in negative territory, April's negative 7.2 percent comp sales were an undeniable improvement over March's negative 8.1 percent, which had been better than February's negative 8.3 percent comp decline. These were incremental improvements from which it was too early to draw any conclusions, but the data were encouraging: Customers were starting to spend a little more money at Starbucks.

Chapter 30

Balance

The first time I walked through
the narrow doorway and into the
unassuming corner shop on Via
Montenapoleone, the most fashionable
and expensive street in Milan, I was
unexpectedly overcome with emotion.
Inside, the unassuming Coltelleria G.
Lorenzi was a silent symphony.
A simple yet unbelievable execution
of nonverbal, visual excitement.

Softly lit displays beckoned me to admire a mind-boggling assortment of handcrafted knives, razors, and cutlery. There were scissors of all varieties—85 for manicuring alone—many forged from steel, some made especially for trimming thick beards, others for cutting delicate fingernails. In all, thousands of items were displayed under glass as if in a museum. I could literally feel the passion, the expertise, that had been put into this space. Such reverence.

"Who *is* this?" I asked my friend Plácido Arango, who had brought me here. Plácido is an accomplished businessman and one of the most genuine people I've ever known; his company, Grupo Vips, operates Starbucks stores throughout Spain. We share a respect for artisans of all kinds. "Mr. Aldo Lorenzi," he told me. "His father opened this shop many years ago."

Every time I returned to Milan, I visited the shop, but I never saw Mr. Lorenzi. Finally, in 2009, Plácido asked an Italian friend, Angelo Moratti, if he would introduce me to Aldo.

"He doesn't speak any English."

"Do you think he's ever heard of Starbucks?" I asked.

"No, he's never heard of Starbucks."

"Do you think I can sit down with him?"

"He won't do it."

"I have to meet him."

"Howard, he's not going to do it." But Angelo agreed to call. Mr. Lorenzi was hesitant, but he kindly acquiesced.

"He'll meet you for a few minutes tomorrow."

It was about 10 a.m. when Plácido, Angelo, and I arrived at 9 Via Montenapoleone. A tall, elegant gentleman, impeccably dressed in a suit and tie, quietly escorted us into his office. We sat down. Angelo translated as I first thanked Mr. Lorenzi for giving me a few moments of his time.

The planned 20-minute visit extended through the afternoon. The three of us listened, entranced, as Aldo Lorenzi spoke with humility and respect about his family and the business his father had founded in 1929—and what it means to him to be a merchant. I took notes on a small pad.

At one point, he asked *me* a question. "How many stores do you have?"

"I'm embarrassed to tell you," I said.

"How many?" he asked again.

"Sixteen thousand." I watched his expression change to disbelief as he heard the Italian translation. "Did he say 16,000 coffee stores?" He shook his head. "I could never even have two."

At the end of our visit, Mr. Lorenzi handed me a gray paperback book translated into English from Italian. I read the title: *That Shop in Via Montenapoleone*, by Aldo Lorenzi. Its thick, textured cover and creamy pages felt as handcrafted as the cutlery encased in glass, and on the flight back to the United States I sat back and turned to the first chapter. "I love our shop . . . ," read the first sentence, written with the conviction of a man who truly knew his trade. I was hooked.

In the months to come, I kept the book close to me. It was one of the few items that took up space on my desk and came with me on business trips. I shared it with friends and partners, but mostly I took tremendous joy in reading Mr. Lorenzi's words to myself. More often than not, a sentence or a paragraph reiterated my own philosophies, but at the same time made me think about retail, our shared profession, in an even more romantic yet practical light:

> *I want to write pages that have their own poetics about the things I make or do, but at the same time I want them to be like the pages of a manual, down-to-earth instructions, exact and useful information about our job. It is a job that has been transformed with the passing of time and yet it has remained the same.*

Despite our differences in culture and business and age, this 73-year-old Italian owner of a solitary knife store spoke my language. He had much to share, and I still had much to learn.

* * *

At the very heart of being a merchant is a desire to tell a story by making sensory, emotional connections.

Once, twice, or 16,000 times.

Ideally, every Starbucks store should tell a story about coffee and what we as an organization believe in. That story should unfold via the taste and presentation of our products as well as the sights, sounds, and smells that surround our customers. The aroma of freshly ground coffee. Interior hues, textures, the shapes and materials of furniture and fixtures, as well as their origins. The art on the walls. The music. The rhythm of the coffee bar and how our partners move and speak behind the counter—and what they speak about.

Each store's ambience is the manifestation of a larger purpose, and at Starbucks each shop's multidimensional sensory experience has always defined our brand. Our stores and partners are at their best when they collaborate to provide an oasis, an uplifting feeling of comfort, connection, as well as a deep respect for the coffee and communities we serve. As Aldo Lorenzi understood, Starbucks Coffee Company's challenge has always been to authentically replicate this experience hundreds upon thousands of times.

When it comes to telling Starbucks' story, my taste for the charm of a neighborhood café might seem at odds with my ambitions for the business. Yes, I have long believed that Starbucks can create authentic, personal experiences while at the same time be a profitable global company. Yes, I want our stores' interiors to personify our values but also to be buildable at scale. Yes, I want our baristas to serve customers with a sincere smile and also with speed, and yes, I believe our flavors and environments can reflect local cultures as well as deliver consistent tastes and quality; a store in Japan that offers lattes infused with the revered sakura flower should also serve brewed coffees whose tastes visitors from the United Kingdom will recognize as Starbucks'.

Whether Starbucks stores could feel small as the company grew big, balancing efficiencies with romance, was a question people constantly asked me, and I was routinely criticized for daring to believe such a balance could be achieved. But striving for balance between extremes is a trait that has long set Starbucks apart from so many other consumer brands. And while over the years my attention has wandered from time to time, at no point have I ever given up my intention that Starbucks should find equilibrium between the personal and the profitable and deliver shareholder value through the lens of social conscience. As Starbucks neared its 40th year, 2011, I was asking everyone at the company, directly and indirectly, to balance an entrepreneurial enthusiasm with the rigor that complex organizations require.

In the summer of 2009, two specific initiatives to enhance our in-store experience were under way. One involved interior design. The other, customer service and partner engagement.

Both initiatives had been percolating in pockets of the company for months, in some cases years, and each promised dramatic improvements if executed well. But change, even when for the better, is sometimes uncomfortable. Sometimes unwelcome. Our partners, customers, and the marketplace were in for some shocks.

* * *

We are proud to have a traditional type of shop, which had remained true to itself over the years, but it must not be forgotten that this creates the need to keep it "fresh." The more that furniture, floor and fittings age, the greater the need for meticulous and periodic maintenance. Old is beautiful, but not if it is neglected.—Aldo Lorenzi, That Shop in Via Montenapoleone

I did not recognize our own store.

Located at the bustling corner of Pike Street and First Avenue in downtown Seattle, directly across the street from the Market, this Starbucks interior space had a familiar yet fresh feel. In spirit it reminded me of our original location, but with a renewed energy. The aura was rustic and earthy but modern. The muted colors naturally warm. As I moved into the space, past customers sitting at a long communal table, some sipping coffee or tea out of ceramic mugs, Arthur Rubinfeld, our president of global development, explained what I was seeing. And what I was not.

The materials used for the store's floor, ceiling, wood columns, cabinets, even door handles had been preserved from nearby buildings and farms, made from fallen trees, or recycled from items like laundry detergent bottles and old wine barrels. The long wood table had once been used in a local restaurant after it was reclaimed from a Seattle-area home. The slate menu behind the bar came from a classroom at Seattle's Garfield High School. Burlap coffee bags lining the walls were from our Kent, Washington, roasting plant. The leather on the face of the coffee bar was recycled from shoe and automobile factories. *Amazing,* I thought.

Above me, LED and compact fluorescent lights were using less energy than regular bulbs. In the restrooms, dual-flush toilets and low-flow faucets reduced water use. Even the paint was carefully chosen to avoid interfering with the store's coffee aroma, and much of the waste generated during construction had been recycled. The entire store was built to be LEED certified—meaning that it meets stringent standards to reduce its environmental impact.

First and Pike was not an anomaly. Eventually, all of our new company-owned stores worldwide would also qualify for LEED certification. And in a few months, July 2009, I would travel to Paris for the opening of our store in Disney Village, where materials had been reclaimed from French wine barrels and old champagne racks and recycled from mobile phone parts and aircraft tires. Coffee grounds from the store, I was told, would likely be donated to the amusement park, where they would be used for composting.

Standing inside the First and Pike store, I looked around. The space was beautiful. So much more than an extension of an existing design, this was a reimagined experience that enhanced the sense of community and reinforced our coffee heritage while demonstrating and encouraging environmental consciousness.

I was extremely proud of what Arthur and his team had brought to fruition in the year since he had accepted my request to return to Starbucks and overhaul our store development.

"We have to let people know Starbucks is coming back," I recall saying to Arthur just before I returned as ceo. I hoped my old friend would accept my offer to head global development. "Arthur, we can do it again," I all but pleaded.

A successful transformation required that I put the right people in the right positions, and I knew upon my return that Arthur would be a linchpin in fixing two significant problems: Starbucks' bloated real estate portfolio and its stale store designs. Given our mutual respect, plus Arthur's balanced approach to business and creative, I felt he was uniquely qualified to resurrect the level of innovative, brand-defining aesthetic that he had brought to Starbucks in the 1990s.

When Arthur first joined as head of store development in 1991, we had only about 100 stores, and Arthur understood better than I did that real estate needed to play a critical role in the company's expansion and branding. For Arthur—an architect with an MBA's perspective and a psychologist's sensitivity to how space resonates with people—a smart store-development strategy was about a combination of mutually dependent elements: negotiating leases for properties in high-traffic, highly visible locales near other desirable retailers; brand-reflective store design; premium yet cost-effective construction; and prudent asset management. For 10 years,

Arthur oversaw the integration of these elements as the company grew.

But after Arthur left, the company deviated from his approach. Store site selection was no longer as deliberate. Designs developed in the mid-1990s were being merely tweaked, not reimagined or even appropriately updated or diversified. Keeping costs low was paramount, and no one was rewarded for intelligent design. Starbucks became the envy of the retail industry for its ability to quickly retrofit a store with one of several "palettes"—a family of colors, furniture, fixtures, and wall graphics—but this core competency also fed our reputation as a soulless, ubiquitous chain.

Meanwhile, competitors old and new went to school on us. McDonald's as well as independent coffeehouses all upped their games, adopting our successes and taking advantage of our shortcomings.

Bringing Arthur back was about reestablishing our coffeehouse authority. I knew he did not need to return. He had a successful consultancy. He'd coauthored a book and was enjoying an entrepreneurial life free from the pressures of Wall Street. What intrigued him, however, was a desire to win back what Starbucks had lost. His aspirations to turn the company around were as optimistic and ambitious as mine. Like other partners who had helped build Starbucks from its infancy, Arthur took the transformation very personally, and when he came back he did so with a vengeance.

His first act was to relinquish the large office he was assigned and designate it a communal meeting room. He tore down the corporate cubicles and turned the department's space into a creative studio. Within months he culled the concept design staff of 60 down to nine and elevated or recruited new talent.

Arthur's initial priority was, with Mike Malanga, to rightsize our portfolio of stores—the difficult process of closing stores and winding down leases.

Simultaneously, his global design team, led by the talented Liz Muller, began birthing Starbucks' new store designs. For artistic inspiration, Arthur and Liz looked to Starbucks' brand and new mission statement, asking themselves how to bring our core principles to life in a manner that, once again, differentiated Starbucks in the marketplace. They found their creative anchor in sustainable construction, which had long been championed by our own Tony Gale, and in Starbucks Shared Planet, the philosophical umbrella for our renewed focus on community, environmental stewardship, and ethical sourcing.

Sustainability. Green. Organic. Recycled. Repurposed. Local. Community. And, of course, coffee. These became the creative watchwords for Starbucks' new store designs.

The dramatic design of First and Pike—along with those of other new concept stores planned for Paris, London, New York City, Hong Kong, and Madrid—would not be replicated but rather used as a beacon to inspire future stores. By fall 2009, Arthur and his team would finalize three new directional designs to be used as creative touchstones and translated to our stores around the world. Each design would, through the mixing and matching of elements, balance sustainability with the comfort and essence of the third place, creating a quieter, simpler, more contemporary approach that showcased coffee and the coffeehouse experience. That meant long communal tables for group conversations and community boards for posting information. Softer colors, exposed architectural features, and less artwork; more symbolic, authentic, and carefully placed pieces would become standard—as would sustainable, recycled, and repurposed materials; more formalized seating arrangements; and child-friendly areas. And under the creative influence of Tim Pfeiffer, senior vice president of global design, unique furniture and lighting were also designed exclusively for Starbucks stores.

I thought our new creative direction, in look as well as philosophy, was exhilarating and truly separated us in the marketplace. But it could not be implemented haphazardly; rolling it out globally to thousands of stores would require a disciplined, phased approach. Once again, we had to marry creative liberty with cost limitations and brand considerations.

Arthur also had more in store.

Without fanfare, Starbucks was also going to open two coffee shops in Seattle that were not like any of our existing stores. Each would serve Starbucks coffee but be unique in design and product mix, offering a heightened local experience. They would not look like traditional Starbucks, nor would they be called Starbucks, but rather named after their street addresses.

The first new store, 15th Ave. Coffee and Tea, would open in July 2009 in a former Starbucks space on a relatively quiet street in Seattle's eclectic Capitol Hill neighborhood. The second store, Roy Street Coffee and Tea, would open a few months later further west, at a busy intersection and kitty-corner from one of Seattle's best independent movie houses. Each store's interior and furniture would be an original design, and on their rather inconspicuous brown-and-white signage, the words "Inspired by Starbucks" would appear below the coffee-house's official name.

There was tension within Starbucks as some people questioned why we would deviate from our identity, in look as well as name. Were we hiding? Trying to masquerade as an independent coffee shop? Did I think Starbucks wasn't good enough?

We were not trying to hide anything, only to explore, and to learn. The idea to experiment with other retail concepts that would further elevate our coffee authority had actually been touched on in early transformation brainstorming sessions, but it was Arthur, as well as our in-house coffee enthusiast Major Cohen, who had run with it. "Break the rules" was my only directive.

Many cities have rich coffeehouse traditions, but during the past 15 years there had been a proliferation of independents in the United States. Their existence, I firmly believed, was an offshoot of Starbucks' ability to foster more savvy and enthusiastic coffee consumers. Many independents had essentially gone to school on us, and I gave them a lot of credit. But I also thought that as we transformed our company, we should continue to explore different ideas and approaches of our own, and to prove to ourselves—not just the marketplace—that Starbucks could deliver a coffee experience on different levels, not just the ones to which we had grown accustomed.

These two mercantile stores, as we referred to them internally, would function as independent businesses as well as learning environments, allowing us to experiment in an active retail setting and gain more insight into what consumers want as their own tastes evolve. It was research. It was creative. It was also a great deal of fun.

The stores operated outside our traditional marketing and supply chain, and many of the rules that allowed a 16,000-store organization to function and prosper did not apply to the mercantile stores. Their managers and baristas and our in-house designers were free to try things that ordinarily Starbucks could not do. At 15th Ave., for example, the pastries would come directly from Seattle's own Essential Baking Company and the soup from the kitchen of local restaurateur Tom Douglas. Wine and beer from regional wineries and breweries allowed us to further vary our menus—which also included salmon, cheese, even a sardine platter—and capture more evening customers.

The stores would sell whole-leaf Tazo teas and more than a dozen freshly scooped whole-bean coffees. Rare, small-batch coffees could also be prepared in one of several ways: Clover, coffee press, or a manual pour-over, where the barista literally pours boiling water in a circular motion through fresh grounds, one cup at a time. The baristas would not wear aprons, but instead could dress however they chose. At 15th Ave., tables and chairs were fashioned from reclaimed wood, and book pages served as creative wallpaper. At Roy Street, some chairs in the sprawling space would be upholstered in plush cranberry fabrics; thick curtains would separate cozy seating sections in the almost 2,000-square-foot space. Both stores would host coffee cuppings and poetry readings as well as movie nights, and even play customers' own CDs. Personally, I thought these stores were beautiful. Exciting. Not better than a traditional Starbucks, just different. A unique expression of the Starbucks Experience. We were learning, innovating, and, again, having fun as creative merchants. And it was likely that some mercantile elements would find their way into our stores around the world.

When the 15th Ave. store quietly opened its doors in July 2009, we anticipated some attention, especially in Seattle, and by now I was somewhat less surprised when news trucks from national TV news outlets actually showed up. When Starbucks acts, people care. Reminiscent of the attention Starbucks had received when we had closed 7,100 stores all at once for espresso training, a vein of shock ran through the initial coverage and critiques, as if Starbucks had somehow disrupted the natural order of things by not using its traditional icons and aprons. Instead of getting credit for taking risks with our business, we were viewed with suspicion.

That said, it was refreshing for me, after the mass store closures a year earlier, to talk about a single store opening instead of hundreds of stores closing. We had come a very long way.

* * *

I believe that the shop can still justify its existence if the staff put their experience and [professionalism] at the disposal of the customer. That is not just a commonplace catchphrase. It is the communication of one's passion for one's work. . . . A presumptuous person lets slip every opportunity to pass on to his workmates the knowledge he derives from his sales activity and interrupts that precious exchange of information that always takes place through contact with the customer. Each one of us is necessary; isolating oneself in the shop is negative.—Aldo Lorenzi, That Shop in Via Montenapoleone

It was barely daylight when I walked into the Starbucks Commerce Center store in Vancouver, Washington, just off Interstate 205, and shook hands with Amy Bernash, the store's manager.

"How long have you been with Starbucks?" I asked Amy.

"Almost seven years." Amy had joined the company as a part-time barista after working for a small investment firm. She is friendly and genuine but has a no-nonsense approach and had quickly been pro-moted. Amy had been a store manager for the past two years.

I looked around at her and the 11 other partners who were either working the drive-thru window or serving customers at the bar. Something about the place looked and felt slightly different from the dozens of other Starbucks stores I visited every month. A little calmer, maybe, and the layout of products and equipment was not typical. Yet everything also seemed to be in its rightful place.

I'd flown in from Seattle early that morning to visit several stores in the Portland area that were conducting experiments to improve customer service and partner engagement.

I'd harbored doubts about this so-called Lean program, which was relatively new to Starbucks but not to the business world. "Lean" is a generic term for a nontraditional way of managing and working that claims to reduce redundancies and waste while making conditions easier for employees and improving product and service quality for customers. Lean has its roots in the assembly lines of the automobile industry, and for decades its principles have been adapted by other industries.

In 2005 one of our partners in Seattle, Scott Heydon, who joined Starbucks as director of North American strategy in 2002 from McKinsey and Company, took it upon himself to learn about Lean and incorporate it into various corners of the company. What most captivated Scott was that Lean's philosophy hinges c employees by asking for their opinions about how to i own work and environment. Scott believes that Lean management telling employees how to do their jobs; rather, its core principle adheres to Starbucks' culture of respect and dignity by asking partners to take more control over their working lives.

Over the years, Scott's work had yielded some small-scale but impressive results. We regularly put together a promotional workbook in Seattle and send it to every store, and Lean techniques helped reduce the book's production time from 23 weeks to 13 and cut its page count from 300 to less than 40. Even though Lean was not widely embraced as a big idea inside Starbucks, Scott continued to champion it as part of his regular job, eventually applying its principles in some stores.

Admittedly, for me, applying a manufacturing-based process seemed cold and impersonal for a business based on human interaction, which was why I had flown to Portland with Scott and a few others. I wanted to see Lean from our store partners' perspectives.

I followed Amy into the back room where, against the backdrop of supply boxes, she talked plainly about the improvements that had taken place at her store since Scott and his team had introduced her to some basic Lean concepts and given her freedom to problem solve.

Amy explained that for years her store had followed protocols, arranging all of their products and equipment—milk, syrups, extra cups—in the exact places the company's manuals and photographs instructed. Her store had also ground all of the whole beans for the day's brewed coffee every morning because the prevailing company wisdom was that it was most efficient to grind coffee in batches.

"I knew there was a lot of waste," Amy admitted to me, but she did not go after it until Scott and her district manager gave her permission to do so.

For a second, Amy stopped talking. "I just wanted to apologize," she said to me. I had no idea what for. She explained. "When I started working with Lean, one of the first things I did was step back and watch my team work. Usually I'm with them behind the counter helping serve customers, but when I took the time to observe from the floor, I saw things, so many things, that were not right. Maybe someone didn't make a beverage correctly, or forgot to hand a customer a straw or shake an iced tea," she said. "I'm sorry that, as hard as we've been working, I missed opportunities around customer service."

I was touched by her dedication. "I like that," I told her with a smile. It meant a great deal to me that she cared as much as I did.

Amy's mood perked up as she described their results. The store's partners had rearranged the supply room, putting the items they replenished most often closest to the door instead of stashed in the back, so they were more accessible. At the cold beverage station, they posted color-coded preparation instructions to ensure consistency regardless of who made a drink. But the most impactful improvement was the decision to stop grinding all brewed-coffee beans in the morning and to do it instead before each new urn was brewed. "In reality it was faster to grind coffee throughout the day," she said. "Plus, the store smells like coffee!" Customers also began complimenting the baristas on the coffee's taste.

Amy said her partners were happier and felt less stress during rush times. In the six months since they had begun piloting Lean to reconfigure their work, their customer satisfaction and quality scores had improved. The store's turnover, which historically had hovered at around 60 percent, went to zero. For six months, not one of the store's 40 partners had left!

My scheduled 20-minute visit turned into an hour as I talked to Amy and her team, peppering them with questions. "How has your job changed?" "Why are you happier?" "What else can be improved?" I was truly impressed by the physical changes they had made in the store, but even more by the pride I heard in their voices.

Amy's store was not an anomaly.

In Portland, another manager testing Lean, Josh Howell, was shocked when he decided to track how many times in a day customers requesting a decaf or a bold brewed coffee were told, "Sorry, we don't have it right now. Do you mind waiting a few minutes?" Josh knew it happened occasionally, but until he counted he had no idea just how often: anywhere from 10 to 30 times. Thirty times a day a barista had the uncomfortable task of telling a customer no. Thirty times, Starbucks disappointed someone and risked losing his or her business.

If the same shortages occurred at other stores, a fairly safe assumption, the company could be losing millions of dollars in sales every year.

For Josh and his fellow partners, fixing the problem became a puzzle they were determined to solve. First, they considered the current situation. Like other stores, they had two brewed-coffee machines and four coffee "shuttles"—each designated to hold a specific brewed coffee throughout the day. An easy solution was to buy more shuttles and heating pads to hold more coffee for customers, but a store's budget and counter space are limited.

The team tried different work-arounds, but nothing stuck until a few of the store's partners sat down, did some creative math, and discovered a system that would eliminate coffee outages without adding costs, equipment, or a lot more work for baristas. First, they undesignated the four shuttles so each one could brew any coffee—bold, Pike Place, or decaf. Second, after some number crunching, they considered brewing a new pot of coffee every eight minutes. They experimented with the rotation and it worked! They called their system the Eight-Minute Cadence, and Josh began sharing it with partners in other stores who also suffered coffee outages. Some adopted it directly, others adapted it to their own store's patterns. Eventually, Scott asked Josh to come to Seattle to help the Lean team more formally introduce the system to all Starbucks stores as a starting place to improve customer service. For baristas, the fact that their peers had voluntarily come up with the idea and were leading its development—and were being supported by executives and engineers—seemed to make it more acceptable.

Cliff, who recognized Lean's potential, had asked Scott to focus on it full-time in the summer of 2008.

Lean was not an easy sell, and many of us in Seattle were on a learning curve as we figured out how to relinquish some of our control by inviting store partners to problem solve as well as adopt new routines. The proposed changes in workflow and thinking could frustrate and intimidate people in the field, but experiencing Lean's effects firsthand could turn skeptics like me into believers. The more our managers and baristas were asked to pay closer attention to the details of their daily activities, the more shortcomings they noticed, voiced, and solved, and the more customer service improved. Their stories found their way to me.

In Chicago, regional director Kristen Driscoll integrated Lean thinking into her coaching and watched, somewhat amazed, as her managers begin tackling various problems. At one store, Americanos were taking longer than necessary to make. At others, carafes of milk at the self-serve condiment bar were going unused and being thrown out. Floors looked dirty no matter how many times partners cleaned them. When pouring brewed coffee, partners turned their backs on customers. People manning the register repeatedly walked away from the machine for any number of reasons, prolonging checkout time. And, in almost every store, pounds of unused ground coffee were being thrown out. Each of these issues was eventually addressed thanks to the persistence and ingenuity of individual store partners.

Kristen summed up Lean's benefit well: "We were spending so much of our time fixing moments, but not actually solving problems. But fixing moments, like mopping a dirty floor, only provides short-term satisfaction. But take the time to understand the cause of the problem—like how to keep a floor from getting so dirty in the first place—solves, and maybe eliminates, a problem for the long run."

In store after store, Lean thinking was producing better ways of doing business, and customer satisfaction began to rise. Not all the so-called repeatable routines, like the Eight-Minute Cadence, were right for every store, but by asking our partners to proactively rethink how they work and to have a hand in improving their own environment, instead of simply coming in and doing their work, we were essentially asking them to act like owners and entrepreneurs. Like independent merchants.

The challenge our leadership faced in formally rolling out Lean was finding a balance between encouraging it and pushing it, between ceding partners more independence while ensuring that they maintained the high standards our customers expect and the performance our shareholders deserve.

For my part, I began posing my own question to partners at open forums around the world: "If this was *your* store, what would you do differently?" If an answer is within the guardrails of Starbucks' values, mission, and quality standards, I encourage them to do it. Inside Starbucks, Lean has become a very big idea.

* * *

What a difference six months can make.

By June 2009, tangible signs that the transformation was taking hold began to emerge:

Our new store designs were being rolled out and lauded.

More of our store partners were embracing Lean principles—though we all still had much to learn—and customer surveys were measuring statistically significant improvements in service and satisfaction. Partner friendliness was up six percentage points, speed of service was up by 10 points, and overall customer satisfaction was up eight points since their recent lows.

In our test markets, VIA was exceeding expectations, and its small team was laser-focused on its nationwide fall launch.

Online, Starbucks had been ranked the number-one most engaging social media brand thanks to our presence on Facebook, Twitter, and nine other outlets.

Our Plan B cost savings were exceeding our quarterly targets and expanding our operating margins.

Monthly comps continued their uptick, from negative 7 percent in April to negative 4 percent in June. At the end of the month, our share price closed at $13.89, up 41 percent from the beginning of the year.

And, much to our pleasure, when the Zagat ratings for best-tasting coffee in our category came out, Starbucks was rated number one.

Despite the fact that many analysts and pundits were still counting Starbucks out, my mood began to shift, and for the first time in a year and a half, I looked forward to hosting our upcoming earnings call. In many ways, July 2009 was looking to be a momentous month for Starbucks, likely full of many pleasant surprises.

Chapter 31

Conscience

It was a late June morning in Rwanda,
the beginning of the dry season,
but the coffee farms nestled in the hills
outside the capital city of Kigali still
looked lush. On the ground, thousands
of farmers and their families were
waiting to greet us.

This was my third trip to Rwanda since Starbucks had begun sourcing coffee beans from the African country in 2004, and as I walked into the sea of people, returning smile after smile that welcomed us to the coffee-farming cooperative, it was hard to imagine, although impossible to forget, that only 15 years earlier Rwandans had suffered horrific acts of ethnic violence and murder in a genocide that turned neighbor against neighbor, ravaged communities, destroyed families, and stole the lives of an estimated 800,000 men, women, and children in barely 100 days. I'd read books about Rwanda's tragic history and had come to know its current leader, president Paul Kagame, whose fight to end the genocide and commitment to healing the country are among the most inspiring acts of rebirth in human history.

I've been to other African nations, and inevitably each has touched me in its own way. But there was something about Rwanda. Something I saw in people's faces, especially in the eyes of the children and their mothers, that grabbed my heart. Their will to move on and rebuild, even to try to forgive instead of dwelling in hate, were incomprehensible yet a testament to the inner strength human beings are capable of. I felt that being in their presence and conducting business together was an honor, especially because coffee was playing an important role in the country's economic and emotional recovery.

Starbucks sources coffee from tens of thousands of farmers in almost 30 countries, mostly from families who work on small farms of only a few dozen acres. Coffee farming requires hard, hard labor. What's more, sustaining a profitable business had been a challenge for them long before Starbucks even existed.

First, harvesting high-quality green coffee beans requires a unique skill set that is acquired over time and often passed down from generation to generation. Growing coffee is indeed a craft.

Second, coffee farmers have a history of not being paid adequately or being charged unconscionably high interest rates to borrow money so they can run their businesses. And too often the money the consumer spends to buy coffee never even makes it to the farmer, but rather gets unfairly distributed among a thicket of middlemen. In my almost 30 years with Starbucks, our coffee buyers had made tremendous progress in ensuring that our farmers are treated and paid equitably. It is a delicate loop that begins and ends with quality. For Starbucks to pay a premium price to a coffee farmer, we have to have a premium product that our customers are also willing to pay a premium for. As such, Starbucks sets high quality standards that not every coffee farmer is capable enough or caring enough to meet.

Starbucks can, however, assist farmers on a number of fronts.

Collaboration between our coffee department and our global responsibility team, as well as our growing partnerships with Fairtrade and Conservation International, was improving the depth of Starbucks' farmer support. We had also committed to increasing the amount of money we make available for loans to coffee farmers from $12.5 million to $20 million per year by 2015. Recently, we had built our second farmer support center in Rwanda—the first has been operating in Costa Rica since 2004—where our own partners help farmers improve the size of their harvests and the quality of their crops.

I was traveling with a group that included Vivek; Darcy Willson-Rymer, who runs Starbucks in the United Kingdom; Peter Torrebiarte, Starbucks director of coffee sustainability; and Christina McPherson, a director of public affairs who had coordinated the trip's back-to-back agenda. Also with us was Harriet Lamb, the executive director of the UK Fairtrade Foundation, and Sheri, who along with Starbucks partner Laura Moix Varma is involved with Foundation Rwanda, an organization founded by photojournalist Jonathan Torgovnik and Jules Shell to provide educational opportunities for Rwandan children born of rape during the 1994 genocide. Jonathan was also with us and would film our group as we toured the co-op, met farmers, and saw a new AIDS clinic.

Our hosts led us into a brick, wood, and tin facility built into a sloped hill. A young man named Gilbert in a button-down striped yellow shirt and khakis described what we were seeing. As he spoke, we walked past rows of wood tables where bushels of raw white coffee beans were drying in the sun. I was impressed by what seemed to be a smoothly run co-op with about 1,800 different farmers.

After the tour, we attended what I could only describe as a jubilant presentation of singing and dancing, and when I was asked to speak I actually found myself at a loss for words. It almost seemed impossible to adequately convey my respect for the thousands of Rwandans sitting in front of me, shoulder to shoulder on the slope of a small hill. I could only begin to understand the trials they had suffered and I was filled with respect for their hard work and commitment. Never before had the human side of the equation that guided Starbucks—a commitment to balancing people and profits—been so palpable. Less than 50 feet from me were thousands of lives that Starbucks had the power to help—or to hinder. Standing in front of a microphone and next to the blue, green, and yellow striped Rwandan flag, I spoke from the heart.

> *As I look out and see all of you, the most honest thing I can say is that it is humbling and very difficult to find the words to express to you the importance of your role with Starbucks. . . . I suspect that most of you have never even heard of Starbucks, so I just want to spend a few moments talking about who we are as a company.*

My intent was to put a story with our faces and to articulate the origins of the company so the farmers and their families might see how their daily work is part of a larger organization with values and purpose. I spoke about the company's history for several minutes, stopping occasionally as my words were translated into Kinyarwanda and broadcast over a loudspeaker.

> *As we look at the future, I think I realize personally more than ever, especially looking at all of you, the deep responsibility that Starbucks Coffee Company has in ensuring that you get the fair price that you deserve. . . . What I can say in closing is that we will be the kind of partner you can depend on, and we will do as much as we possibly can to help you and your families.*

Earlier that day, I'd had a more private conversation with a small group of farmers whom I'd wanted to hear from directly about how things were going. Some 20 people had gathered in a long, narrow open-air room, and I took a seat on a bench against a brick wall with Gilbert to my left, who translated the farmers' comments into English.

The room as well as the farm was very quiet, and other than the voice of an individual speaking, all we heard was the occasional chirping of birds. I listened as a dapperly dressed man in a white collared shirt and gray sport jacket posed a question.

"What is Starbucks going to work on so that they can help the farmers eliminate some of the challenges they are experiencing?" Embedded in his question was an issue that is not unique to Rwanda and that we need all of our farmers, in every country, to understand.

"A reason we are successful as a company is our ability to source the highest-quality arabica coffee in the world," I answered, stressing that quality is paramount. "One thing we want to try and do with the coffee here in Rwanda is help you become more efficient in how it is being grown." I looked across the room at Peter Torrebiarte who oversees the farmer support centers and ensures our C.A.F.E. Practices are implemented around the world. I asked him to elaborate and passed the floor to him.

> Starbucks recognizes that we have to pay the best price for the best coffee, but helping you is not just about the price we pay. Myself, I am a third-generation coffee farmer, and what we can do through the farmer support center is help you make more money through sharing what we have learned from some of the best farmers around the world who faced similar problems. . . . We are coffee roasters, not farmers, but we can share with you better, cheaper solutions that will provide you with higher quality and higher yields. Some of the farmers we have helped through our first support center have reduced the cost of their fertilizers by 80 percent and increased their yields by 20 to 30 percent, and that means more money for you.
>
> The final objective is for you to be able to have more of your coffee with our stores by helping you establish a high-quality, consistent, and cost-efficient coffee so you can focus on farming and not worry whether you will sell your crops.

After Peter spoke, I felt the need to reiterate our commitment to helping the co-op's farmers be the best they could be. "Starbucks is here to stay in Rwanda," I stated succinctly. "We are deeply committed to Rwandan coffee and Rwanda. We are going to be buying Rwandan coffee for many years." It was our shared responsibility, Starbucks' and the farmers', to ensure both fairness and quality, which would increase the amount we were able to purchase, the price we could pay, and the profit the farmers could realize. "We recognize the opportunity for the future," I added. "We also see something in the hearts and minds of the people here, and we want to bring that to life in our stores all over the world."

As the meeting neared an end, Harriet from the Fairtrade Foundation smiled and posed a question to the half-dozen female farmers in the small room.

"We would like to know, what are your dreams for your futures?" The question was a good one, significant because honoring Rwandan women—thousands upon thousands of whom had survived brutality during the genocide and now solely supported themselves and their children—was of utmost importance to the country. I listened intently, and the first response I heard through our interpreter was not what I had expected. The female farmers, said Gilbert, hoped to produce their own coffee one day, without men, and to prove to others that, as women, they could do a great, even better job on their own because of their patience and attention to detail. Several people in the room clapped.

Then Harriet asked a young woman with blue heart earrings dangling from her lobes the final question of the session. "Can this lady tell us what is her dream for her family?" The woman, whose name was Mukamwiza Immaculate, responded clearly and quietly, and I sensed Gilbert was slightly taken aback as he translated her words. "She would like to make an income so she can buy a Friesian cow so she can get more milk for her family. That would be her dream." I, too, was taken aback.

"I just want to understand," I said, leaning forward and looking at the woman. "What will a cow do, just so I understand?"

Gilbert explained. "From cows you get milk, so the kids will obviously have better nutrition, but local breeds do not produce as much milk as Friesians, which have enough milk for consumption and more milk to sell, so the milk also becomes additional income for the family."

A cow. I mouthed the words silently, trying to wrap my head around just how difficult this woman's life must be. I closed the meeting with a final thought. "I believe very strongly that all of us are responsible for what we hear and what we see. We have heard your words, and we understand some of the issues and some of the challenges. We will not forget. We will understand, remember, and work hard for you." I waited patiently as Gilbert interpreted my words, and then I looked at Mukamwiza. "And we're going to try and get you a cow."

A single cow, I was later informed, costs $500.

"It is wonderful that you are helping her," a government official who was accompanying us said to me, "but there are so many others . . ."

That sentiment weighed heavily on my mind during the long flight back to the United States. How much could one person, or for that matter one company, really do? I did not have an answer other than that doing nothing was unconscionable.

* * *

Returning to Seattle was a bit like landing in another world, and it took a while to mentally and emotionally transition. But I was eager to share what I'd seen and heard in Rwanda. In an open forum, I told the story of our visit to the co-op, and when I finished speaking I asked, as always, if anyone had questions. In the back of the room, a woman I didn't recognize raised her hand.

"My name is Linda O'Brien," she said. "Five months ago, when I was out of work and needed a job, Starbucks gave me one. I would like to pay it forward and buy that woman a cow."

Linda not only donated money to purchase a cow, but within weeks her comment motivated us to initiate a relationship between Starbucks and Heifer International, a nonprofit that provides livestock to impoverished populations around the world. Through Heifer, more Starbucks partners—as well as the Starbucks Foundation—donated funds to send Friesian cows to Rwanda. Equally important, Heifer attended to the complexities of buying, delivering, and maintaining the livestock, training recipients like Mukamwiza how to properly care for them so they thrive.

Our partners' support of Rwanda further confirmed for me that, despite all of the trials the company had been through, we were living up to our responsibilities as well as our values.

* * *

Starbucks' stock was below $10 and the economy grim the day I took a call from a manager at one of Starbucks' institutional shareholders, an organization whose leaders I had known for quite some time.

"Howard, we've owned this stock for a long while. We know you're under tremendous pressure, and we feel very strongly that this is the time to cut the health-care benefit." He went on. "You've got all the cover and the license in the world. Everyone will understand you had no choice."

I knew instantly that the call would be short. Of course we had a choice.

The degree of health-care coverage that had become a hallmark of Starbucks was, however, an expense that was rising significantly, to the point that it felt like a runaway train. In 2009, providing health coverage for our partners would account for almost $250 million of costs, up almost 50 percent per partner compared to 2000.

This was not the first time I'd been pressured to eliminate or significantly reduce our partners' health-care coverage. Doing so would have an immediate effect on profitability, but at much too high a cost. The very foundation of Starbucks, our true competitive advantage, is our culture and guiding principles. That reservoir of trust that we have established with our people had already been drained to some degree. This would sap it dry. While the company would have to ask our people to share in the rising expenses of health care, eliminating it was unthinkable.

At the same time, I also knew that I needed to do more for our partners around the world. I'd spent the majority of my time during the past year and a half focusing on our customers and stabilizing US operations; the time was coming to turn our attention further inward and reinvent the partner experience by innovating compensation, benefit, and incentive approaches in ways that mattered to our people. Olden would soon leave his temporary post as head of Starbucks' partner relations, and I needed to fill that tremendously important role with someone who would bring deep experience as well as an unequivocal understanding of our unique priorities.

How leaders embody the values they espouse sets a tone, an expectation, that guides their employees' behaviors. As ceo I am responsible for large-scale decisions about giving our partners stock in the company, for instance, and maintaining health-care coverage. But I am only one man. It is up to each partner to bring Starbucks' values to life in ways beyond what even I can imagine, such as partnering with Heifer International, and in the summer of 2009 I received several e-mails that similarly touched me for different reasons.

One from Suzy Wolford, a district manager in California, demonstrated how our partners were actively integrating our values into running their stores.

Howard,

Yesterday we held (RED) Friday in our stores, an idea we got from our neighbors to the south. Our whole bean sales were not where we wanted them to be and we thought this would be a fun way to engage the partners, boost our sales and donate to a very worthwhile cause. We allowed our partners to wear red: red t-shirts, red aprons AND decorate their stores in red. The focus for the day was to sell anything from the (RED) platform but primarily (RED) whole bean.

The store managers loved the idea and decorated their stores with red balloons, red streamers, red tablecloths, even red carpet runners for the customers as they entered! (RED) facts were posted throughout the stores. Partners engaged each customer in conversations around (RED) whole bean and (PRODUCT) RED in general. There was an energy and electricity in the stores that I have not felt in my six years with Starbucks. Many customers lingered longer than usual just to soak up the atmosphere. The engagement, passion and energy was AMAZ-ING and inspiring.

What was the result? The stores sold 1,666 lbs. of whole bean coffee in ONE DAY! I honestly could not be more proud to be a Starbucks partner than I am at this moment. (Quite frankly I was speechless this morning when I saw the results.) The pride and passion each of our store partners and customers demonstrated yesterday was inspiring and you can be assured that the Spirit of Starbucks is alive and well in San Diego!!

This and other stories brought on the same feelings of accomplishment that I experienced as our stock price and financial performance improved. They demonstrated to me that Starbucks, despite being in the fight of its life, had not lost its conscience or its soul as we worked to reestablish our financial health. Achieving this balance had long been my definition of success.

Chapter 32

Winning

Sitting in the familiar New York City offices of Kekst and Company—where almost two years earlier, I'd talked about Starbucks' downfall—I waited to begin what I felt would be the most important earnings announcement the company had made since going public.

Starbucks' profits were growing again.

Our performance in the third quarter of fiscal 2009 had defied everyone's expectations, marking our first earnings growth since the first quarter of 2008. The company earned $152 million, compared to losing almost $7 million a year earlier. In terms of earnings per share, we posted a 20-cent profit, up significantly from the penny loss we had reported the prior year. Wall Street had not seen the spike coming, and while we would not say so on the call, Starbucks' performance had beaten analysts' consensus forecast by five cents.

As the story of our transformation continued to unfold, this quarter was a definitive sign that it was gaining more traction. Our work, of course, would never end, but the company had turned a corner and the news would surprise our critics, please investors, and be a psychological turning point for many of our partners who were working so hard.

Personally, for the first time in a long time, I felt as if we were winning. Not that we had won, because there is never a finish line, but that despite the odds, the brand and our partners were prevailing.

Publicly, however, I needed to balance my enthusiasm and pride with caution.

The earnings call began at 5 p.m. sharp eastern time.

Over the past 16 months, Starbucks has faced both the headwinds of the global economy, just as all businesses have, and our own unique set of challenges. Today, I am pleased to report results for the third quarter that point to positive momentum from the comprehensive set of actions we've taken to transform the business.

Now at the outset, let me just say that a lot of hard work still lies ahead. One quarter does not make a trend, but I speak with you today with a sense of confidence based on results, results that give us tangible evidence that our transformation initiatives are beginning to be reflected in our financial and operating performance.

Overall, sales were still down from a year earlier, to $2.4 billion from $2.6 billion, but comp declines had been steadily improving since December 2008, when they hit a low of negative 11. In short, we were trending back toward positive comp territory. Most importantly, our fixed costs had drastically decreased—we were spending less money to operate the business, especially in the United States—which meant that in the months to come, as the company's sales continued their incremental rise due to a collection of consumer-facing initiatives, bottom-line earnings would continue to grow.

In the United States, the business unit we had had to fix first and foremost, comps across the country were improving month by month, and our operating margin, now at 13.4 percent, had jumped from 8.8 percent the previous year due to the permanent operational improvements. As for the competition that people had predicted would fuel our demise, it was having the opposite effect.

As you know, extraordinary advertising dollars have been spent by fast-food companies trying to attract coffee consumers. Many commentators and industry watchers have been concerned that this marketing spend would have a negative impact on Starbucks.

To the contrary, it appears that the various marketing campaigns and all the media coverage about coffee has created unprecedented awareness for the coffee category overall and has actually had a positive result on Starbucks' business.

It helped that Starbucks had stopped playing defense. In May 2009, we had launched our own multichannel marketing campaign with BBDO—full-page newspaper ads, billboards, and an exclusive deal with CNBC's *Morning Joe* news program. Combined with the ongoing dialogue we were having with three million fans on Facebook—which made Starbucks a top brand on the social networking site—the company was driving brand awareness, loyalty, and traffic, finally telling our story directly to consumers.

My presentation on the conference call was much more than a quarterly review, it was an 18-month synopsis of the choices and initiatives that had, collectively, brought us to this moment. Dramatic cost reductions and process improvements. Better beverages due to espresso training, the Mastrena, Pike Place Roast, Clover, and, soon, VIA. Value offerings and loyalty programs. Improved customer service. Tastier, healthier food. Strategic social networking. Spontaneous marketing events. Traditional advertising. Lean thinking and fresh, relevant store designs.

I also attributed our financial performance to actions whose benefits were hard, if not impossible, to quantify—activities or intangibles that Wall Street and cynics easily discounted but that I believed were intrinsic to the reason Starbucks had been able to do so much heavy lifting over the past year and a half: the Transformation Agenda. Immersive creative retreats. The new mission statement. Open forums and memos. New Orleans. Shared Planet initiatives. And, most critical, the care, talent, and commitment that tens of thousands of store managers and baristas had brought to their work and to their customers every single day to create the Starbucks Experience.

Just as no one thing had led to the company's spiral, no one thing was leading to its resurgence. Even failures such as Sorbetto had taught us, had taught me, valuable lessons that would aid us going forward. My leadership continued to evolve, and perhaps more than ever in my career, I was effectively balancing entrepreneurial vision with patience of execution, paying the same degree of attention to the back end of the business that I was hardwired to pay to the front end. By no means was I doing it alone: Starbucks was also on the verge of having the strongest leadership team in its history.

This quarter's performance was momentous not in and of itself, but in what it suggested for Starbucks' future: that we had a future.

Before handing the call to Troy, I concluded my comments:

I am really pleased to report the transformation of Starbucks Coffee Company is well under way. The Transformation Agenda we laid out 16 months ago has helped us focus on the most important success factors for our company, while also enabling us to continue nurturing and building our brand. Yet as I told our board of directors last week, while we are quite pleased with our performance and results this quarter and encouraged by the improving store traffic and average ticket trends we are seeing, we know we have more work to do to build on recent momentum and accelerate our progress. While we remain cautious about the global economic recovery, our plan is built to ensure that Starbucks is well positioned to benefit as economies improve. In the meantime, we will remain laser-focused on what Starbucks Coffee Company is and always has been about—coffee excellence, our customers, our partners, our values, and now an even greater rigor around operational improvement.

In the question-and-answer portion of the call, the analysts' questions were predictably diligent as they tried to interpret the implications of line items in our quarterly release. While I by no means expected

Wall Street to enthusiastically praise the company for its progress to date, this call was the first in what seemed like years in which I heard the word "congratulations" from several members of the financial community.

Analyst notes put out after the call were tempered. They were "reassured" by our sales and "impressed" by our stabilization of the business, acknowledging that our ability to manage against competitive and economic pressures was "better than expected." Overall, the Street gave Starbucks credit for improved earnings, but remained cautious about our future growth.

Investors, as measured by the stock price, cheered. By the end of the week, on Friday, July 24, our share price closed just above $17, a jump of 17 percent from the price prior to the earnings announcement.

A shadow over the day, however, was the still-stinging pain of layoffs and store closures that we'd incurred along the journey, undoubtedly the lowest points in Starbucks' history. Our current partners' sacrifices and contributions had been great, and I wanted to acknowledge them with more than just words of thanks. On the Monday after earnings, the company announced a decision that I considered a personal victory.

Back in December 2008, we had made the difficult decision to make our annual matching of the funds that partners contributed to their 401(k) retirement plans discretionary instead of automatic, knowing there was a very real possibility that there would be no match. Many companies had made a similar choice as a precaution to ride out the unpredictably weak economy, and while I believed it was the right thing to do fiscally, I also had every hope that, as our performance improved, Starbucks would be strong enough to eventually go ahead and make the match in 2009. Not doing so would, by my own standards, be a failure. Helping partners build their futures and care for their families is a core value of mine as an entrepreneur, an employer, and a son who watched his own family struggle. So in July 2009, when we concluded that Starbucks would indeed be able to match the contributions of eligible employees, I was elated. The news would not make headlines or mean much to shareholders, but for me, the ability to match funds was as important as anything we were able to accomplish all year.

In addition, we also announced that Starbucks would, unlike many companies that had indefinitely capped employee pay, increase our partners' salaries according to merit. The amount of the increase would vary depending in part on individual performance, but again I was happy that we were in a position to reward people. Still, I knew our partners deserved even more, and that we would have to deliver.

In the next few days after the earnings announcement, I read headlines that had tones I had not heard in a long time. "Starbucks Swings to Profit." "Starbucks Climbs as Profit Beats Estimates on Cost Reductions." "Starbucks Shares Soar Following 3Q Profit Beat." I also received e-mails from a handful of people who knew, more than most, what the quarter's results meant to me personally.

"It was a very good day. For Starbucks. For its shareholders. And you. Keep it up," wrote Jim Fingeroth, whose counsel had been so instrumental in setting the stage for my return as ceo. "Turnarounds are not easy, but very satisfying when they're done."

Mellody Hobson, a perceptive board member whose support had buoyed me many times, sent a quote attributed to Harriet Beecher Stowe:

> *When you get into a tight place and everything goes against you, till it seems as though you could not hang on a minute longer, never give up then, for that is just the place and time that the tide will turn.*

Those words took me back to December 2007, when I was helplessly watching our comps plummet day by day, and then to December 2008 and the angst-ridden dinner in New York City with Billy the night before our analyst conference, when more than at any other moment, doubt had engulfed me.

Yes, Starbucks' tide had turned. And now I had absolutely no doubts that its performance would continue to trend upward. This quarter was not a peak, but rather the beginning of a climb to create a new kind of company.

The time was coming to turn our attention beyond the United States and beyond our stores to profitable growth via new revenue streams that would have been unthinkable without successfully transforming the foundation of our business.

No longer was Starbucks a flailing house in need of mending. We were a stabilized global organization that could refocus on growth—with all the opportunities and risks that that implied.

Chapter 33

Nĭ Hăo

I've come to think that I am at my best as a leader when Starbucks is being challenged or fighting for survival. I'm comfortable with, and in a way enjoy, the rugged, steep ascent. That is my nature. And while I would not want to constantly battle against the odds, the raw feeling of accomplishing something that others did not think possible, or leading people beyond where they thought they could go, is extremely gratifying.

Still, rarely do I stop to celebrate a milestone. It is also my nature to look around the corner for what must come next.

In the fall of 2009, after we reported our third-quarter earnings, Starbucks was by no means taking a victory lap, but I was confident that our business would continue to improve. Each week, same-store sales and our revenues in the United States were on the rise, and the fourth quarter's performance shaped up to be even better than the third. It was nice to once again look forward to the earnings call.

As our fiscal year neared its close, I wasn't feeling a sense of success so much as a sense of relief that the pressure was no longer as intense as it had been during the past year and a half. As much as I thrive on being an underdog, I did welcome a shift from survival to growth mode. Focusing on proactive growth was a right we had earned by virtue of transforming the US business, a privilege I would never again take for granted.

"Starbucks deserves an 'A' for turning itself around during the recession. But it will take work to stay at the top of the class," read an August column in *The Wall Street Journal*, its title warning, "Starbucks Faces Growth Challenge." That was correct. Returning Starbucks to disciplined, profitable growth was my next priority, and my immediate and first focus was on Starbucks Coffee International, the unit that included all of our stores and consumer packaged goods businesses outside the United States.

International was by far the company's most exciting and largest prospect. That was why, in early September 2009, I flew to China. I was anxious to ignite our future.

* * *

Joyful shock. That was the look on Helen Fei's face.

I was in Shenzhen, China, attending an open forum with about 200 of our Chinese partners. I'd only just arrived in the country and had spent the morning visiting Starbucks stores on what was a brutally hot, humid September day. Today's was the first of several open forums I would attend in three cities during the trip. I was still catching up to the time zone difference—Shenzhen is 15 hours ahead of Seattle—but the energy in the room enlivened me.

In the back, half a dozen baristas in green aprons stood holding trays of small paper coffee cups while other partners from Starbucks' 34 stores throughout Shenzhen—China's third-largest city, which, amazingly, was a small fishing village only 30 years ago—filled the rows of chairs.

When I stood up to talk to the group, I knew the first thing I had to say:

It's important for me to be very transparent, and I feel like I need to apologize to all of you because I have not been to China in over a year and a half. During that time, we have been incredibly focused on fixing the US business. And that has taken all of our time and our energy—and one of the things that has suffered is the close attention we in Seattle have paid to the exciting growth and development in China. We're very sensitive to that and apologize for it.

But those days are over, the US business is now in very good shape, and we're going to return our focus, attention, and discipline to make sure we do everything we can to accelerate the growth and development of Starbucks China.

After I spoke and answered questions, I took my seat in the front row. There was local business to attend to, and I listened as a translator told me that a partner in the room was about to receive the coveted recognition of being designated store manager of the quarter.

"Helen Fei!" someone announced.

I turned and looked around the room to see a woman in a black short-sleeved polo, her dark hair pulled back from her face, stand up, cup her hands over her mouth, and somewhat shyly walk to the front of the room to receive a framed certificate. It was clear from her expression that she was surprised, and clear from the sound of the applause that she was widely liked and respected. I clapped as she walked to the front of the room.

Later, I learned that Helen was 30, married, and has a son. In 2003 she had moved from her small village to work as a barista for Starbucks in Shenzhen. After two years, she had had to move back home for family reasons, but she stayed in touch with her colleagues at Starbucks and rejoined the company when she was able to return to the city.

Then, in another unexpected announcement, Helen was told in front of the group that in addition to being named manager of the quarter, she was also being promoted from her current position of store manager to district manager. As the tears in her eyes welled up,

I sensed that working at Starbucks was more than just a job to Helen.

"Congratulations," I said a few moments later.

"*Xie xie*," she replied, thanking me in Chinese and smiling as we posed together for a photo. I stepped back as others patted her on the back. So many of Helen's generational peers had, like her—and for that matter like me—left their families and come to a big city to make their own way. In some cases, to make their mark. I was proud that Starbucks is an employer China's young people strive to work for. There was so much energy and excitement here, not just in this room, but in almost every Chinese city I visited—a palpable sense of possibility, most notably among young people. The entrepreneurial spirit is alive and well in Greater China, and every time I return I am amazed by just how much change the cities have undergone since my prior visit.

China is, of course, the world's fastest-growing major economy, and with a gold-rush mentality, companies from all over the globe have been flocking here to reach the country's 1.3 billion consumers. We opened our first store in China in Beijing in 1999, and year after year our stores have continued to post positive comps, and profits have improved. Now, in our 10th year, our almost 700-store presence in Greater China is still relatively small compared to what the market can sustain. The booming country offers huge possibility for Starbucks' retail and consumer packaged goods businesses, and it was now a top priority for the company.

In the near future, China would be Starbucks' largest market outside of the United States.

The Chinese had embraced Starbucks for the same primary reason that customers in the other 52 countries we operate in had. Quite simply, there has always been a universal appeal in our ability to elevate the coffee experience by creating a connection. In China, people were not only enjoying Starbucks coffee, but also using our stores as an extension of their homes or workplaces—perhaps even more so than in the West. With China's homes being particularly small and apartments remarkably tight, Starbucks' clean, spacious, safe, comfortable environments are a welcome destination, especially during afternoons and evenings, when our stores tend to be most crowded. And whenever we open a new store, it is not unusual to see a line out the door and down the block.

The third place experience that we had nurtured in the United

States is as relevant in Oman, Jordan, as it is in Dublin, Ireland. Or São Paulo, Brazil. Even Paris. In that sense, Starbucks is no longer a Western brand. We've created something that has universal acceptance and fulfills a universal need.

The main challenge we face abroad is, of course, a different one than we had faced in the States and Canada. As Starbucks now knew all too well, growth for growth's sake is a losing proposition. We had to expand with diligence and attention to detail. And in other countries, the details are about being locally relevant and respectfully reflecting the cultures our stores are operating in. Making Starbucks locally relevant without diluting the brand is an ongoing issue that we have to address to a degree that we did not have to in the past. While there are many aspects of the transformation that would be applied to our businesses and stores around the world, creating products that honor regional tastes and traditions is not something that can best be accomplished in Seattle and simply exported. Locally relevant products, to resonate, have to be invented and executed by local talent and leaders.

* * *

"Welcome to Starbucks' INNOVATION Store."

The bright, hand-chalked sign welcomed several of us into a mock store at Starbucks' business offices, which serve as the support center for all of our stores in China. It was lunchtime, and our small group was seated at a long rectangular table dressed with a white tablecloth. I was not sure what to expect, but I was hungry and, looking at the small porcelain plates and silverware in front of us, I had a hunch that scones, blueberry muffins, and breakfast sandwiches were not on the menu. I leaned forward on the table, head resting against my hand, just smiling as I listened to our local partners explain what we were about to taste. I almost felt relaxed. After the past 18 months of rapid-fire problem solving, it was a pleasure to sit, listen, and wait to be pleasantly surprised by our partners' self-directed innovation.

Our China team had spent the past few months experimenting with new recipes, infusing local flavors into foods and beverages that, one day, Starbucks might serve in its Greater China stores. During the next hour, a parade of new drinks and dishes were placed in front of me, one after the other, many with ingredients Starbucks had never used.

Peanut Mocha Frappuccino.

Iced Oriental Beauty with Aloe.

Then, a thick green drink called Black Sesame Green Tea Frappuc-cino. I took a sip. Delicious. It was a local twist on one of Starbucks' best-selling beverages, Green Tea Frappuccino, that had been created in Japan.

"Green tea is an essential ingredient in Chinese culture," the woman immediately to my right explained to me. "And black sesame is another ingredient that the Chinese use in cooking." I nodded. Annie Young-Scrivner was the newest addition to the Starbucks leadership team. I had just hired her to be global chief marketing officer, and it was her first week on the job. She was a dynamic presence.

Annie came to Starbucks from PepsiCo, where she had most recently been chief marketing officer and vice president of sales for Quaker Foods and Snacks. A smart, charismatic leader, Annie is someone who I believe will bring to the team the global, multibrand experience the board had been urging me to acquire, as well as deep international perspective, most notably in China. Annie was born in China, and her parents moved to the United States when she was in grade school. She is fluent in Chinese and, over the course of her career, had lived in Shanghai, where she served as region president of PepsiCo Foods for Greater China, and worked in 27 other countries. The thickness of Annie's passport rivals any I have seen. She understands the Asian market as well as the culture to a degree few people in Seattle currently do. Annie elaborated. "In China, black sesame is looked at as a product that has efficacy. It helps your skin, and the women think that it keeps their hair from turning white as they age. The sesame itself is used in a lot of breads, pastries, and as a cooking ingredient for flavor."

Next, lunch's main course. As each small plate was placed before me, it was obvious that our partners were truly thinking outside of the box. Sesame noodle salad. Spicy Thai beef wrap. Soup. Lasagna! Everything tasted fresh and flavorful, and while I knew our Asian stores probably would not serve noodles—research already told us that our customers in China did not want Starbucks to serve food they could easily get on any street corner—I was impressed by the creativity I was experiencing.

As was Michelle, who sat to my left. She had joined me on the trip, although not purely in a Starbucks capacity. In the past few weeks, I had made the decision to go ahead and unleash one of the company's other brands: Seattle's Best Coffee, or SBC. The 550-store retail and packaged coffee business had been a stepchild quietly operating in Starbucks' shadow. I chose Michelle as its president and gave her unspecific marching orders: Unlock SBC. Here in China, she was researching SBC business prospects.

Finally, dessert. A single scoop of ice cream *affogato* with a thick black sesame sauce. At the center of the table sat fruit kebabs and plates of small chocolates and pastries, even mini-sandwiches. Most notably, these dishes were meant to be shared in small group gatherings, social occasions that Starbucks' food offerings currently did not cater to. But sharing is an intriguing idea, especially for crowded Asian cities such as Shanghai, where personal space is rare and people chose to entertain and gather in public spaces, like Starbucks.

Such sensitivity to regional lifestyles and palates is a critical piece in how Starbucks shows up around the world. Yet I knew that we had to resist the obvious. When we opened in Switzerland in 2001, we had been pressured to put the regionally favored beverage known as *kaffe crème* on our menu, but on opening day we sold dozens of Frappuccinos and barely any kaffe crèmes. Our international customers, we were coming to understand, wanted to taste Starbucks, not the store next door. But they were delighted when we put a Starbucks twist on their traditions. In Taiwan, when our partners created a product called coffee jelly, a gelatin made with coffee, the popular cool beverage migrated around Asia and became one of the region's best-selling seasonal products.

So even though every food and beverage we sampled in Shanghai that afternoon would not make it into Starbucks' stores in China, I left our offices encouraged by the possibility that every country where Starbucks operates might exhibit the same entrepreneurial drive. Somewhere on the day's menu was another coffee jelly. Perhaps another Frappuccino. Or VIA.

For me, it had also been great fun to stop for a few moments to taste and ponder what could be.

★ ★ ★

At its core, I believe leadership is about instilling confidence in others, and being in China at this juncture as Starbucks turned a corner was an opportunity for me to allay fears about the company's stability and then get our people excited about what is possible. About dreaming big. And then bigger.

I also wanted to instill a comprehensive understanding of the lessons learned from Starbucks' trials. In the earlier years of the company, it was my job to imprint Starbucks' mission to ensure the brand's consistency across cultures, but now my role is to imprint our most recent wisdom, and in some respects to translate the leadership's new operational mind-set. I am very conscious of not making the same mistakes in China or anywhere else in the world that we made in the United States, and we will proactively share our new tactics and techniques.

As time and resources allowed, we would roll out our new point-of-sale system and the Mastrena to our stores in other countries. Clover, too. Our experts from Seattle would share our new store designs, Lean techniques, and social networking knowledge with managers and our joint-venture partners. We would instill a new level of cost discipline and use our more efficient supply chain to improve distribution around the globe. And we would continue to ensure that each barista knew how to pour the perfect shot of espresso: like honey pouring from a spoon.

I've said often that every enterprise and organization has a memory. And those memories create a path for people to follow. As I see it, the transformation was a brief but specific period in Starbucks' history, and our memory of its collective lessons will inform our future. They are already informing my leadership:

Grow with discipline. Balance intuition with rigor. Innovate around the core. Don't embrace the status quo. Find new ways to see. Never expect a silver bullet. Get your hands dirty. Listen with empathy and overcommunicate with transparency. Tell your story, refusing to let others define you. Use authentic experiences to inspire. Stick to your values, they are your foundation. Hold people accountable but give them the tools to succeed. Make the tough choices; it's how you execute that counts. Be decisive in times of crisis. Be nimble. Find truth in trials and lessons in mistakes. Be responsible for what you see, hear, and do. Believe.

In the lakeside city of Hangzhou, I stood up once again to speak to our baristas and store and district managers. Almost a year ago, Starbucks' stock had tumbled to $7.17, its lowest close since 2001. Yet this week, in America, our share price hit an 80-week high, more than $20 a share. While I rarely talked about our stock price, I did mention this to our partners who had gathered on the second floor of one of Hangzhou's 13 Starbucks.

I stand before you today to say that the momentum in the US business continues and I feel we will end fiscal 2009 strongly, going into fiscal 2010 with as much confidence about the future as we've ever had.

But the courage, the creativity, and entrepreneurship that we need in China must come from you. We have to establish a very healthy balance between the Starbucks history and heritage and your own Chinese culture. I encourage you all to challenge the status quo, to start thinking about what we can do to become more relevant. Let's really demonstrate the hunger, the excitement, the entrepreneurship that made this company great. However, we can't turn Starbucks into a company that we don't respect and don't recognize. We must do it in a balanced way.

Starbucks' transformation was being achieved not simply because we were effectively responding to external economic, technological, and social challenges, or correcting the problems we had brought upon ourselves. Rather, it was being achieved because of *how* our partners tried to solve these problems.

If Starbucks is to be a company my father would have felt proud to work for, a company that my wife and children and our partners' families will hold in high regard, we have to maintain balance on many fronts. Balance between the emotional and the disciplined. Between instinct and information. Between global and local. The personal and the professional, and, of course, between profit and humanity. Doing so will not be easy as we expand our brand and businesses around the world. But the sheer power that Starbucks Coffee has to positively affect the lives of tens of millions of people—partners and their families, customers, farmers, shareholders—is as invigorating for me as opening my very first store.

★ ★ ★

Before leaving Shanghai, we visited a beautifully designed store in the center of People's Park, a tree-filled oasis surrounded by traffic and office buildings. As we left and made our way across the park on yet another hot, humid afternoon, the store's manager, Li Yan, ran to catch up with us, holding something in her hand. She reached us and handed me a flat wrapped gift. I opened it right there to find, encased in a box, laminated documents in Chinese. At first I did not know what they were, but Li spoke and someone translated. "These are four copies of China's very influential newspaper, *People's Daily.*" Then Li pointed to the date of one of the newspapers. I squinted a bit to see what she was referring to. July 19, 1953. My birthday. She had presented me with an original copy of a newspaper from the day I was born. The three other newspapers were from special dates in Starbucks' history: the day the company went public (June 26, 1992), the opening of our first store in Taiwan (March 28, 1998), and when we opened our first store in Shanghai (May 4, 2000). As we each held a side of the box and looked at the newspapers, Li explained that it was a present to me on behalf of her partners. I was beyond touched. Truly taken aback by the thought and effort behind such a personalized gift. "*Xie xie,*" I said. She thanked me as well and returned to her store.

Some people wondered why I returned to Starbucks as ceo. And why I stay. "He doesn't need to do this. Why is he so motivated?" Quite simply, I love this company and the responsibility that goes with it.

Onward . . .

Tribute

Even after all these years, coffee still has the power to surprise me.

In January 2010, I sat down with Dub Hay and Andrew Linnemann from our coffee department and asked them to create a very special blend for our 40th anniversary year. I wanted a coffee that captured the essence of our history and honored our most unique qualities as a company and a coffee purveyor and also had a taste profile that would resonate with our most loyal partners and customers. I requested a blend that was distinctively Starbucks yet like nothing we'd ever produced. A flavor that, unlike the easy approachability of Pike Place Roast or even the intensity of our coveted Christmas Blend, would pack an unequivocally bold punch.

The brainstorming to choose the beans began.

First, the coffee team selected aged Sumatra, because aging our own coffee to reveal its rich cedar and spice notes has become a defining Starbucks trait. Next, Colombian, because the dense, high-grown beans of that country's southern Nariño region are a cornerstone of our most popular blends and because Colombia is where Starbucks first began actively contributing to social programs and practices that improve the lives of farmers. Next, naturally sun-dried beans from Ethiopia, because the beans' intense berry aroma reveal even before tasting that the coffee is unlike any other. Finally, the complex beans from the remote coffee farms of Papua New Guinea, which have been on our menu from the very beginning.

It was a risky combination. The Ethiopian beans would be particularly difficult to procure at the speed and in the quality and quantity we needed for global roasting and distribution in early 2011. And rarely, if ever, had a blend of coffee mixed aged beans with beans that were dried naturally in their cherry skins. The tastes could conflict on the palate. But after five months of experimenting with small batches, the coffee team landed, as always, on just the right process—they roasted the Ethiopian beans separately, and the Papua New Guinean beans provided the needed balance. In October 2010, the final shipment of Ethiopian beans arrived and to everyone's relief met our high standards.

I stood in the cupping room across from my office and tasted the new blend for the first time. The coffee hit my tongue with a beautiful aged cedar note that gave way to a robust fruitiness and ended with a balanced acidity.

"This is exactly what I was looking for," I said to Dub, Andrew, and Doug Langworthy, who had led the development. "This is a big, bold, knock-your-socks off coffee." It really was spectacular. We hugged and shook hands, and I took a sample home to make for Sheri and me in my French press. Sipping the coffee the next morning, I knew it was exactly what I had hoped for and like nothing I'd ever experienced.

"I have had two extraordinary cups of coffee in the last 24 hours, one was in the tasting room yesterday and the other was at 5:30 this morning," I wrote in a thank-you e-mail to the coffee and Starbucks leadership teams. "I am so proud and so respectful of the work put in to produce something so special and fitting for this celebratory event."

Perhaps even more fitting, we named it Tribute Blend.

★ ★ ★

As I write these words in the fall of 2010, just weeks after tasting Tribute, Starbucks and I find ourselves at a moment of culmination.

First, the process of documenting our transformation period for this book has come to an end. Reliving these two years has given me a chance to reflect on a remarkable ride. I truly hope the telling has been informative and that it inspires others to consider the untapped potential within their own organizations as well as within themselves. Yes, it is possible to rise, fall, and rise again, recapture lost dreams, dream bigger, and succeed in our ever-changing, complex world—without abandoning what matters most. And at Starbucks, what matters most are our guiding principles and the culture that supports them.

Starbucks has regained a healthy balance with a culture that celebrates creativity and discipline, entrepreneurship and process, as well as rigorous innovation. But perhaps the most vital thing that came out of the past two years has been the confidence we gained knowing that we could preserve our values despite the hardships we faced. Holding fast to those values steadied us throughout the tumultuous journey, and the ways in which we conduct our business will continue to bring our partners pride and fuel their engagement as we continue to grow.

People will always be our most important assets and Starbucks' competitive advantage, which is why, on the cusp of celebrating our 40th anniversary, foremost on our minds as we head into 2011 is how to mark the occasion in ways that honor our partners. Developing Tribute Blend was just one of the many ways we will do so.

A New Blueprint for Profitable Growth

In fiscal 2010, Starbucks revenues increased to a record $10.7 billion, and our operating income increased by $857 million to $1.4 billion, up from $562 million in fiscal 2009. Our full-year operating margin of 13.3 percent represented the highest consolidated operating margin in our history, surpassing the previous high of 12.3 percent achieved in fiscal 2005. These results enabled us to share a special bonus with nearly 100,000 of our store and roasting plant partners.

The record fourth quarter of 2010 was not just a triumphant end to a single year, but also an exclamation point capping a defining period in our shared history. I could not be more proud of Starbucks' partners. And although I have never been one to bask in celebration, our company's performance gives me pause, a reason to step out of the day-to-day business and reflect on choices and lessons and what they mean for the future. Today we see new possibilities on the horizon, possibilities that will continue to grow the company, further enhance the culture, and evolve present-day Starbucks in ways few can imagine.

Growth, we now know all too well, is not a strategy. It is a tactic. And when undisciplined growth became a strategy for Starbucks, we lost our way. But no longer are we growing the company the way we did in the past.

In short, Starbucks today aims to be a very different type of company.

Sourcing, roasting, and serving the highest-quality coffee will remain our core, of course. And we will continue to invest in our retail stores and the Starbucks Experience. The stores are our foundation. But now we are going further, in a way that only Starbucks can.

For more than 20 years, I've said that every company must push for self-renewal and reinvention, constantly challenging the status quo. For Starbucks, doing so means we are once again thinking big and dreaming big, embarking on a road we have not taken before. Creating innovative growth platforms that are relevant to our core and worthy of our coffee was a critical element of the Transformation Agenda—it was one of the seven goals we announced in March 2008. Not only are we achieving this today, but we are also engaging in new product innovation, as well as extending coffee to other forms inside and outside our stores. All are key to our growth.

Our experience with Starbucks VIA proved we can create new product categories, while raising the bar on quality. In just 10 months on the market, VIA's US sales reached $100 million. To put that in context, only about 3 percent of US products generate more than $50 million in sales during their first year on the market, and only 0.3 percent ever makes it to $100 million in sales, according to SymphonyIRI Group, a research and consulting firm that specializes in retail and consumer products. VIA, however, is not just a product, but also a brand platform, and by September 2010 we had launched VIA decaf, iced coffee, and flavored VIA in vanilla, mocha, caramel, and cinnamon spice. Perhaps most surprising, even to us, has been consumers' overwhelming adoption of VIA as a single-serve solution, in place of home-brewed coffee and pods. Single-serve is a huge category where Starbucks has lagged in the past, but today we are becoming a significant player—and not just with VIA.

Although my friend Don Valencia was definitely a visionary, I don't think he ever imagined that the product he once called JAWS would one day reach $1 billion in worldwide sales.

In this respect, VIA will not be alone. Starbucks envisions building a portfolio of $1 billion brands, which will also include Seattle's Best Coffee. Less than a year after we unleashed SBC in 2009, the brand's look and feel and its strategy had already been overhauled. Under Michelle's leadership, SBC is adding more retail concepts and packaged products, and aggressively expanding its distribution. SBC is now offered in more than 40,000 locations, up tenfold since fall 2009, including Subway, Burger King, and AMC movie theaters, as well as in 550 retail outlets such as Borders.

And just as we had yet to tap SBC's potential, Starbucks also had not taken full advantage of, nor had we exerted enough control over, our consumer packaged goods (CPG) business, which includes Starbucks branded products such as packaged coffee, ready-to-drink beverages, premium ice creams, as well as Tazo teas.

In 2010, CPG was a $700 million global business. Respectable, but nowhere near the size it could or should be. Now, under the leadership of Jeff Hansberry, whom I named president of our consumer products business in June 2010, CPG is poised to grow in pace and size, significantly more than it ever has. With Jeff's prior experience at E. & J. Gallo Winery and his 17 years of working for Procter & Gamble, Starbucks is finally building a global consumer products organization that mirrors our retail footprint in terms of capability, reach, and consumer understanding.

Most crucial, however, is how we are integrating Starbucks' consumer goods business with our retail stores and our powerful customer engagement tools and resources. Consider:

There are companies that operate huge global networks of retail stores, like us.

Others distribute their products on grocery shelves all over the world, like us.

And a few do an extraordinary job of building emotional connections with their customers, as we have learned to do.

But only Starbucks does all three at scale, and we increasingly see a future where each complements the others, forming a virtuous cycle that allows us to go to market and grow the company in a unique way.

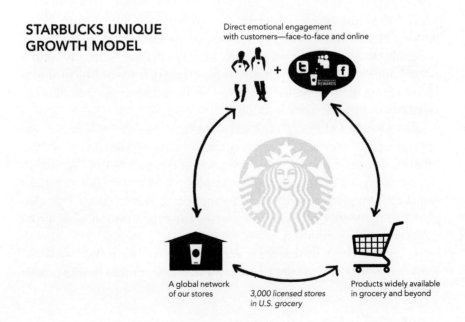

STARBUCKS UNIQUE GROWTH MODEL

Direct emotional engagement with customers—face-to-face and online

A global network of our stores

3,000 licensed stores in U.S. grocery

Products widely available in grocery and beyond

The engaging customer relationships that we create through our partners in our thousands of stores—plus the customer connections we foster in digital venues and with our loyalty cards—are paving the way for us to introduce new consumer products and rituals to consumers, in our retail stores and in other distribution outlets such as grocery.

Again, we saw this play out with VIA. Our customers' trust in our coffee and our partners—and the relationships they have with our brand online and through our loyalty programs—yielded trial, acceptance, and sales of VIA in our stores and in other venues. With one voice, we marketed VIA through multiple, complementary channels.

Few, if any, other retail brands have been able to create a significant global footprint through multiple channels of distribution outside of their core stores. Yet this, I believe, is Starbucks' destiny.

So it is with this strategic vision that we embark on the next chapter of Starbucks' story. We could not, however, turn the page without having first transformed and stabilized the retail business and the brand in the United States. That is the foundation from which our growth will always spring.

A Transformation Realized

Just as no single product, person, or initiative is determining Starbucks' future, no one thing is responsible for having transformed the company to be in a position to grow as never before. Since my return as ceo, many sustaining initiatives have taken root and blossomed, each helping us to meet the goals of the Transformation Agenda that we articulated back in early 2008.

To conclude *Onward*, I want to revisit these goals as well as provide a snapshot of the progress we continue to make on the initiatives that supported them. Doing so, I believe, brings this part of our company's story full circle, illustrating how the plans we created and executed not only brought about the transformation of our business, but also continue to solidify our ability to pursue the type of sustainable, profitable growth we envision.

Revisiting these initiatives is also a fitting tribute to our partners' hard work and diverse talents; without them, Starbucks would not be here today.

BEING THE UNDISPUTED COFFEE AUTHORITY

From day one, I knew we could not transform the company if we did not excel and lead in our core business, and so a goal that began with Espresso Excellence Training evolved into innovative products and practices that continue to improve the quality and delivery of our brewed and espresso beverages. Today, customers tell us that our brewed coffee and espresso-based drinks taste more consistent and significantly better than they did two years ago. The proof of Starbucks' coffee authority will always be in the cup.

Pike Place Roast Since launching Starbucks' signature approachable blend in April 2008, we've served one billion cups of Pike Place Roast to customers. Today, the breakthrough brew is our top-selling whole-bean coffee.

We also no longer send any preground coffee beans to our stores, instead grinding all beans, including bold and decaf, just prior to brewing a batch. That means our coffee tastes fresher and, much to the joy of the merchant in me, the rich aroma of freshly ground coffee once again permeates our stores throughout the day.

The Mastrena With this elegant espresso machine now in almost 70 percent of all of our US company-owned stores and its rollout continuing throughout the world, our baristas have more control over each shot and the steaming of milk, and once again they can more fully connect with customers by making eye contact and conversation with them as they wait on the other side of the espresso bar.

Clover The transcendent little coffee machine born in Seattle's Ballard neighborhood produces one of the top five best-selling beverages at the more than 100 stores that serve it in cities in the United States and Canada. Clover is finding its way into more locations, giving customers an opportunity to enjoy the nuances of our traditional blends and the flavors of our exotic, smaller-batch Starbucks Reserve coffees.

IGNITING THE EMOTIONAL ATTACHMENT
WITH OUR CUSTOMERS

People continue to come to Starbucks for coffee *and* human connection, and we have put our customers back at the center of the Starbucks Experience by addressing their needs, providing value in a manner congruent with the brand, and developing programs that recognize and reward our most loyal customers.

Starbucks' Loyalty Program Our customers have thanked us for thanking them. In December 2009 we rolled the Rewards and Gold Cards into a single new program called My Starbucks Rewards. Customers cite the program as a reason they are visiting our stores more frequently. To date, more than $1.5 billion has been loaded onto Starbucks Cards. It is hard to overstate the value of our loyalty program, to our customers and to the company . . . and much more is planned for its future.

MyStarbucksIdea.com Since launching in March 2008, the site's 250,000 registered members have submitted 100,000 ideas. We've launched 100, including enabling a customer to remotely buy someone a drink, selling reusable cup sleeves for our hot beverages, and bringing back salted caramel hot chocolate. As long as customers talk, we'll continue to listen and respond.

Social Media With more than 27 million fans around the world, Starbucks is currently a top brand on Facebook. One million people follow Starbucks on Twitter, and each month our website receives 12 million visitors. Popular applications that people download to their mobile devices allow them to locate the nearest Starbucks store, get nutritional information, even pay for your purchases. More than just a marketing tool, our digital presence further engages our customers, which is an essential element in our growth model going forward.

Digital Ventures In the fall of 2010, in partnership with Yahoo!, we launched the Starbucks Digital Network, finally tapping into the value of our vast Wi-Fi network by bringing community information and free premium content to our customers on laptops and mobile devices in our US company-owned stores. Even at its nascent stage, the Starbucks Digital Network has amassed an impressive collection of carefully selected providers that includes: *The Wall Street Journal, The New York Times,* and *USA Today*; free music downloads from Apple's iTunes; educational games from Nickelodeon; exclusive book excerpts from major publishers; career and job information from LinkedIn; Zagat restaurant reviews for local eateries; and health and wellness tips. The Starbucks Digital Network is designed to be a meaningful differentiator that will dramatically enhance the Starbucks Experience for our customers.

Lean Techniques In our stores, Lean techniques have put us on a path to achieving operational excellence, finding new ways to deliver world-class customer service and perfect beverages while keeping costs in line and our partners engaged. As we continue to formally implement and share better routines with our baristas, they continue to problem solve and swap their own ideas. Today, our stores report that lines move faster, operations run smoother, and partners have more time to connect with customers. And, in 2009, our partners named Lean their most valued program of the year.

EXPANDING OUR GLOBAL PRESENCE—WHILE MAKING EACH STORE THE HEART OF LOCAL NEIGHBORHOODS

Starbucks continues to accelerate our retail presence around the world while striving to connect with and support the neighborhoods and cultures that each store serves.

Starbucks Coffee International Starbucks' businesses outside the United States remain our biggest source for future growth—another $1 billion business in and of itself as we open more stores and refine a more disciplined, profitable business model. Eventually, half of all our stores will be located outside North America. Perhaps the most significant move I've made in securing the success of our international model happened in December 2009, when I asked eight-year Starbucks veteran John

Culver to oversee our global expansion as president of Starbucks Coffee International. John is familiar with our international markets, having lived and worked in Hong Kong for years, and he has the rare ability to connect with people across cultures. During John's first year on the job, our international business revenue and operating margins were up well ahead of our targets, a testament to his leadership skills and the deep focus he has brought to the business.

Expansion in China In September 2010, when Starbucks opened two new stores in Changsha, a city of six million—relatively small compared to other cities in China—customers were lined up out the door and down the block. In the rain.

Without doubt, Greater China is destined to become Starbucks' second home market as we open thousands more stores across the country. Already, the majority of our stores throughout China are delivering double-digit profit margins, a far cry from their performance just two years ago.

As part of our long-term strategy to be locally relevant on many fronts, Starbucks will soon open its first research and development center in China, and—in partnership with the Chinese government and working closely with local universities—we have already begun to grow coffee in the country's beautiful Yunnan province. And as for the Black Sesame Green Tea Frappuccino I tasted at our Shanghai innovation store, it is now being sold in Starbucks throughout China. It's a hit.

New Store Designs and Concepts Our new designs continue to find their way to stores around the world. By working with regional materials and collaborating with local craftsmen, we are creating thoughtful spaces that allow customers in every culture to feel at home in their neighborhood Starbucks stores and to experience a sense of discovery when they visit our locations around the world.

Mercantile Stores Our two stores in Seattle continue to experiment with new products like beer and wine as well as new coffee preparation techniques, such as individually brewed coffee by the pour-over method, which has become one way of serving single-cup decaf coffee in Starbucks stores, helping to eliminate the waste from unsold decaf. As a result of the lessons learned with these stores, we opened a very special store on East Olive Way in Seattle that incorporates some of the mercantile stores' best design elements and product offerings—including wine and beer after 4 p.m.—with our sustainable construction practices. As must-see destination spots for Starbucks' partners and customers who visit Seattle from around the world, these three unique shops showcase our willingness to take forward-thinking risks in the same way that the Pike Place store symbolizes our respect for our roots.

BEING A LEADER IN ETHICAL COFFEE SOURCING AND SUSTAINABILITY

Starbucks expanded our partnerships with Fairtrade and Conservation International and is reducing our stores' environmental impact. We also do a much more effective job of sharing with others our extensive efforts on this front.

Sourcing In 2009, 81 percent of our coffee purchased was C.A.F.E. Practices–verified, up from 77 percent in 2008. And with the purchase of almost 40 million pounds of Fairtrade coffee that same year, Starbucks became the largest buyer of Fairtrade coffee in the world in 2009. In Rwanda, the Starbucks farmer support center is now complete and actively assisting coffee farmers throughout East Africa. Five months after my visit to Rwanda, Starbucks partners raised $55,700 to send cows to coffee-growing communities. In the summer of 2010, 30 heifers arrived in Kigali and were placed with families, including Mukamwiza Immaculate's, who were trained in how to best care for their new animals. Since August, three calves have been born into the group.

Serving Our Communities Starbucks partners and customers contributed almost 186,000 hours of service in neighborhoods around the world in 2009; our goal is to one day contribute one million hours each year. In New Orleans, a city that is always on our minds, we honored our pledge to give $5 million over five years, and we continue to stay engaged with the city's revitalization effort. In 2010, we awarded $100,000 to three nonprofits based on customers' suggestions about where Starbucks should donate funds.

Environmental Impact Efforts continue to make our company-owned stores more environmentally friendly. As space, municipal regulations, and local recycling services allow, our stores can recycle paper, cardboard, cups, compost, glass, and/or plastics, as well as offer customers free coffee grounds for gardening. Since 2009, Starbucks has convened two "cup summits" with local governments, cup manufacturers, and recyclers, as well as competing retailers, to help us identify what's required to make our cups recyclable. Because of these collaborative efforts, on November 30, 2010, Starbucks and its suppliers announced that we had found a way to recycle used paper cups. This brings us one step closer to our goal to have 100 percent of Starbucks' cups be reusable or recyclable by 2015.

We also continue to work toward a goal of having all new Starbucks company-owned stores LEED certified in 2011, and to date more than 200 of our stores have either achieved or are currently registered for LEED green building certification. We are currently retrofitting all of our stores with high-efficiency lighting and are on track to reduce water consumption by 25 percent in 2015. And as of 2010, Starbucks has purchased renewable energy certificates equivalent to 50 percent of the electricity consumed in our stores. These and other sustainability efforts will also positively affect thousands of Starbucks' joint-venture and licensed stores around the world as they follow suit.

DELIVERING A SUSTAINABLE ECONOMIC MODEL

As we set out to do, Starbucks has drastically improved how we operate our business by reducing costs, building a world-class supply chain, and creating a culture that drives quality and speed and manages expenses on an ongoing basis.

Cost Reductions The $400 million we told Wall Street in

December 2008 that Starbucks would cut from its cost structure for fiscal 2009 ultimately grew to $580 million, much to
the surprise of the financial community. The cost cuts are permanent, and in 2010 we have preserved them and continue to
achieve additional savings, as evidenced by ongoing improvements in our operating margin. The work to keep costs in
check will never end, and the challenge ahead is to sustain
what we have achieved and strive for more while continuing
to wisely invest in our people, in growth, and in innovation.

Supply Chain Back in 2008, only three out of every 10 orders
were delivered perfectly to our stores. Today, nine out of 10
orders to 16,500 stores are delivered on time, with every item
included and no errors. SCO's safety performance has improved
by 90 percent, we are recruiting talent from top-ranked supply
chain schools, and in the last two years SCO realized cumulative savings of $400 million.

Store Technology In fall 2009, US store managers received
laptops loaded with software that automates and eases once cumbersome processes like scheduling, hiring, and performance
reviews. Our more intuitive point-of-sale system hit company-
owned stores in the United States and Canada in 2010, and pilots
are planned for our international stores. Once the rollout is complete, we will be able to cut an estimated 700,000 annual hours
off our customers' wait-in-line time in the United States alone.
To ensure that we stay relevant to consumers' lifestyles, our new
systems will be optimized for mobile technologies, allowing our
customers to eventually order, pay, and connect with us using
smartphones and other mobile devices.

Building Our Senior Leadership Team Of the dozen individuals currently on Starbucks' leadership team, the majority
have joined the company or the team since I returned as ceo.
Since the fall of 2009, in addition to appointing Annie Young-
Scrivner, John Culver, and Jeff Hansberry, I also found the right
person to head partner resources in Kalen Holmes, who joined
Starbucks that November, bringing almost 20 years of human

resources experience, most recently at Microsoft. In June 2010, we added two more members to the senior leadership team: Mary Egan from Boston Consulting Group now serves as senior vice president for global strategy, and SYPartners' Dervala Hanley came on board as vice president of corporate initiatives and planning.

Our team meets weekly as well as monthly, and as a group we are open to building consensus, we welcome creative tension, and we always try to learn from our past.

Today's Starbucks leadership team is by far the most talented and collaborative group I have had the honor of working with in my history at the company.

Biennial Analyst Conference On December 1, 2010, two years after we last presented to Wall Street in our most desperate hours, Starbucks senior leaders and I took the stage in New York City to tell a very different story, one no longer based on predictions of our transformation, but on irrefutable proof of record financial results. Starbucks performance was ". . . nothing short of remarkable," wrote Marc Greenberg from Deutsche Bank, "and quite honestly the most significant business turnaround we have witnessed." The day after the conference, compared to December 2008, Starbucks' stock closed at $32.76, up almost 400 percent.

★ ★ ★

The leadership team gathered around the huge roasting machine—each of us wearing a yellow safety vest, goggles, and green hard hat—and waited. Behind us stood about 50 partners who were among the 163 working at Starbucks' coffee roasting plant in Kent, Washington, located about 30 minutes from our offices. I'd requested that we hold part of our monthly senior leadership team meeting at the plant on this special day.

It was the first time in 40 years that Starbucks was roasting beans not just from Ecuador, but from the Galapagos Islands, that cluster of volcanic islands in the Pacific Ocean that is home to an amazing variety of species. The beans being roasted today came from the island of San Cristobal. They were rare—organic, shade grown, even bird friendly—and the coffee—we named it simply "Galapagos"—would be sold in less than 700 Starbucks stores in the fall of 2010. Galapagos was the first product in Starbucks Reserve, our new line of premium whole-bean coffees that we roast only in small batches and make available for a limited time.

Standing not far from pallets that transport some 65 million pounds of green coffee beans into the facility each year, I was reminded of Starbucks' earlier days, when my office was located in the former roasting plant. Back then, at the end of every day and before I headed home for the evening, I would walk the plant's floor. The partners always expected me, knowing I would make the rounds, usually stopping at the roasters' cooling tray to rake my hands through the beans and feel the coffee between my fingers before saying goodnight and thank you to everyone. At that time, the company was small enough that I knew each partner's name. Small enough that I knew their families. Two people from those days still work for Starbucks, Michael McNulty and Dave Seymour.

Visiting our Kent roasting plant is often bittersweet. No longer do I have time to walk the floor daily or even to come by as much as I would like. But I never forget the partners in our roasting facilities around the world who are responsible for bringing our coffee to life; they are the critical link in every bean's journey from farmer to cup. Without their expertise, passion, and daily dedication to excellence, Starbucks simply could not succeed.

"Reserve could not happen, *it would not happen*, if roasters were not putting the final touches on the coffee here at Kent," announced Tom Barr, vice president of global coffee, whose team sourced the beans for Reserve. Tom has been with Starbucks for 10 years.

So even though we had come to Kent to celebrate a new coffee, this day was really about celebrating people—including the roasters, mechanics, operators, technicians, managers, and devanners (the first partners to handle and then prep the beans when they arrive from afar). An impressive amount of people at Kent have been with Starbucks well over a decade, having stayed with the company during our roughest times and as we transformed.

"We are using 11 different roast curves to meet the unique roast and flavor profiles of some of the coffees that we roast here," Ruben Maglaya told us. Ruben has worked for Starbucks for *18 years*. I reached through a group of people to shake his hand.

Finally, it was time. Everyone watched and listened as the rush of coffee beans spilled from the silo into the large, flat, round, rotating roaster. As the beans slowly churned, the rich aroma of coffee filled the air.

Moments like this are among my favorite. When the past and the present overlap. When I am at the heart of Starbucks' operations. And when I cannot contain my smile because I am quite literally witnessing the magic that happens behind the scenes.

Times such as this, surrounded by people who think of each other as family, solidify my belief that Starbucks' best days are ahead of us.

Acknowledgments

Writing a book, like building a company, is a collaboration, and I am grateful to many people for helping me tell Starbucks' story.

Most important, to my wife, Sheri, and my two children; nothing in my life would be possible without your love.

The research, writing, and editing processes were made almost seamless by the extraordinary talent and grace of Joanne Gordon, who was able to find my voice on the page. She routinely and unselfishly accommodated my own busy schedule. I am so proud of the book and could never have done this without her.

Joanne and I would both like to thank everyone at Rodale, especially Maria Rodale, for their passion and commitment to this project from day one. Colin Dickerman and Karen Rinaldi were true editorial partners, and we were blessed to benefit from their intelligence, respect, humor, and ability to balance the needs of readers with the intentions of authors. Also, a special thanks to Steve Madden for his support.

At William Morris Endeavor Entertainment, Jennifer Rudolph Walsh was, as always, a tireless advocate who routinely steered us in the right direction.

More than 150 partners from throughout Starbucks candidly shared their memories and expertise, helping us to even more authentically re-create the company's shared history. A special thank-you to Starbucks' senior leadership team and board of directors for their time as well as their trust in my decision that publicly telling a difficult part of Starbucks' history would make us a stronger organization.

In my office, Nancy Kent, Tim Donlan, and Carol Sharp provide knowledgeable support every day, responding to each request with a calm smile and always delivering. Thanks to Chris Gorley for her discretion and precision in noting every word; Gail Resnik for her diligent legal review; and Gina Woods, whose leadership, expertise, creativity, and candor make her the ideal partner to manage *Onward*'s unusually complicated production and marketing processes. Thanks also to Vivek Varma, Corey DuBrowa, and Dervala Hanley for their honest editorial insights; and to Heidi Peiper, Trina Smith, Christina McPherson, and Deb Trevino for their research and attention to details throughout the process. The book's elegant design is due to the talents of Christopher Riggs, Kelly Clark, Nichole Guy, and Lisa Maulhardt at SYPartners. We are also grateful to the many people who read early drafts and final versions of the manuscript and provided feedback, including Jeffrey Hoffeld, Betty Sue Flowers, Richard Tait, Suzanne Sullivan, Bill Bradley, Mike Ullman, Mellody Hobson, Billy Etkin, and Len and Nancy Kersch.

Thanks also to Beth Lamb, Aly Mostel, and Yelena Nesbit at Rodale, as well as the team at Edelman and Mark Fortier.

For their friendship and support over many years, I want to acknowledge, in addition to those mentioned in the book, Plácido Arango, Ana Maria van Pallandt, Warren Bennis, Walter Robb, Amy Kavanaugh, Bill Campbell, Tony La Russa, Tim Ingrassia, Daniel Auerbach, Kenny G., Sharon Waxman, John Yamin, Steve Kersch, Colin Cameron, my cousin Alan Cohen, my sister Ronnie Schultz, and my brother, Michael Schultz. And to my mother, who has always been and continues to be a tremendous influence in my life.

Onward was primarily about Starbucks' transformation period and thus the story heavily focused on our US business even though the company's ongoing success is also due to our joint-venture partners and licensees around the world, many of whom I have known and called friends for years: in Japan, Yuji Tsunoda of the Sazaby League; in Spain, Plácido Arango's Grupo Vips; in Mexico, Alberto Torrado of Grupo Alsea; Starbucks' business partner for the Middle East, Turkey, and Russia, Mohammed Alshaya's M. H. Alshaya; in the Philippines, Jun and Menchu Lopez, owners of the Rustan Group; the Marinopoulos Group in Greece, Cyprus, Austria, Switzerland, and Romania, run by Panos Marinopoulos; in Hong Kong and parts of China, Michael Wu and the Maxim Group; in Taiwan and other regions of China, John Hsu of UniPresident Group; in Indonesia, V. P. Sharma of P. T. Mitra Adiperkasa; in Perú, Alfredo de Ferrari Morello's Delosi Group; and Henry McGovern of AmRest, Starbucks' business partner for Central Europe. Also, Fred Hazelwood of the John Bull Group in the Bahamas; I. C. Hur from Shinsegae Corporation in South Korea; Russel Creedy of Restaurant Brands New Zealand; and in Malaysia, Francis Lee with Berjaya.

Finally, not a day goes by when I do not think about Starbucks' tens of thousands of partners. Their hard work and fortitude transformed the foundation of our business, and the values, the passion, and the ideas that they show up to work with every day are what makes us such a special organization. For all they do, my heartfelt thanks.

From the coauthor

In addition to the above, I would like to thank my parents, David and Virginia Gordon, for that little blue typewriter and a lifetime of unconditional love. My son, Theo, for his laughter and patience. And Matthew, for his support in every season of our lives.

For helping me find my own balance, thanks to my loving sister Susan and her husband, Howard; my surrogate Seattle family Katie Bedford and Sherri, Tom, and Maggie Brothers; as well as dear friends Kim B., Adrienne K., Caroline R., Julie Z., Mary Anne S., Lynn H., Lori S., Jamie K., Cari S., Lindsay P., Leigh G., Sam K., Cate H., Ben D., Dan M., Lois W., Ilysa G., and, as promised, Ellen A. A special thanks to Tonya Kimbrough of Pronto on eight, whose smile brightened my days.

I am grateful to my literary agent Stuart Krichevsky for years of wise counsel, commitment to excellence, and understanding. Stuart is a true professional in the publishing world.

Finally, to Howard Schultz. His honesty, focus, generosity of spirit, compassion for others, trust in me, and desire to tell Starbucks' story for all the right reasons made collaborating on his book one of the most rewarding experiences of my career. Howard gave me unfettered access to Starbucks' partners, whose high standards, intelligence, and kindness are, I believe, reflections of his leadership. After more than a year of sharing Howard's past and present, I feel compelled to paraphrase the talented writer Dori Jones Yang, who worked with Howard on his first book: Howard Schultz truly is the man he set out to be.

Photo credits

Where it all began, in 1971
1   Jeff Corwin
2   Nick Gunderson
3   James McFarlane

Rwanda
1, 5, 6   Jonathan Torgovnik
2, 3, 4,   Riccardo Gangale
7, 9

8   Chris von Zastrow

The proof is in the cup
1, 5   Geoffrey Ellis
2   Paul J. Richards/Getty Images
3, 4   Keith Bedford

Returning to our heritage
6, 7   Young Lee

Ethically sourced coffee
1   Jonathan Levine
2   Martin Thiel
3, 7   Michael Hanson Photography
4, 9   Sam Knight

5, 6   Stanley Hainsworth
8   Starbucks Coffee Department

The Starbucks Experience
1   Young Lee
2   Rob McDougall
3a, 4b   Aaron Leitz
3b, 3c   Major Cohen
4a   Armstrong Photo
5a, 5b   Touch Worldwide

6, 7   Zhang Tong
8   Kirsha Baldwin
9   Martin Coles
10   Árpád Földházi
11, 12   Colm Pierce

Taking it personally
1, 2, 3,   Touch Worldwide
6, 7, 8

4   Kevin Mazur/Getty Images
5   Matt Peloza

Reimagining our future
1, 7   Rubin Photography
2, 3, 5, 6   SYPartners
4   Matthew Mar

Innovation
1, 13   Young Lee
2   Aaron Leitz
3, 4b   Starbucks Coffee Company
4a, 7b, 12   Armstrong Photo
5   Geoffrey Ellis
6   Haley Munro

7a   Courtesy of the Valencia Family
8   Courtesy of Starbucks Japan
9   Courtesy of Concord Music Group
10   Iridio
11   Ralph Alswang

Onward...
1   John Keatley
2   Gregg Segal

Automat photo (at front of book)
Courtesy of the Hardart Family

Index

An asterisk (*) indicates that photos are shown in the insert pages.